GLOBALIZATION
AND DEMOCRACY

GLOBALIZATION

Series Editors

Manfred B. Steger

*Royal Melbourne Institute of Technology
and University of Hawai'i–Mānoa*

and

Terrell Carver

University of Bristol

"Globalization" has become *the* buzzword of our time. But what does it mean? Rather than forcing a complicated social phenomenon into a single analytical framework, this series seeks to present globalization as a multidimensional process constituted by complex, often contradictory interactions of global, regional, and local aspects of social life. Since conventional disciplinary borders and lines of demarcation are losing their old rationales in a globalizing world, authors in this series apply an interdisciplinary framework to the study of globalization. In short, the main purpose and objective of this series is to support subject-specific inquiries into the dynamics and effects of contemporary globalization and its varying impacts across, between, and within societies.

Globalization and Sovereignty
John Agnew

Globalization and War
Tarak Barkawi

Globalization and Human Security
Paul Battersby and Joseph M. Siracusa

Globalization and the Environment
Peter Christoff and Robyn Eckersley

*Globalization and American Popular
  Culture, 3rd ed.*
Lane Crothers

Globalization and Militarism
Cynthia Enloe

Globalization and Law
Adam Gearey

Globalization and Feminist Activism
Mary E. Hawkesworth

Globalization and Postcolonialism
Sankaran Krishna

Globalization and Media
Jack Lule

*Globalization and Social Movements,
  2nd ed.*
Valentine Moghadam

Globalization and Terrorism, 2nd ed.
Jamal R. Nassar

Globalization and Culture, 2nd ed.
Jan Nederveen Pieterse

Globalization and Democracy
Stephen J. Rosow and Jim George

*Globalization and International Political
  Economy*
Mark Rupert and M. Scott Solomon

Globalization and Citizenship
Hans Schattle

Globalization and Money
Supriya Singh

Globalization and Islamism
Nevzat Soguk

Globalization and Urbanization
James H. Spencer

Globalisms, 3rd ed.
Manfred B. Steger

Rethinking Globalism
Edited by Manfred B. Steger

Globalization and Labor
Dimitris Stevis and Terry Boswell

Globaloney 2.0
Michael Veseth

 Supported by the Globalization Research Center at the University of Hawai'i, Mānoa

GLOBALIZATION AND DEMOCRACY

STEPHEN J. ROSOW AND JIM GEORGE

ROWMAN & LITTLEFIELD
Lanham • Boulder • New York • London

Published by Rowman & Littlefield
A wholly owned subsidiary of The Rowman & Littlefield Publishing Group, Inc.
4501 Forbes Boulevard, Suite 200, Lanham, Maryland 20706
www.rowman.com

16 Carlisle Street, London W1D 3 BT, United Kingdom

British Library Cataloguing in Publication Information Available

Library of Congress Cataloging-in-Publication Data

Rosow, Stephen J.
  Globalization and democracy / Stephen J. Rosow and Jim George.
    pages cm. — (Globalization)
  Includes bibliographical references and index.
  ISBN 978-1-4422-1808-6 (cloth : alk. paper) — ISBN 978-1-4422-1809-3 (pbk. : alk.
paper) — ISBN 978-1-4422-1810-9 (electronic) 1. Democracy—Developing countries.
2. Democratization—Developing countries. 3. Neoliberalism—Developing countries.
4. Globalization—Political aspects—Developing countries. 5. Developing countries—
Politics and government. I. George, Jim, 1946– II. Title.
  JF60.R674 2015
  321.8—dc23

                                                                                   2014008574

♾™ The paper used in this publication meets the minimum requirements of
American National Standard for Information Sciences—Permanence of Paper
for Printed Library Materials, ANSI/NISO Z39.48-1992.

Printed in the United States of America

CONTENTS

ACKNOWLEDGMENTS

In many ways, this book got its start in the conversations between us over many years. I would like to thank Jim especially for sharing his work on the neoconservatives and on neoliberalism, which I have found especially inspiring. I thank him also for nominating me for a distinguished visiting professorship at Australian National University (ANU) in May and June 2011 and then for joining this project so enthusiastically. Many at ANU's School of Politics and International Relations created a welcoming, stimulating, and critical environment in which to work and willingly listened and commented upon early versions of ideas that have gone into this book. Special thanks to Michael McKinley, John Ravenhill, Tom Chodor, Guy Emerson (thanks again for the tour of Melbourne), and Barry Hindess, as well as those faculty and students who attended and commented on my lectures. While in Australia Manfred Steger and Anne McNevin graciously invited me to try out some of the ideas that went into this book at the Globalization program at the Global Cities Institute at RMIT. Without Manfred's invitation, and prodding, this book would not have happened.

I also owe a debt, collectively and individually, to an extraordinary group of scholars, interlocutors, friends, and fellow travelers of many years that can never be fully repaid. Danny Warner, Michael McKinley, Annette Freyborg-Inan, Judy Hemming, Peter Vale, and Clinton Fernandes have provided constant intellectual sustenance, friendship, and criticism of all of the thinking that I have brought to this book. To colleagues and students at the State University at Oswego, thanks for making it possible to work and think in spite of the neoliberalization of the university: Walter Opello, Bruce Altschuler, Craig Warkentin, Lisa Glidden, Stephon Boatwright, Miriam Jimenes, Jennie Han, and Christina Dragomire. I also thank the School of International and Public Affairs at Columbia University, and especially Michael Doyle, for hosting me during my sabbatical in 2012–2013, and SUNY Oswego for granting it. Finally, to Ellen Goldner, whose friendship, trust, forbearance, love, and critical thinking have sustained me for more than thirty years. I dedicate this book to Julian, Gabriel, and Ben, who are and will be harbingers of global worlds.

—Stephen J. Rosow

I want to thank Steve for the invitation to join the project. It was an enjoyable and rewarding experience. It was particularly interesting for me because, after years of working on sometimes quite esoteric theoretical issues concerning the ways we think about and behave in the international-relations sphere, this book gave me the opportunity to concentrate on some specific empirical issues—in Africa, India, and Latin America—and on the implications for peoples in these regions of adhering, simultaneously, to democratic politics and neoliberal economics. This has been a topic of conversation with many friends and colleagues in many places since the 1980s and the Thatcher/Reagan eras. In particular, Michael McKinley and I have sought to evaluate the implications for both global "winners" and "losers" in this context, and I thank Mike more generally for his friendship and always-stimulating perspectives on any number of issues. I also want to thank Tom Chodor and Guy Emerson for their insights on the Venezuela chapter in this book. I dedicate the work to my daughter Sara and brothers Alan, Frank, and Robert.

—Jim George

This book has been influenced, as all are, by numerous conversations between the authors and with others, especially those involved in critical international political theory. None is responsible for the ways the ideas in this book have emerged from our thinking about those conversations, but this book would not have happened without them. Some will no doubt recognize their influence, and others will certainly scratch their heads in puzzlement at what we have done with ideas they contributed to our conversations. Still others will not recognize that their generosity in sharing their thinking with one or both of us has challenged and shaped our thinking. Whether they agree or disagree with our arguments and lines of thought in this book, we hope it at least repays their generosity with a text worthy of continuing dialogues and conversations about how to think about democracy and possibilities for a better world.

INTRODUCTION

ONE OR MANY FORMS OF DEMOCRACY?

DEMOCRACY: ONE OR MANY?

In November 1989, the wall separating East and West Berlin, that massive symbol of the Cold War, was breached, and Germany was reunited by a conservative prime minister, Helmut Kohl. Also in 1989, Francis Fukuyama, then deputy director of the Policy Planning Staff at the U.S. State Department, declared in a much-read article that not only had the "West" won the Cold War but also that the victory of Western liberal democracy marked "the end of history." More specifically, Fukuyama suggested that the post-Enlightenment ideological conflict between liberalism and its major alternative (socialism) was over, and liberal capitalism, grounded in the doctrine of free trade and political democracy, would shape the global future.[1]

Skip ahead to the beginning of the new millennium. In his inaugural address for his second term in 2004, President George Bush declared: "It is the policy of the United States to seek and support the growth of democratic movements and institutions in every nation and culture."[2] At first glance there was nothing terribly unusual about such a statement; U.S. presidents since Woodrow Wilson have articulated the American global project similarly, as part of an "exceptionalist" presumption integral, seemingly, to American cultural and political identity. But in the post–Cold War era, and driven by the desire to transform the end of (modern ideological) history into the beginning of a triumphant "American century," a number of advisers to President Bush insisted on the need to grasp the historical moment for a "muscular" form of global liberalism, even if this meant imposing U.S.-style democracy, particularly in strategically sensitive regions of the world (e.g., the Middle East). From this perspective (paradoxes aside), the strong imposing democracy on the weak was considered legitimate, strategically and philosophically, in the quest for a stable, ordered, global environment in which a U.S.-inspired political and cultural value system and a commitment to free-market economics might indeed incline the global future toward such a "democracy."

In fifteen years, thus, the mainstream discourse of democracy in the United States had shifted significantly, from a celebration of freedom from (perceived) intellectual and political oppression to the global clarion call for regime change. Accordingly, in his State of the Union address in 2004, President Bush proposed doubling the budget for the National Endowment for Democracy (NED), a government-funded organization created by the Reagan administration in 1983 as part of a global Democracy Project, initially tasked with "creating" democratic societies in the U.S. image in places where this image had become tarnished (e.g., in Latin America). The NED has been authorized and funded by Congress since 1983. Its aim is "democracy promotion" throughout the world.[3]

At least two other articulations of the democracy-promotion theme have become influential in the contemporary period. One is derived from an important intellectual source known as democratic peace theory.[4] Inspired initially by two influential articles on Kantian liberalism and its impact upon international relations by Michael Doyle,[5] and afforded a measure of "scientific" credibility in the works of behavioralist political scientists, such as Bruce Russett, democratic peace theory argues that since liberal-democratic states do not go to war with one another they are foundational in any project designed to create the systemic conditions in which capitalist markets might flourish and a range of associated social freedoms and political liberties might become possible.[6] We engage the issue of democratic peace theory and its significance for orthodox political discourse on global democracy in chapter 5.

The second and even more influential invocation of the democracy-promotion theme has a related but somewhat different origin but is very much aligned with an orthodoxy that represents the socialist age as historically and intellectually over and that celebrates the age of market freedom, individual liberty, and capitalist democracy. Derived from the strict economic rationalism of the 1920s Austrian school and given more accessible and familiar dimensions by Nobel Prize winners such as Friedrich Hayek and Milton Friedman, this *neo*liberalism has become integral to the orthodox democratic debate since the 1980s. Since this time, and most powerfully invoked as part of the Washington Consensus during the 1990s, the neoliberal perspective on democracy has taken on hegemonic status in global affairs. As Milton Friedman insisted in the 1960s and 1970s, the connection between capitalist free markets and democracy is direct and logically insurmountable—free markets require social and political liberty in order that individuals are free to (rationally) choose the means to their economic ends—and this means/ends process is only available to all within a genuinely free-market environment.[7] Political participation, in this context, is necessarily of the minimalist variety (e.g., self-interested rationality in the ballot box) with more direct "economic" behavior of much greater significance. This is an issue for detailed analysis in chapter 2.

There are, of course, a range of alternative perspectives to this global orthodoxy that effectively reject this neoliberal logic and are inherently skeptical of the U.S.-led democracy-promotion project. At the more moderate end of this alternative spectrum, social democrats, mainly in Europe, have articulated their concerns with neoliberal globalism and any forceful imposition of democratic freedoms. This has seen a renewed interest in "cosmopolitan democracy" in which a broader, more humane form of liberalism underpins an image of the global future founded not just upon economic rationality and "market" democracy but also on a concern for human rights and international law and the democratizing influences of a range of global civil-society institutions. As David Held puts it, "The possibility of democracy today must be linked to an expanding framework of democratic institutions and procedures."[8] This is a view supported by others, such as Jan Aart Scholte, who emphasizes the need to make international organizations democratically accountable as part of an expanded arena of global governance.[9]

The works of Jürgen Habermas have been significant in shifting this critical literature onto more radical terrain, primarily via the development of the theory of "discursive democracy," in which orthodox strictures concerning notions of rationality and rational action are loosened somewhat from their instrumentalist and strategic parameters and reconceived in terms of an emancipatory thematic that offers hope for democratic dialogue across borders, cultures, and ideologies.[10] A similar purpose infuses the contribution of scholars such as Andrew Linklater, whose work resonates with critical concerns about the possibility for new forms of democratic identity in the age of neoliberal globalization, as intellectual and territorial borders break down and as a democratic ethic emerges within the global community.[11] Another dimension of this multilevel citizenship ethos is to be found in the work of William Connolly, in terms of the notion of "agonistic democracy," which refuses to reduce the complexity and multiplicity of democracy in globalization to a single form, focusing instead on the tensions and ambiguities that promote global/local forms of a democratic ethos.[12]

Over the past two decades or so, increasingly radical forms of democratic theory and practice have also become part of the political and intellectual landscape. Indeed, in the twenty-first century, the meanings and practices associated with democracy around the world are in many respects defying TINA ("There Is No Alternative") in favor of more heterogeneous and heterodox, multiple and critical realities. Some brief examples might indicate the nature and variety of this heterodox response:

1. In August 1992, Subcommander Marcos in Chiapas, Mexico, wrote: "Collective work, democratic thinking, and subjection to the decisions of the majority are more than just traditions in indigenous zones. They have been the only means of survival, resistance, dignity, and defiance [for indigenous peoples]."[13] Accordingly, in this and many other writings, speeches, and political action, the people of Chiapas have sought to resist neoliberal capitalism with local forms of "indigenous democracy."

2. In 1956 in the Basque region of Spain, a movement of "collectivist democracy" emerged among peasants, workers, and artisans. It has subsequently become the Mondragon Corporation, owned by workers and underpinned by democratic principles in the decision-making process and in the everyday workplace. Its aim in this regard is to "combine the core goals of a business organization competing on international markets with the use of democratic

methods . . . the creation of jobs, [and] the human and professional development of workers."[14] It has grown into the seventh-largest corporation in Spain, with operations in eight countries outside of Spain. We discuss its democratic credentials and its implications for the TINA principle in more detail in chapter 6.

3. Since the 1990s, several states in Latin America have invoked radical "people's democracy" responses to neoliberalism and U.S. involvement in the region. There have been significant differences in the nature and extent of the radicalism associated with these "pink tide" movements, but in their different ways, the late Hugo Chávez in Venezuela, Evo Morales in Bolivia, Inácio Lula da Silva and Dilma Rousseff in Brazil, and Rafael Correa in Ecuador have all articulated their antipathy to neoliberalism and a commitment to an alternative democratic future for their peoples and societies.

We investigate these and related themes in more detail in chapters 3 and 4.

The point, for now, is that democracy is being thought about and practiced in a range of ways in the contemporary era, some of which we have already noted: as U.S. geostrategic globalism, as hegemonic neoliberal political economy, as radical alternatives to neoliberalism and U.S. dominance, in grassroots and indigenous movements seeking to create or sustain social and political collectivism, as the participatory struggles of ostensibly liberated peoples (from structural and ideological imperialisms), and at the heart of a liberal cosmopolitanism concerned to infuse the global status quo with humanitarian and ethical dimensions.

This, we suggest, is not at all surprising, even in an age where TINA principles are invoked to essentialize and universalize particular forms of political and economic organization. Indeed, to propose there can be no "real" alternatives to the current hegemony of theory and practice on democracy is to miss the point regarding the intellectual and political process by which hegemonic reality is created and sustained. More precisely, it ignores the always temporary, contested, and unstable nature of hegemonic power and the political and intellectual flux associated with struggles for hegemony.[15] In the current context, most specifically, it ignores the contestation and contestability concerning the very meaning of democracy that is evident in so many spaces and places in the current era and that underpins and directs a range of alternative democratic practices.

This is not to suggest that "anything goes" in relation to alternative democratic meanings and the various democratic resistances to the global status quo. In principle, democracy is, for example, effectively incompatible with racism, Fascism, Soviet-style socialism, fixed social hierarchy, and religious and political fundamentalisms. There is, nevertheless, a good deal of nuance left in the contestation over democracy as a politics of becoming—as both an aspiration and a practice—carried out in conditions of social and political struggle, or, as Marx put it, as the distinctive actions of people struggling to govern themselves, albeit under conditions not of their own choosing. "Democracy" remains a contested concept, in spite of the attempts to naturalize and globalize particular forms and practices.

A cursory view of the multiple invocations of democracy in political theory can be seen to reflect this contestability. "Democracy" invokes (1) *a type of constitution* that embodies popular sovereignty—rule by all of the citizens as opposed to rule by one (monarchy, tyranny) or by a few (aristocracy, oligarchy); (2) *a form of government* that refers to two fundamental governmental principles, representation and majority rule; (3) *a type of society* in which, as Tocqueville described America, a relative equality of the condition of the citizenry and a spirit of individual freedom and equality prevail; (4) *a way of making decisions* that stresses deliberation, rational debate, and dialogue; (5) *an ethos* as a way of orienting one's life ethically amid the inevitable agonism of political life in multicultural and pluralist societies; (6) *as an ideal and ideology* as in the triumphalist discourses of global democracy promotion mentioned above. This is not an exhaustive list, but the sociolinguistic diversity concerning the meaning of democracy attests to the contestability and instability of any attempt to naturalize or globalize a particular kind of democratic regime—including the neoliberal version of democracy promoted so confidently by advocates of the global free market since the 1980s.

In the remainder of this introduction, consequently, we seek to illustrate further this conceptual instability in the contemporary notion of a globalized democracy.

THINKING ABOUT DEMOCRACY "IN" GLOBALIZATION

Democracy is traditionally imagined as contained within states, as a bounded community legitimated by a particular constitution of popular sovereignty and a self-contained governmental apparatus. Conversely, globalization generally refers to reterritorializations of social life in more distant relations that cross, transcend, and subtend national and state borders. Globalization, in this regard, is comprised of spatially expansive and indeterminate networks whose vectors of power operate at speeds that undermine the spatial and temporal forms of social relations that make democracy possible. Consequently, both as concepts and historical phenomena, democracy and globalization are most often thought to be effectively independent of one another, not as having historically constituted and infused one another. However, this dichotomy of inside (democracy) and outside (globalization) is false. Just as the dichotomy between the state and the international system belied the complexity of the mutually constitutive relations of states and international orders,[16] the dichotomy between democracy and globalization acts to narrow our understanding of a complex arena of reciprocation and symbiosis. Indeed, as Benedict Anderson indicates, the modern print media was essential to the formation of both the nation-state and the international system as it informed, educated, and created ties among diverse people within and across states. Similarly, the new age of digital media, with its more fluid networks of communication, would seem to hold out new possibilities for democratic "imagined communities" within and across national borders.[17] More obvious examples of this intersection of inside/outside are evident in, for example, the shared fate of global citizens confronted with environmental problems requiring something more than "national" interests to solve them or peoples in many parts of an economically interdependent world having to face together the implications of global commodities networks and the global division of labor in contemporary capitalism.

In these cases, and many more, it becomes clear that rethinking democracy and its relationship to globalization is a necessary and important feature of any contemporary analysis of twenty-first-century politics at all levels, from the individual to the state to the global. As indicated above, the dominant neoliberal framing of this relationship promotes a particular view of it, which suggests that a limited "liberal" form of democratic society can be successfully transferred to a global form as long as the more socially radical dimensions of the democratic tradition can be subordinated to the logics and dictates of global capitalism. This particular image of democracy "in" globalization, we suggest, is too narrowly ideological to be successfully applied for long in a diverse and volatile global context. Thus, while neoliberal theory and practice has been accorded hegemonic status since the 1980s, we argue in this book that both in thought and action it is effectively blind to the vulnerable and unstable nature of its hegemonic rule and to the multiple and heterodox forms of democratic response, both local and global, that its ideological narrowness is provoking.

GLOBALIZATION, DEMOCRATIC INSTABILITY, AND CALLS FOR CHANGE

All political and social formations presume particular configurations of space and time. Democratic political formations are no different. Democracy presumes a bounded community that enables distinctions between citizens and noncitizens and that enables a sense of a unified "people" to form and that liberal democracy has assumed continuity with the modern territorial state. We develop this theme in more detail later in emphasizing how democratic regimes are constituted by particular configurations of inclusion and exclusion—their "domestic" inside being constituted significantly by their "foreign" outside.[18] It stands to reason thus that the more intensive and extensive flows of people across state borders in the contemporary era of globalization will lead to important reconfigurations of inside and outside, domestic and foreign. Accordingly, we do not think of globalization as "outside" of democratic domesticity (as the "international" has traditionally been represented) but as an increasingly integral feature of everyday social life around the world that is prompting a range of conceptual and structural tensions in the workings of democracy as the imperatives of global capitalism create new institutional and politico-cultural relations.

There has always been tension and the potential for instability in democratic systems, of course. Indeed, from its very beginnings, democracy was considered replete with such characteristics. Plato argues (in book 8 of the *Republic*) that democracy cannot lead to stable, lasting institutions because it allows too much freedom to individuals who are not responsible or knowledgeable enough to create political and social stability. Rather, democracy, as Plato understood it, creates a "democratic man" who believes himself free to live any kind of life he chooses, most often without regard for the public good. Because of this freedom, however, democracy will inevitably deteriorate into anarchy and tyranny as the masses seek security and public order and give their support to any talented demagogue who promises them stable and secure government. The Platonic specter of anarchy, disorder, and ungovernability through "too much democracy" and his solution based on political elitism have continued to shape much conservative thinking on modern democratic theory.[19]

In the modern liberal era (post–seventeenth century), nevertheless, the idea of representative government, together with the notion of the rationally acting individual capitalist as the personification of "hidden hand" stability and public order, appeared to resolve the tensions between the ever-expanding desire for democratic freedom and the concerns for social and political tranquility. And the achievements of liberal-capitalism have been significant in this regard. Democratic agency was manifest, for example, in the often-intense struggles for inclusion and justice by marginalized populations within liberal-capitalist states. Democracy for these groups—women, workers, the poor, slaves and former slaves, immigrants—often meant a way to a better life and relief from the indignities and oppressive conditions fostered by entrenched immiseration and prejudice. But representative government, centered on liberal individualism and market logic as the ultimate public goods, never fully absorbed the social and political desires of modern democratic subjects. This was most powerfully evident in the world-changing eras of the eighteenth century (e.g., the French Revolution) and the nineteenth century (e.g., the Industrial Revolution). In the contemporary era of global neoliberalism, it remains evident as alternative forms of democratic political subjectivity—agitating for democratic worker control, infused with issue-specific activism, or driven by new forms of citizen forums—increasingly challenge the boundaries of liberal representative democracy, perceived as fundamentally inclined toward political elitism and economic exploitation. It is very evident, too, in the attempts to expand the Bolivarian Revolution and pink-tide phenomenon in Latin America into organizations of democratic regionalism; in the village, town, and city collectivism of Kerala, India; and in the subaltern political associations within and across poor communities in South Africa, South Asia, and elsewhere. In all of these places, and many more, the calls for a more meaningful democracy and a change to the poverty and social injustice have been heard.

Other voices from within the broader liberal tradition have been heard also challenging democratic orthodoxy. These appeals for a cosmopolitan world order and for new forms of transnational democratic constitutionalism tend to share the broad concerns, about the rich getting richer and the poor, poorer, that characterize much critique from the global South, but they emphasize, too, some of the major structural discontinuities now apparent between representation and democratic political activism under globalization—a discontinuity that has become more pronounced as far-reaching policy decisions are taken in international organizations and transnational corporations whose decision-makers are not democratically accountable through the representative system and whose economic and political interests are often directly at odds with the great majority of state-based citizens.

Of concern, too, in this regard, is the compression of time and space associated with democratic governmentality in a globalized world order. Aristotle argues that, above all, democratic citizenship requires leisure because serious deliberation among groups of people takes time. Democratic citizenship, he thus concludes, must be restricted to wealthy men who can afford the time to leave the household for extended periods of time, which of course, rendered women, slaves, and metics (resident aliens) unsuitable for democratic citizenship. Aristotle's fifth-century-BCE restrictions on the composition of the citizen body are no longer acceptable, of course, but his concern about the issue of time as intrinsic to the process of democratic deliberation has become an issue of analytical significance again at a moment when governments, corporations, and individual citizens increasingly measure achievement and success in terms of blinding speed—of instantaneous communication, of electronic wizardry concerning deliberations over people, money, and global crises. For some, indeed, the movement toward a "global village" centered on extraordinary advances in communication technology is the harbinger of a new age of global democracy.

We acknowledge the positive dimensions associated with the compression of time and space integral to the "global village" notion while keeping in mind, more firmly, the interests this new time/space continuum mainly serves—global capitalism and political elitism—and the democratic deficiency this situation necessarily implies. We discuss this theme and "cosmopolitan" responses to it later in the book when we address the problems of democratic governability under globalization as it relates to a range of contemporary issues—for example, the rapid movement of people across borders and associated questions of inclusion/exclusion and of democratic citizenship. At other moments in the book, albeit indirectly, we touch on the fundamental question in all of this—the question of what precisely democracy might mean in a globalized age of blurring techno-speed and "casino capitalism."[20]

This, however, is not a book on democratic theory but a theoretically informed account of democracy "in" globalization. Thus, our focus is on how specific democratic regimes in the age of globalization are taking the new conditions into account and how new democratic imaginaries are forming. In chapter 1, we touch on some of the ways in which democracy has been imagined up to the present day, via a series of historical vignettes that situate democratic theory and practice in specific times and spaces. Chapter 2 looks more directly at the present and globalized neoliberal democracy, exploring its intellectual antecedents and the ways, in practice, it seeks to order the global world through a managerial and limited form of "market" democracy. Chapters 3 and 4 look at how neoliberal democracy as a global form has generated critical challenges in ostensibly very different parts of the world (Latin America, Africa, India, and post-Soviet Russia), primarily in the form of alternative democratic movements invoking the need for political emancipation and social justice rather than just economic forms of "liberty." Chapter 5 turns to questions of how the current global order is prompting a widespread reassessment of democratic community beyond state boundaries. Chapter 6 then presents several more radical challenges to traditional democracy in the form of non-statist democratic experiments.

CHAPTER 1

DEMOCRACY IN HISTORICAL CONTEXT

TOWARD HETERODOXY

In this chapter, we introduce democratic theory historically in order to stress the historicity and heterodoxy of democratic possibilities. Each of the brief vignettes on the historical development of democracy presented here seeks to contribute further to an understanding of how historical experiences of democracy that have come to form a tradition of Western democratic thought have come to significantly influence a twenty-first-century globalism dominated by doctrines of liberal individualism, the free market, and political minimalism. In particular, they seek to illustrate that intellectual contention and political volatility always surrounded democracy's core principles, that attempts to universalize and essentialize these principles were always challenged, and that, therefore, tendencies toward democratic heterodoxy in an age of neoliberal global hegemony are best understood not as utopian or heretical but as part of an ongoing struggle for social and economic justice and meaningful political participation.

The first examines ancient Athenian democracy from the point of view of contemporary interpretations that seek to recapture its value for pluralizing contemporary democracy against the traditional opposition of modern and ancient, representative and direct democracy that has been taken for granted in dominant liberal-democratic understandings of democracy. The second examines popular sovereignty's emergence in populist claims in the debates of the English Civil War, prior to its formation of modern democratic government in order to suggest that popular sovereignty is never fully assimilated to the form of the state. The next focuses on how liberal skepticism about popular sovereignty and "too much democracy" generated a new form of liberal democracy. Finally, we turn to the interpolation of neoliberal globalism into liberal democracy, which becomes the focus of the next chapter.

VIGNETTE 1: ANCIENT OR CLASSICAL DEMOCRACY: ATHENIAN EXPERIENCES

The traditional narrative of modern democracy, from the eighteenth century on, has largely viewed classical Greek democracy as ill suited to the modern world. It has, consequently, showed little interest in seriously investigating how ancient democracy actually worked. Ancient or classical democracy is thus most often characterized as "direct" democracy and therefore as outmoded, suited only to small city-states. From this perspective, classical or direct democracy is characterized as governed not by reason but by demagoguery, as allowing "too much freedom" to those incapable of dealing with the responsibilities and complexities of life in a free society. Modern democracy, on the other hand, is of the representative kind, thus once removed from this demagoguery and irresponsibility and imbued with post-Enlightenment liberal sensitivities that guarantee the protection of individual rights and the rule of law. The founding fathers of the American Constitution shared this perspective to varying degrees,[1] as did a major democratic theorist of the 1950s and 1960s, Robert Dahl, who proposed that the political ideas and institutions of Greek democracy, innovative and crucial as they were in their time, were (rightly) rejected during the development of modern representative democracy.[2]

Dahl's conclusions on this issue are correct as far as they go. Mainstream liberal and conservative thinkers have largely rejected the classical Greek model in their considerations of what is possible and desirable in the contemporary world, invoking instead variations on the capitalist democracy model touched on above, which, since World War II in particular, has been largely articulated in American cultural, geopolitical, and economic terms. But more critically inclined thinkers have been skeptical about the reasoning behind the mainstream position, suggesting that while "direct" democracy of the classical kind might indeed be illogical in large, complex modern societies, this is not the major reason for the repudiation of the Greek democratic scenario. Rather, the repudiation of the Greek experience is less about any historical irrelevancy per se and more about a deeply embedded conservative fear of "too much democracy," and an ongoing concern in the modern era about maintaining traditional order and control in a situation where the "mob" has political power.[3] Accordingly, a range of critical scholars have refocused attention on the historical-political and intellectual context of the classical Greek era (sixth–fourth centuries BCE) in seeking broader insight into the current contestation about the nature, meaning, and future of democracy and democratic society.[4]

The best historical evidence we have is that Athenian democracy was born in the struggles of peasant farmers to escape "from any form of servitude or tribute to lord or state" in the sixth century BCE.[5] The term itself combines *demos* (the people) with *kratia* (rule) as *demokratia:* "rule by the *demos*, the mass of ordinary adult male natives."[6] It seems to have arisen primarily as a derogatory term, used by the aristocracy as a term of contempt for the abilities of the "ordinary" people to rule themselves. The struggle for Athenian democracy nevertheless resulted in the "emancipation of the serfs" during Solon's reforms in the 590s BCE, and the creation of a "Council of 400," which afforded the small landowners and the *thetes,* the non-landowning foot soldiers, some influence over government decision making.[7] The main governing council, the Areopagus, remained restricted to the richest (male) citizens, but Solon's reforms helped to constitute the nascent Athenian *demos,* creating a sense of the people as a collective body whose allegiance was not just to kinship or religion but also to the constitution of the community as a collective political entity.

Moreover, Solon (638–558 BCE) created a criminal court, in which any ordinary citizen could seek justice against any other, regardless of class or kinship. The importance of this court cannot be overstated. As Ellen Wood puts it: "Crime was now defined as a wrong committed against a member of *the civic community,* not necessarily a kinsman; and the individual Athenian had the initiative as citizen, while the civic community, in the form of citizens' courts, had jurisdiction."[8] The point is that these early concessions to the democratic sensibility created a sense among the lower orders in Athens that they were citizens, together with the wealthy, that in formal terms at least they were equals to those who had traditionally ruled them.

This gave added momentum to the struggles between the *demos* and the elites, which continued long after Solon's initial reforms. Athenian politics, consequently, saw aspiring political rulers increasingly seeking the support of the "people" in order to consolidate their power base in society. One of these rulers, Cleisthenes, allied himself with the *demos* for this purpose and in so doing instituted constitutional reforms that strengthened the role of ordinary citizens, furthering their sense of themselves as a political entity and weakening the role of the traditional ruling caste. Cleisthenes's most important reform was the division of the polis into "tribes," based not on kinship or blood but on geography. These "tribal" areas were then subdivided into *demes*, essentially local districts in which citizens could meet and debate public matters.[9] The *demes* then became the basis of elections to the "Council of 500," the body that set the agenda for the ruling assembly, which met around forty times a year (as many as 6,000 citizens may have attended any particular session), while the council met almost daily. Cleisthenes also expanded the jurisdiction and importance of the "people's court," which would develop into the primary institution for checking the power of ambitious politicians (for example, through the practice of ostracism in which the fall from favor would be met with removal from office and exile) and into one of the most important democratic institutions of the fifth century BCE. Cleisthenes's reforms are thus perceived as "the single most powerful push towards the concept of participation in the history of Athenian democracy."[10]

For the next two centuries, this democratic structure and its participatory ethos was a significant feature of Athenian life, with only two brief oligarchic revolutions (in 411 and 404 BCE), both primarily reactions to defeats in the Peloponnesian Wars. Under Pericles (495–429 BCE, in power 461–429 BCE), power was shifted away from the more oligarchic Areopagus to a "Council of 500" and the court system, and the latter took on increased political functions. Moreover, Pericles initiated pay for the council and the juries, thereby making it possible for poorer citizens to participate. In this way, the jury courts became especially important in holding the political leaders and magistrates accountable to the *demos*.

In this broad context, the Athenian democracy of the fifth and fourth centuries also produced a remarkable body of philosophical and systematic reflection, including a number of literary genres engaging in the examination of politics and government.[11] It saw, for example, the Sophists, a diverse group of teachers and philosophers, traveling from city to city teaching people how to think democratically, how to use rhetoric to make strong arguments for their views, and how to think about the crucial philosophical issues underpinning the great political issues of the day—in particular the question of law in a democratic society, for example: if a democracy has the power to make laws that people are obligated to obey, what does this mean for natural and religious law? Questioned too was the capacity of social and political beings to control their own fate in a democratic society, for example: what are the possibilities and limits of human agency? Raised also in distinctive ways were questions of ethics, of how one might live a virtuous, ethical life in a democratic society. Religion continued to occupy an important space in the Athenian democracy, but it no longer represented an unquestioned, unchallengeable ethics. Participation in political decision-making processes also now created ethical quandaries, obligations, and principles. In a democratic society, therefore, was "virtue" not something that could be understood in different ways, in ways no longer limited to the superior knowledge and reason of the elite?

Many of these questions continue to characterize the democratic debate in the contemporary era in one form or another, and an ethos of social and political equality continues to animate much democratic practice around the world in the twenty-first century. But as indicated above, from its Athenian beginnings, the theory and practice of democracy was an issue of fierce contestation. Pericles—whom Thucydides describes as the foremost and most powerful Athenian of the classical democratic era[12]—spoke in positive terms of its significance in creating both a moral and a political community concerned with democratizing public life. In his Funeral Oration, thus, he proposed:

> We are the only people who regard a man who takes no interest in politics to be leading not a quiet life, but a useless one. We are also the only ones who either make governmental decisions or at least frame the issues correctly, because we do not think that action is hampered by public discourse, but by failure to learn enough in advance, through discourse, about what action we need to take.[13]

From this perspective the good democratic society is underscored by the practice of participatory politics and when ordinary citizens, not just the elite, take an active part in how society is governed. For Pericles, this also helped in the creation of a more educated and politically astute populace and a more inclusive and complete society in general. Aristotle (384–322 BCE), an admirer of Pericles, would echo this point and indicate further its broader social benefits when he argued, in the *Politics*, that the deliberation of everyday citizens was more likely to produce better decisions for society as a whole than a reliance on an elite, no matter how educated or knowledgeable (despite restrictions on citizenship to free adult males with the leisure to participate in deliberations, effectively ruling out not only women, slaves, and metics (resident aliens) but also much of the producing classes).[14] On the other hand, Plato, regarded as the "father" of the conservative (and reactionary) perspective on the Western democratic narrative, responded to the democratic ethos and the prospects for political participation of the *demos* quite differently. In book 8 of his *Republic*, for example, he describes the Athenian democratic culture as one centered on a major misperception about both the nature and capacity of the *demos*, a misperception that led not to an enlightened citizenry and sound government but to destructive notions of equality and social freedom, the elevation of ignorant opinion over truth, and the tyranny of the uneducated mob.[15]

This ancient contestation goes on in regard to the meaning and implications of democratic ideas and practices, with many influential "democratic" thinkers continuing, to one degree or another, to maintain the skeptical Platonic view on the "democratic ethos" and the political rule of the majority. We touch on some elements of this thinking below (e.g., in Tocqueville). Suffice it for now to say that this brief sojourn into classical terrain is meant to indicate something of the historical and intellectual context within which the struggles for democracy began in the era of the Greek enlightenment. It is important to note also that, for the most part, this struggle was effectively lost for "democrats" for millennia, as modern Europe came to be through seemingly endemic conflicts involving feuding elites, territorial disputes, religious wars, and so forth. The notion of the "people" (as menacing mob or as vehicle of historical emancipation) remained visible through all of this,[16] but it is not really until the early modern era (seventeenth century) that the democratic ethos and the agitation for political democracy again becomes a significant historical and intellectual factor.

VIGNETTE 2: DEMOCRACY AS A MODERN ETHOS OF POPULAR SOVEREIGNTY

For really I think that the poorest he that is in England has a life to live as the greatest he; and therefore truly, sir, I think it's clear, that every man that is to live under a government ought first by his own consent to put himself under that government.[17]

This was the view of Colonel Rainsborough, a spokesman for the Levellers, proclaiming the principle of popular sovereignty during the Putney Army Debates in 1647.[18] The Levellers were a group of writers and political activists connected to Oliver Cromwell's New Model Army during the English Civil War. In addition to engaging in the Putney Debates (in which army officers debated the new constitution), they published and distributed numerous books and pamphlets, including the influential *An Agreement of the People* in 1647. The Leveller group was quite soon after stripped of its power and influence, but its significance in the present context is clear enough—as modern articulators of the democratic ethos and of the striving for a democratic political structure as the necessary foundation of the "good" society.

For Rainsborough, the good English society of the seventeenth century was one that included "the poorest he" and "the greatest he" as part of a single community and with all imbued with the right to consent to the government under which they lived. This was still by no means a comprehensive democratic appeal—there was no mention of the poorest "she"—but there is a sense here of the crucial part to be played in the good modern society by the "common people" as a political collectivity capable of, and deserving of, the rights and obligations of citizenship. For all this, Rainsborough, in seventeenth-century England, did not argue for either political or economic equality per se, but emphasized rather the need to respect the ordinary people as an integral part of the collective body politic—as the foundation of a "Commonwealth," in Hobbes's terms, that would come to inspire ways of thinking and behaving in society that might be fashioned into a democratic expression of popular sovereignty. In this sense, the perspectives of Rainsborough and the Levellers represent another historically specific and culturally infused articulation of the democratic ethos and its possibilities in a complex, volatile social setting.

Likewise, Montesquieu, writing in early and middle eighteenth-century France, defines democracy in terms of its principle—equality—and its spirit—civic virtue. In *The Spirit of the Laws*, consequently, Montesquieu stresses the significance of a "civic virtue" in the pursuit of a democratic society based on liberty, freedom, and equality. This is no easy task, he acknowledges, because it requires as its guiding principle the willingness to sacrifice individual self-interest for the collective interest of "the people" as a whole—an idea that was threatened in the eighteenth century by a thrusting bourgeois culture and an emergent liberal-capitalism that was for many Enlightenment thinkers the keystone of the democratic future.[19] Realizing the call to civic virtue, the revolutionary events of 1789, and the aftermath, prompted both a more radically tinged invocation of the democratic ethos and a more profound sense of the problems it faced in modern political practice. For the more conservative Montesquieu, the best that one could hope for in this modern context was a freely elected liberal republic, founded upon a binding constitution that ensured a separation and balancing of administrative powers (between the executive, the legislative, and the judicial) in order that the influence of any one power or class or set of interests could not exceed that of the others.[20]

A century later, another French aristocrat with democratic sympathies, Alexis de Tocqueville, thought he had seen the ultimate model of a republican democracy in action in the United States, where, he believed, an individualist ethos and a democratic ethos were indeed being successfully fused in a "new world" context beyond the class stratification and feudal mind-sets of the European ancien régime. The United States became, for Tocqueville, the new symbolic reference point for the democratic imaginary. Citizens in America manifested a democratic spirit within them, he wrote, while praising their passionate belief in both individual liberty and social equality as intrinsic to their great republican adventure. But he, like Montesquieu, maintains that the very characteristics that gave such substance and strength to the U.S. republic could also undermine and destroy it without powerful and respected institutions to ensure "civic virtue."

The problem with the democratic ethos of social equality and the "sovereignty of the people," he proposes, echoing Greek skeptics from the ancient era, is that it leads to the notion that the "people" must rule, and, therefore, any dissent to the rule of the majority must be suppressed—to maintain "democratic" order. The solution for Tocqueville, as for Montesquieu, lay in cultivating civic virtue, which he considered difficult to cultivate among the lower classes, and therefore, he argues that "universal suffrage is by no means a guarantee of the wisdom of the popular choice."[21] The best solution was visible in New England, "where education and liberty are the daughters of morality and religion, where society has acquired age and stability enough to enable it to form principle and hold fixed habits," and therefore, "the common people are accustomed to respect intellectual and moral superiority and to submit to it without complaint."[22] Otherwise, governmental institutions need to be balanced and calibrated to ensure rule by the indirectly elected Senate, of "eloquent" and "distinguished" men as an important counterweight to the "vulgarity" of the directly elected House of Representatives. This kind of social and class balance, he maintains, is important more generally in reducing the risk of the "tyranny of the majority" in modern societies and of the American republic "perishing miserably among the shoals of democracy."[23]

Marx, of course, took a more radical approach to all of this in the nineteenth century and, amid the social misery of the industrial revolution in Europe, had little time for the views of French aristocrats on what the good democratic society should be like. Nor was Marx persuaded by the argument that the millennia-old struggles for liberty, freedom, and equality depended upon a system of checks and balances in either liberal republican or parliamentary systems. Indeed, for Marx, these systems, and these institutions, actively worked to enhance class privilege and an ethos of market exploitation and, as such, sought to undermine democracy rather than to protect it. In Marx's early critiques of German liberalism, for example, he castigates liberal parliamentary reformers who sought democratic political emancipation on the basis of free parliamentary elections.[24] A genuine "sovereignty of the people," he contends, can only be achieved when notions of "civic virtue" are infused with class consciousness, when there is radical social restructuring, and when the economic means of production are in the hands of the working class. And Marx had more faith in the democratic commitments of the (class-conscious) majority, following its defeat of the liberal-capitalist system, to resist any descent into tyranny under the "dictatorship of the proletariat."

There is a good deal of ambiguity in Marx's writings on this postrevolutionary phase, but given the dialectical framing of his thinking in general, the move to proletarian democracy is perhaps best understood as a first step in an enhanced intellectual and political trajectory for humankind—from the basic struggles of the masses for democratic freedom to increasingly higher forms of communal solidarity—in which social and productive relations would be increasingly infused with a democratic ethos. For some, of course, this is simply utopian speculation, for others, including some of those touched on above—the Zapatistas in the mountains of Chiapas, the peasants and workers in the Basque collectives, and the millions of poor barrio and favela dwellers throughout the pink-tide states of Latin America—it provides a democratic imagery of aspiration and opportunity and collective triumph over great odds and, in particular, over the perceived "false democracy" of the neoliberal world order.

VIGNETTE 3: THE ACCOMMODATION OF DEMOCRACY AND LIBERALISM

As indicated above, the liberals and republicans who came to power through the revolutions of the seventeenth and eighteenth centuries viewed democratic agitation based on popular sovereignty with skepticism and concern. They endorsed the principle that all legitimate political authority derived from the consent of the governed but were loath to endorse fully the proposition that "the people" therefore had a right to govern per se. Instead, liberals accepted the reality of modern democratic politics but only if their interests were protected by republican constitutions of the kind envisaged by Montesquieu and Tocqueville. In fact, most of the thinkers whom we now think of as constructing the modern tradition of American democracy felt this way. James Madison, for example, was concerned that direct political participation by the people would threaten the principles of private property and would lead to intolerance of minority opinions. Thus, half a century before Tocqueville's conclusions on the issue, Madison was echoing Plato's misgivings about the rule of the majority, proposing in *Federalist* no. 63 (1788) that the indirectly elected Senate was "necessary as a defense to the people against their own temporary errors and delusions" and acted as "a safeguard against the tyranny of their own passions."[25] More immediately, Madison and other U.S. "founding fathers," such as Alexander Hamilton and Thomas Jefferson, were following the intellectual lead of John Locke, in particular, who in his influential writings on the new liberal world of the seventeenth century had endorsed an indirect representative form of democratic legislature that above all protected private property.[26]

This was a theme that was even more evident by the nineteenth century as liberal-capitalist societies sought to pay due respect to the principle of popular sovereignty while diluting the passions and energies of the masses that Marx and other radicals sought to capture for revolutionary purposes. Here the notion of "representative democracy" had both structural and ideological significance, in splitting up the "mob" into geographical (electoral) districts and in placing greater emphasis on the role of political parties as the primary conduits through which their interests and desires might be coherently channeled into government. But liberal government could not contain the energies and passions of popular sovereignty so easily. Most obviously, while democracy implied equality, capitalism required inequality, and increasingly, as the promise of "trickle down" proved illusory for the great majority of people, the demands for equal rights and more equality in the distribution of wealth also increased. Nor was it as easy to resort to the notion of "the rule of the law" as an objective foundation for ameliorating this democratic surge or, indeed, to the "neutral" or "balancing" institutions of the state. For *homo economicus* (capitalism's "economic man"), the law was understood as a bulwark against threats to private property and a protector of liberal civil society within which market relations and the pursuit of individual self-interest could be legitimately carried out. For some of those reimagining themselves in democratic terms, however, the law was simply an ideological mechanism by which the capitalist state ensured minority privilege and free-market exploitation. For many others, less radically inclined, the law acted as Solon and Cleisthenes intended it should, as the institution that most obviously manifested the ethos of democracy—ensuring that, all other evidence to the contrary, "Jack (or even Jill) was as good as his master."

Either way, liberal capitalist governments were forced to respond to the demands and expectations of the poor and the working classes as they became increasingly imbued with the democratic ethos. And, much to the chagrin of Marxists, in particular, liberal capitalism adapted, to become a more inclusive form of "social democracy," which saw "mixed economy" systems emerge to (partially) regulate the capitalist market while introducing progressive social policies and welfare programs to ameliorate its worst excesses. This proved to be a highly successful strategy in staving off the ideological extremes of left and right, and after World War II in the United States, the UK, and parts of Western Europe, variations on Keynesian social democracy were instituted as a means of simultaneously accommodating the desires for democratic collectivity and free-market individualism. It was this Keynesian compromise that effectively defined the social democratic world order until the mid-1970s, when, confronted by the twin specters of stagflation at home and a multitude of problems globally (e.g., Vietnam and OPEC), there was a powerful and ultimately successful challenge to the social democratic compromise in the major Western states—from neoliberalism—and an agitation for a return to a minimalist "market democracy."

As indicated at the beginning of the chapter, neoliberalism views democracy and the democratic ethos as dependent upon market principles and an individualist, entrepreneurial attitude to the complex issues of modern society and politics. This perspective has become evident, too, as neoliberalism has become a major influence on the theory and practice of the global political economy since the 1990s and increasingly since the end of the Cold War.

GLOBALISM AND "NEOLIBERAL DEMOCRACY"

In the wake of the Cold War, neoliberals invoked democracy as the keystone of the triumph of modernity, capitalist economics, and Western political culture—associating democracy with a mode of thinking and behavior in which a free-trade value system provides the necessary conditions for individual and social freedom. In more philosophical terms, neoliberal democracy seeks to save the modern world from the disasters that befell it at the end of the Keynesian era (too much: public spending, welfare, state involvement in the economy) by formalizing and attenuating it, that is, by stripping it back to individualist "economistic" foundations. The core values of democracy, thus, liberty, freedom, and equality, can, in neoliberal terms, be best realized in (neoclassical) economic terms, in the realm of private choices, freely and rationally made. Consequently, democracy becomes synonymous with capitalism and free-market principles and collectivist approaches with antidemocratic "tyranny" (the USSR) at worst and "failed" (Keynesian/socialist) societies at best.

We discuss this issue in more detail in chapter 2. For now, the metaphorical flourishes of Michael Mandelbaum indicate the nature of the neoliberal imagination when it comes to democracy in the current era. Thus, in Mandelbaum's terms, the people of the world have chosen the free market and Western-style democracy since the end of the Cold War because they believe that "the market is to democracy something like what a grain of sand is to the pearl that an oyster contains: the core around which it forms."[27] More prosaically, capitalism and democracy go together because "the effective workings of free markets produces wealth, and wealth supports the two principal features of democracy: liberty and representative government."[28]

At the core of this image of "representative democracy" is the election process, the crucial legitimating agency of neoliberal democracy because it gives the ordinary people what they want—the opportunity, at regular intervals, to participate in the modern political process in the way that modern democratic theory insists upon. More precisely, from a neoliberal perspective the electoral process—minimally understood—is all the modern *demos* wants from its representative system. Or, as Mandelbaum puts it, "representative democracy avoids, for most citizens, the problem that Oscar Wilde identified with socialism—that it takes too many evenings."[29] This presumption, about the political passivity of the contemporary masses, is not derived from the "false consciousness" notions associated with Marxism nor the more sophisticated hegemonic theme of Gramsci. Instead, from the perspective of Friedrich Hayek or Milton Friedman, the modern aspirational voter is naturally less interested in "political" participation, per se, than in "economic" activity, in the pursuit of a materialist self-interest that satisfies a more immediate and more profound rationality in the ongoing pursuit of security and prosperity. What is "irrational" from this point of view are the attempts by people seeking to overturn this natural order by radically changing the political system that affords so many people the opportunity to engage successfully with the free market. On this basis, a naturally functioning democracy has a particular meaning for neoliberals, and not surprisingly, it is a minimalist meaning. More precisely, neoliberalism favors a "polyarchic form of democracy"—a minimalist form that effectively allows a small political elite and powerful corporate sectors to rule, while emphasizing the electoral process and the competition between (liberal capitalist) political parties as integral to the "sovereignty of the people" theme. We explore this process and its ideological legitimation a little further in chapter 2, in relation to twenty-first-century American society in particular but also in terms of the globalizing of the polyarchy model in U.S. foreign policy (e.g., in Iraq) and in neoliberal globalization per se.

In this regard, the long-standing concern about the "irrationality" of more emancipatory forms of democracy is readily apparent, as indeed they have been in Western engagements with the global periphery for decades. It was integral, for example, to the findings of the Trilateral Commission in the 1970s, which concluded that the end result of "radical" democratic thinking, and the misplaced desire for rule by "the people," had seen modern societies faltering under an "overload of democracy," which effectively destroyed economies and created political expectations that could not be fulfilled—thus leading to social dislocation and governmental crisis. This was a particularly acute problem in the Third World, it was argued, where "socialist" influences were stirring up radical democratic expectations and anti-Western sentiments. If order was to be restored in such circumstances, insist Samuel Huntington and his Trilateralist colleagues, the tendency toward "too much democracy" needed to be thwarted and elite rule restored. This would then improve the conditions by which capitalist markets might operate unhindered and respect might be increased for Western (particularly U.S.) power and global leadership.

The work of Huntington and the Trilateral Commission in the 1970s is important in the present context, as a thematic bridge between the dominant Cold War meaning of democracy in the West and the post–Cold War neoliberal representation of it. It actually is of enhanced significance because it is located also at the intersection between neoliberalism and the neoconservatism that was to become so crucial to the U.S. global "democracy promotion" strategy during the Reagan era (1981–1989) and, most explicitly, during the presidency of George W. Bush (2000–2008). The neoconservative critiques of democracy, particularly U.S. democracy, were already evident in the early 1970s as part of an ongoing confrontation with the counterculture movement, those protesting the Vietnam War and the "new left" in general.[30] The neoconservative position, simply put, was that throughout Western societies the generation of the 1960s, prompted by the delusions of grandeur associated with democratic notions of social and political equality and the "people's" right to rule, had descended into a hedonistic, disrespectful "mob" that was now threatening traditional (elite) rule, American and Western culture, and the systemic dominance of Western power and status in the world.

Integral to this critique was the view that capitalism, as a core Western and democratic value, was crucial to the resuscitation of the good modern society, that while its "autonomous individual" theme could, as Tocqueville and others noted, threaten "civic virtue," its entrepreneurial discipline and aspirational philosophy were important in channeling mass behavior away from political radicalism.[31] This is a theme that has remained intrinsic to the globalizing of neoliberalism (and a less influential neoconservatism) in the current era, as advocates of neoliberal globalization have reworked the neoclassical imagery of the good "economic" society popularized by Milton Friedman and others and the "triumphalism" of post–Cold War neoconservatives such as Fukuyama. This has been the case most notably in the support given to regimes around the world that have embraced the neoliberal free-market doctrine while retaining political control in (often brutal) minority hands in variations on the polyarchy theme (e.g., China, post-Soviet Russia, Saudi Arabia). On the other hand, there has been condemnation and relentless intervention in the affairs of societies that have sought to break down elite rule and replace it with a form of democracy that takes the "sovereignty of the people" notion more seriously (e.g., Venezuela, the pink tide generally).

In the introduction, we touched on some of the negative reactions around the world to this kind of discrepancy in neoliberal democracy. At the core of the neoliberal world order, for example, in the United States and the UK, there has been disquiet by a whole spectrum of people concerned by another discrepancy—between the extraordinary wealth and increasing privilege of minorities favored by a free-market environment—and the fate of great majorities structurally and ideologically abandoned by the neoliberal system. In the midst of the resultant social dislocation, serious questions are again being asked about what democracy means in such a situation. The protests of the Occupy movements with their representation of a society split between the rich "1 percent" and the struggling "99 percent" pose this question in simple but profound terms, as do the many challenges to the neoliberal model of democracy from areas far beyond the core neoliberal states. In Latin America, the meaning of democracy has been a question of particular significance in the continent-wide rejection of the neoliberal invocation of it. Consequently, different kinds of democratic imagery have been invoked from that to be found in the neoliberal "economistic" variant, and different kinds of democratic ethos (radical, collectivist, indigenous, etc.) have been expressed in the ongoing contestation with neoliberal globalization. In chapter 3, the "Bolivarian" ethos integral to Venezuela's contestation over the real meaning of democracy will receive detailed examination. In chapter 4, we examine three more situations—in post-apartheid South Africa, in the "shining" India of the post-1990s period, and in post-Soviet Russia under Yeltsin and Putin—as further examples of the struggles over democracy in the neoliberal era. In the chapter now to follow, however, we turn in much more detail to the theory and practice of neoliberal democracy in order to explain more precisely what it stands for, what some of its implications are in practice.

CHAPTER 2

NEOLIBERALISM AND DEMOCRACY

DEBATE, CONFLICT, AND CONTESTATION IN THE CURRENT ERA

This chapter examines some of the most significant current debates on democracy. It suggests, as an organizing principle for the discussion to follow, that democracy has always been and remains a contestable concept and practice and that to understand democracy one needs to understand this contestability in its historical, intellectual, and political context. Consequently, in the current era, the nature and implications of democratic politics and democratic governance must necessarily be located as part of a larger contemporary debate over neoliberalism and the neoliberal world order within which, to an overwhelming degree, the debate over democracy now takes place.

The fate of democracy under neoliberalism is particularly complex, and its contestability is particularly fierce. This is because neoliberalism projects its theory and practice as entirely compatible with democratic principles and practices while its critics argue that neoliberalism is, by definition, antithetical to these principles and practices. The critical argument, more precisely, is that the neoliberal image of democracy is, at best, severely limited, and that for the most part it represents the interests of corporate capitalism, of the major states in the global community, and of a transnational elite able to take advantage of the educational, cultural, and market opportunities intrinsic to neoliberal globalization.

The neoliberal attitude toward democratic freedom, for example, was captured most incisively by Karl Polanyi more than sixty years ago, when he spoke of the perspective of Friedrich Hayek, one of the founding voices of neoliberalism, as ultimately, the "freedom for those whose income, leisure and security need no enhancing," as against those looking to "democratic rights to gain shelter from the power of the owners of property."[1] Another dimension was added to this debate by Franklin Delano Roosevelt, who, pondering the devastation of the Great Depression of the 1930s, affirmed a particular meaning to democratic society, in which social justice is an intrinsic factor and in which democracy is "meaningless in the face of economic inequality."[2]

In taking a similar stance in this book, we do not seek for a moment to idealize democracy. We acknowledge that it has never existed in a pure form, devoid of power politics, ideology, or social injustice. We acknowledge too that an idealized notion of direct or classical democracy is unfeasible, even though our preference is for a "popular" democracy with broad emancipatory goals and practices. From this perspective, democracy can be said to exist where the dispersal of political and economic power is dependent upon the decisions made by an informed and freely participating majority and where democratic participation is understood as part of a process designed to change unjust political and economic structures and relationships.

We therefore agree with Lakoff and Smith, who emphasize the shared social responsibilities and obligations of a functioning democracy in the twenty-first century. Democracy, they insist, must be a public enterprise, not a private enterprise. What this means, more precisely,

> is that there is no such thing as a "self-made" man or woman or business. No one makes it on their own. No matter how much wealth you amass, you depend on all the things the public has provided—roads, water, law enforcement, fire and disease protection, food safety, government research, and all the rest. . . . Public life depends upon recognition of our equal humanity. This is why Democracy is, and must remain, public.

To the very rich, they suggest, "the only question is whether you have paid your fair share for all we have given you."[3] It is in this broad context that we suggest here that while neoliberal democracy represents itself in the participatory and social-justice terms often associated with it, this is neither its purpose nor its actuality. Instead, we suggest, a neoliberal democracy is both intellectually and structurally designed to serve the interests of the capitalist market and of a systemic status quo that dominates global society in the early twenty-first century, a status quo that does not seek to privilege genuine political participation and social justice but profit maximization and corporate elitism. In this regard, democracy in a neoliberal context is, at best, a severely limited form of "market democracy" and is riven with antidemocratic tendencies and motivations.

In this regard, neoliberal globalization is not only an economic ideology but also a broad political project that aims to create a social and cultural environment supportive of corporate interests. It is, in this sense, a political and normative project designed to create a particular kind of world and particular kinds of democratic citizens. As Wendy Brown puts it, "Neoliberal rationality . . . involves extending and disseminating market values to all institutions and social action," and "all dimensions of human life are cast in terms of market rationality." Further: "Neoliberalism does not simply assume that all aspects of social, cultural, and political life can be reduced to such a calculus; rather, it develops institutional practices and rewards for enacting this vision . . . through discourse and policy promulgating its criteria, neoliberalism produces rational actors and imposes a market rationale for decision making in all spheres." Brown goes on to argue that neoliberalism seeks to transform democracy into a formal shell, in which individual citizens become effectively passive recipients of an economic rationality as political "common sense." A neoliberal democracy thus encourages

> the extension of economic rationality to all aspects of thought and activity, the placement of the state in forthright and direct service to the economy, the rendering of the state tout court as an enterprise organized by market rationality, the production of the moral subject as an entrepreneurial subject, and the construction of social policy according to these criteria.[4]

Integral to this neoliberal perspective, unsurprisingly, is the desire to globalize its economic rationality, its entrepreneurial subjectivity, and its limited market democracy. And while democracy has many times before been globally prescribed (e.g., via colonialism and modern "just war" doctrines), neoliberalism utilizes the great technological achievements of the current era to radically compress time and space in the quest for a single global-market society in which free trade and free movement across borders of people, goods, services, and ideas are seen as the foundation of liberty and freedom and in which the nation-state becomes the facilitator and protector of market freedom. In this global quest, the traditional liberal discourse of democracy and the promise of participatory politics is a crucial legitimating factor. How else, for example, can the diminishing luster of the "trickle down" theory be sustained among peoples, cultures, and communities witnessing the widening gaps between rich and powerful minorities and poverty-stricken majorities?

This is a theme we will return to, in detail, in chapters 3 and 4 in particular. In this present chapter, we touch upon it shortly in relation to a form of democracy known as "polyarchy," which, we suggest, following Sheldon Wolin's lead, is most appropriate when considering the issue of democracy in the United States, in many ways the exemplary site of neoliberal power and influence in the world. Suffice it to say for now that when the U.S. political elite speak of democracy promotion and when its economic elite enthuse about the globalizing of democracy, it is the polyarchal form of democracy they refer to—a limited, "managed" democracy in which minority interests are protected and enhanced even while a formal and often extravagant fealty is paid to the rule of the majority, primarily via the election process. We look at events in Iraq, in particular, as an example of a globalized polyarchy in action as part of the U.S. democracy-promotion strategy.

More immediately, the discussion to follow explores the neoliberal phenomenon and its attitudes to democracy in detailed intellectual terms. It asks what its major ideas are, how it operates in practice, and how it came to its hegemonic status in the contemporary era.

NEOLIBERALISM: THEORETICAL FOUNDATIONS

Like everything else concerning the debate over neoliberalism, the issue of its nature, origins, and rise to global prominence is contentious. But in theoretical terms, the character and motivation of the neoliberalism that has dominated the global political economy since the 1970s can be usefully gleaned by reference to the influences upon it of Friedrich Hayek and the Austrian school of free-market economics (e.g., von

Mises), which represented its position as a corrective to socialism in the 1920s and 1930s, and, since the 1950s, by the "monetarism" of the so-called Chicago school of economics, which was implacably opposed to Keynesianism and interventionist perspectives of all kinds in the post–World War II era. The influence of Milton Friedman is particularly significant in this latter context.

The foundational philosophical components of neoliberalism are perhaps best articulated in von Mises's *Human Action* (1949), which is grounded in an epistemology of methodological individualism and in a praxeology of human decision making, which seeks to explain how individuals satisfy their fundamental needs for security and prosperity via economic calculation, that is, via the application of economic rationality to decisions matching means to ends. This essential human action is expressed most naturally and effectively, von Mises argues, in a modern capitalist system, where informed cost-benefit decisions can be made against a market-based criterion for success and failure—monetary profit. In other words, the capacity to make profit from decisions made in market competition (calculated in regard to the competitive market price) is the foundation of individual rationality and social freedom in modern societies.

Economic rationality thus (the efficient matching of means to given ends through rational calculation) is also, from this perspective, the marker of democratic progress more generally because it provides a natural and objective social space within which all market actors might operate, irrespective of their social background. Macroeconomic social planning, such as that engaged in by the Soviet Union, would distort these natural calculations, suggest von Mises and others, such as Milton Friedman, who insisted in the 1960s and 1970s that the connection between free markets and democracy is direct and logically insurmountable—free markets require social and political liberty in order that individuals are free to (rationally) choose the means to their economic ends—and this means/ends process is only available to all within a genuinely free-market environment.[5]

Governments should not intervene in this free-market environment because such intervention distorts the processes by which the natural prices of goods and services are set in competitive markets. Without genuine market competition, thus, there can be no genuine pricing system in a complex economy and no rational and efficient means to allocate capital goods productively. For von Mises and Hayek, and those subsequently to become neoliberals, this is why socialism and/or interventionist approaches are bound to fail in the long run and end up in the corrupt inefficiency of bureaucrats and central planners imposing ideological decisions upon issues of allocation and distribution and, simultaneously, upon individual liberty and democracy. This, moreover, is why the standards of living in societies that do not practice free-market principles are invariably lower than those that do and why, in Hayek's terms, collectivism, central planning, and interventionism are important features on *The Road to Serfdom* (1944) rather than democracy.

Integral to this perspective, then, is an insistence upon the marketplace as the only site in which the essential capacity for economic calculation might flourish, and in which the self-interest of competitive individuals might produce both a natural economic equilibrium and an equivalent social and political equilibrium, based on the differing entrepreneurial capacity and effort of individuals confronted with the profit imperative. The very limited notion of (market) democracy that underlies neoliberalism is perhaps best appreciated in terms of the "sovereignty of the consumer" theme, which one finds in Austrian-school debates on the correct balance between supply and demand and wages and prices in an efficiently functioning capitalist society.

Here, one encounters an image of the ultimate "consumer democracy" in which supply-side capitalism responds to the demand preferences of rationally acting individuals driven by the profit imperative. In this context "Consumers determine precisely what should be produced, in what quality, and in what quantities," and modern individuals

> are merciless egoistic bosses, full of whims and fancies, changeable and unpredictable. For them nothing counts other than their own satisfaction. . . . In their capacity as buyers and consumers they are hard-hearted and callous, without consideration for other people. . . . Capitalists . . . can only preserve and increase their wealth by filling best the orders of the consumers. . . . In the conduct of their business affairs they must be unfeeling and stony-hearted because the consumers, their bosses, are themselves unfeeling and stony-hearted.[6]

There is arguably no better statement in the neoliberal literature of a view intrinsic to it, that those living in market-based societies should not expect the kind of social justice or equity in the marketplace that socialists and liberal progressives demand. The argument instead is that this should not be expected of market-based societies. Instead, the capitalist marketplace—as the preeminent rationalized articulation of the modern human condition—is designed to allow the most entrepreneurially astute individuals to successfully achieve security, prosperity, and profit, while those less capable in this context fall behind and must take responsibility on themselves to improve their condition. Markets thus naturally produce "winners" and "losers," and while government might have a minimalist role in allaying the worst implications of this natural process (e.g., social and ideological volatility), its primary role (apart from its responsibilities on national security) is to facilitate the efficient functioning of a market democracy.

This neoliberal characterization of the rationality of the market is not necessarily a reiteration of the "unfeeling and stony-hearted" nature of capitalism invoked above. It is infused with elements of the classical liberal narrative, derived from a linear reading of modern (post–seventeenth century) Western history, in which market capitalism, despite its selfish individualistic inclinations, produces open societies committed to social and economic freedom and democratic politics. Where neoliberals tend to diverge from their traditional liberal counterparts is in their harderline adherence to market purity and their extreme skepticism regarding "mixed economies." Indeed, as the attacks increased upon the Keynesian era and "embedded liberalism" in the late 1970s, neoliberals insisted that interventionist and regulatory systems, per se, are, at best, idealistic distortions of liberal economic theory and practice and are bound to fail (as in the stagflation era of the 1970s) or, at worst, are authoritarian and totalitarian exercises in social engineering, designed to destroy the right to choose and impose collectivist ideologies, as in the Soviet Union.

For most of the Keynesian Wirtschaftswunder (economic miracle) period of rapid and sustained growth in Western societies (1945–1973), this neoliberal perspective was considered an exaggerated and rather archaic polemic and, within university-based economic communities, as the ranting of a heretic fringe unable to cope with its marginalized status. But from the mid-1970s on, as governments and analysts desperately sought answers to the questions raised by stagflation, a major shift in economic theory and practice became evident. Indicative of this shift were the presentations of the Nobel Prize in economics to Hayek in 1974 and then to Friedman (1976) and the growing influences of neoliberal approaches to government-market relations and to public policy and governance more generally.

By this time, with Friedman as its most prominent advocate, a neoliberal "monetarist" approach emerged that represented the ideas of von Mises and Hayek, and others, in contemporary terms, insisting that the seeming complexity of the historical moment had a very simple solution—the repudiation of the mixed economy and a return to market forces as the basis of the modern good society. After three decades of government interventionism, neoliberals argued, governments must get out of the marketplace in order that ailing economies might be resuscitated and a crucial entrepreneurial spirit rekindled within struggling and confused societies. Control of the money supply rather than government-induced initiatives to provide full employment must become the principal goal of budgetary policy and market competition the basis of a fair and democratic society.

In policy terms, the neoliberal mantra was again simple enough, established as it was upon three fundamental and universally applicable policy goals—the reprivatization of major sectors of the economy (e.g., transport, mining, telecommunications, manufacturing, health, and education) and of publicly owned companies and firms, the deregulation of the economic system and its key institutions (e.g., banks, industrial relations, stock market), and the general shifting of legislation and attitudes toward free-market capitalism at all levels of society. If these fundamental principles were put in place, if strict limits were imposed upon "unproductive capital" spending (e.g., on welfare programs), and, importantly, if the "distorting" power and influence of trade unions upon wages and prices were curtailed, it would be possible again, proposed neoliberals, to unshackle the genius of capitalism for the benefit of national and global communities.

A quite remarkable shift in intellectual and policy emphasis has since taken place, with many of those societies most closely associated with Keynesian mixed-economy ideas and practices (e.g., the UK and the United States) rapidly adopting the neoliberal mantra and its "radical" policy prescriptions. What was once hegemonic in economic and policy circles has been repudiated theoretically and discredited in practice. And what was only a few years before regarded as fringe-dwelling extremism has been installed at the center of the economic profession and the decision-making processes of the political class.

Since the 1980s, consequently, neoliberal theory and practice has become dominant in the global political economy. Actually, it's more precise to say that the earliest articulation of neoliberal principles, in practice, was in Chile in 1973, when the CIA helped orchestrate the overthrow of a democratically elected president (Allende) in favor of a right-wing general (Pinochet) perceived, correctly, as far more amenable to the free-market doctrines of Friedman and the Chicago school. The antidemocratic underbelly of neoliberalism was evident elsewhere in Latin America too, in the often-brutal regimes in Brazil and Argentina in particular.

In the 1980s, however, the "formal" neoliberal surge was most evident at the core of the Anglosphere—in the UK under Margaret Thatcher (1979–1990) and the United States under Ronald Reagan (1980–1988). It dominated analytical and policy agendas, also, in Australia, New Zealand, and Canada. And during the 1980s, neoliberalism became hegemonic within the major institutions of the global political economy (e.g., IMF, World Bank), where Keynesian perspectives were discarded and the original Bretton Woods regulatory institutions became the most powerful sites of a globalized free-market agenda. This agenda became commonly known as the Washington Consensus, representing the neoliberal policy prescriptions for the reconstruction of economies in the developing world, emanating from the Washington-based IMF and World Bank and the U.S. Treasury Department. Aligned with the economic "radicalism" of Thatcherism and Reaganism and imbued, philosophically, with Hayekian and Chicago-school principles about the correct relations between states and markets, it sought to privatize, deregulate, and open to market competition, economies, societies, and cultures around the world.

Intrinsic to the Washington Consensus model of development, consequently, was an insistence on the need for fiscal discipline via significant cuts to public spending (e.g., welfare, health, education programs), tax reform (via cuts to personal and corporate tax—to stimulate entrepreneurialism), the deregulation of financial markets, floating and competitive exchange rates, the opening up of developing economies to foreign direct investment and multinational corporations, and the privatization (selling off) of government-owned industries. Following the implosion of the USSR and the end of the Cold War, this neoliberal agenda was at the core of the "shock therapy" programs of the 1990s, invoked as essential to the transition from socialist central planning to free-market capitalism, in Russia and elsewhere in Eastern Europe.

The rise to global hegemonic status of neoliberalism has not resulted in the demise of the state, as some of its more zealous advocates have claimed. In the advanced economies, in particular, governments remain the agency of last resort for a whole range of societal demands and, consistent with neoliberal thinking, the crucial agency of facilitation and protection for the efficient functioning of the free market. But since the 1980s, many of the most powerful national governments around the world have severely limited the scope and range of their direct involvement in the market, adhering to the neoliberal mantra on privatization, deregulation, and market forces. In the wake of the Keynesian interventionist hegemony, therefore, governments everywhere have also embraced this mantra, disposing of trillions of dollars of state-owned assets in the charge toward privatization and market competition.

Summarizing this phenomena as it took place in the 1980s and 1990s, Yergin and Stanislaw speak of the "greatest sale in the history of the world," in which governments around the world began to privatize that which had been "public" property for so long—from steel plants to phone companies and electrical utilities to airlines and railroads. Moreover,

> all around the globe, socialists are embracing capitalism, governments are selling off companies they had previously nationalized, . . . Marxism and state control are being jettisoned in favour of entrepreneurship; the number of stock markets are exploding and mutual fund managers have become celebrities.[7]

At one level, at least, this neoliberal world order has been successful. There has been a massive expansion of financial sectors around the world, financial markets have seen significant growth, particularly in the major states, and there has been an acceleration in the process of economic globalization, as more and more domestic economies have been integrated into a global-market system of "turbo-capitalism." In this process, however, the financial growth lauded by neoliberals has largely occurred outside of "real" economies, in the world of electronic currency trading, hedge funds, and "derivatives." In the 1980s, Susan Strange and others warned of the dangers of this, emphasizing the "casino capitalism" characteristics of a financial system in which billions of dollars are traded almost instantaneously and the capacity of investors and speculators to destabilize and effectively destroy economies and societies via financial contagion (e.g., in Asia, 1997–1998).[8]

In the wake of the global economic crisis of 2008, which saw investment banks and mortgage corporations succumbing to bankruptcy and stock markets in freefall, neoliberal capitalism in general, and the celebrity status of fund managers in particular, have undergone something of a reappraisal. Indeed, since the 1990s, there has been a range of critical reappraisals going on concerning neoliberalism and its market zealotry and a number of reconfigurations of the neoliberal mantra. Some have sought to modify and humanize it and ameliorate its social consequences (e.g., in Scandinavia, Australia, Canada, etc.); some have engaged it more pragmatically, integrating collectivist philosophies with individualistic ones to best promote capital accumulation and economic growth (e.g., Singapore, South Korea, and China, in particular).[9] There are also more radical reappraisals now evident within the neoliberal world order, with some states and peoples seeking to confront and overturn its conceptual and structural influences (e.g., in Latin America; see chapter 3). In recent times, too, there has been a widespread critical response to the neoliberal age in its Anglo-American heartland, as the recent Occupy movements and continuing antipathy to neoliberal global institutions (IMF, World Bank, WTO) indicate (see chapter 6).

NEOLIBERALISM IN PRACTICE: IMPLICATIONS FOR DEMOCRACY

Much of this antipathy has to do with the increasing levels of unemployment, inequality, social dislocation, and deep insecurity associated with neoliberalism since the 1980s. Thus, whatever growth there has been in the neoliberal era, it has gone overwhelmingly to the rich world. Indeed, the gap between the richest 10 percent of the world's states and the poorest has increased by almost 50 percent over the past thirty years. In 2007, consequently, the richest 2 percent in the world owned more than 50 percent of the world's wealth, while 50 percent of the world's people owned less than 1 percent.[10] Moreover, during the period of neoliberal dominance, there has been an extraordinary concentration of wealth and power in a diverse range of states and regions around the world, from the small, mega-rich oligarchy in Russia that emerged following the neoliberal "shock therapy" of the early 1990s to the incredibly wealthy minority in China who have gained much from the "neoliberalism with Chinese characteristics" evident since the 1980s to the rise of fantastically rich entrepreneurs in Latin America and other areas of the developing world that characterized the neoliberal surges of the 1980s and 1990s.

This is not only a trend evident in developing societies. Within the major neoliberal states, the gap between rich and poor has also increased significantly under neoliberalism. There have been some winners, in the

financial sector, within the corporate CEO community, and among educated minorities capable of taking advantage of the new service industries,
in particular. However, income inequality in the OECD, for example, has
increased in seventeen of the twenty-two states (1985–2008), where the
average income of the richest 10 percent is nine times higher than the bottom 10 percent.[11] These gaps are even starker at the Anglo-American core
of the neoliberal world order. In the UK, for example, the top 10 percent
of the population is now one hundred times richer than the poorest 10
percent.[12] In broader social-justice terms, it's worth recording that approximately 10 percent of UK citizens were designated as living in poverty
in the pre-Thatcher era. But following the Thatcher neoliberal regime, in
1999, 25 percent of Britons were living below the poverty line, and 33
percent of children were in this category.[13]

The result of all this is that British political culture, as well as its
economy, underwent significant reconfiguration under the first wave
of neoliberalism in the 1980s. The political environment shifted to the
right, the unions were "tamed" following the brutal conflict with the
coal miners in 1984, belligerent nationalism again became a vote winner
(after the Falklands War), and while Britain as a whole arguably became
more affluent, in financial terms, it now had an underclass of Dickensian
proportions. The ideological point, summarized by Andrew Gamble, is
that "poverty, unemployment and disadvantage are no longer conditions
demanding remedy through government programs," even at the core of
the democratic world. The ultimate legacy of the neoliberal reconfiguration, suggests Gamble, has been a rejection of the British social democratic
tradition and an acceptance that social and economic inequality is now
"welcomed and praised, and promoted through fiscal policy."[14]

The Blair and Brown Labor/neoliberal governments sought to ameliorate this situation, with only moderate success, and even in the wake of
the financial crash of 2008 and the devastating exposure of market logics
and attitudes entailed within it, nothing seems likely to change. On the
contrary, the current Cameron government has introduced a hard-line
austerity plan for Britain's future, including further cuts to welfare provisions and social-security benefits for the poorest. The social implications
of all this were apparent enough in the Tottenham riots in 2012, and in
the various Occupy protests around the UK in 2013, where a sense of
alienation and anger at the system was palpable.

In the United States, the scenario is even starker. Between 1947 and
1979 (during the Keynesian era), the income of the bottom 20 percent of

American workers rose by 122 percent as U.S. productivity rose by 119 percent. Since 1979, however, in the age of neoliberalism, U.S. productivity has risen by 80 percent, while the income of the bottom 20 percent of American society has fallen by 4 percent. But, most significantly in this period, the income of the top 1 percent has risen by 270 percent.[15] The salary gap between workers and corporate CEOs in the United States (from a ratio of 30 to 1 in 1970 to 500 to 1 in 2000) starkly illustrates the growing gap between winners and losers in the neoliberal system and the phenomenal rewards going to the small minority of winners in this system.[16]

The more general scenario is one in which neoliberalism has accelerated in the United States. The result has been "substantial levels of social exclusion, including high levels of income inequality, high relative and absolute poverty rates, poor and unequal educational outcomes, poor health outcomes, and high rates of crime and incarceration."[17] Comparing the United States with other neoliberal societies in 2012, Timothy Noah finds that

> Among the industrial democracies where income inequality is increasing, it's much worse in the United States than it is almost anywhere else. Among 34 nations recently surveyed by the OECD, the United States got beat only by Turkey, Mexico, and Chile. That's as measured by the Gini coefficient, and including taxes and government transfer payments.[18]

Summarizing this directly in regard to U.S. democracy, Lakoff and Smith argue that, in the neoliberal era, democracy has increasingly come to mean that "nobody should care about anybody else, or take responsibility for anyone else." This, they argue, is a real threat to everything that American democracy is said to stand for and to the public goods and services that all citizens can democratically share. The results could be catastrophic for U.S. quality of social life, with "public roads and bridges: gone. Public schools: gone. Publicly funded police and firemen: gone. Safe food, air, and water: gone. Public health: gone." Under the unregulated free market and a "winner take all" mentality, the American dream is thus becoming a nightmare for increasing numbers of Americans.[19]

And yet neoliberal advocates and commentators, many from the United States, continue to represent its theory and practice as the basis of "real" democracy, indeed necessarily so. As Mandelbaum puts it, "The remarkable success of democracy, particularly in the last quarter of the twentieth century, is due to free market economics." Free-market capitalism, he argues, is the keystone of any genuine democracy, and the potential for justice, liberty, and freedom in democracies can only really be fulfilled within a free-market environment. Likewise, the desire for egalitarianism and social justice are only genuinely possible within liberal societies infused with modernist rationality and capitalist logics and attitudes. Thus:

> Genuine democracy, and in particular liberty, requires supporting [market] institutions. These cannot function properly unless the people operating them have the necessary skills and habits, which are underpinned by a particular set of [liberal-capitalist] values.[20]

And as a neoliberal cheerleader such as Thomas Friedman has made clear, neoliberal globalization necessarily speaks with an American accent. This is because in the globalized neoliberal narrative, the United States is the ultimate success story, in its casting off of stifling old-world tradition and imperialism and in its embracing of individualism, political freedom, and market forces as a liberal-capitalist superpower. Recent events (e.g., the 2008 global financial crisis) have seen even Friedman speaking in more muted terms about capitalist globalism, but his enthusiasm in *The Lexus and the Olive Tree* (1999) continues to infuse orthodox U.S. perspectives on the neoliberal global order. Friedman is aware that a perceived triumphalism concerning the relationship between the United States and globalization has raised the ire of many around the world. But, as he puts it, they should either "get on or get out of the way" as American capitalism leads a historical surge in global affairs analogous to the rise of the United States to the apex of geopolitical and social modernity. In typically pithy style, he announces, "We [the United States] want 'enlargement' of both our values and our Pizza Huts. We want the world to follow our lead and become democratic [and] capitalistic."[21]

As indicated above, Friedman's proselytizing on behalf of American capitalism and democracy is, at best, highly problematic if one ponders critically the fate of millions of ordinary Americans under neoliberalism since the 1980s. But it is important to note that while the neoliberal world order might well speak with an American accent, the global success story of neoliberalism is not totally encompassed within the American telling of it. Indeed, even where the Western developmental narrative has no historical or cultural purchase (e.g., post-Soviet Russia, China) the central premises of the neoliberal story are, nevertheless, represented as crucial to future global growth, prosperity, and "democracy."

Thus, while the United States has been the major beneficiary of it, the neoliberal world order cannot be reduced to the interests of a single state per se (however powerful), or a single elite or ruling class. A more precise comprehension of the winners in the neoliberal context would focus on a transnational or global elite who, in their various spaces and places, are able to take advantage of the social and political conditions intrinsic to a neoliberal democracy. The neoliberal variation on the Western democratic narrative is thus useful not only to U.S. ideologues invoking the "manifest destiny" theme as its rationale for global leadership but also to any number of ruling regimes in the Middle East, Asia, Africa, and Eastern Europe who can easily and successfully manipulate the free-market promises of neoliberalism to their own (antidemocratic) advantage (see chapter 4).

In this context, a major neoliberal tension becomes apparent on the question of democracy. It is that neoliberalism, in practice, is much less committed to the classical democratic narrative than it is in theory. Indeed, in practice, neoliberalism functions most effectively within a particular kind of "managed" democratic structure, while remaining inherently suspicious of and opposed to democratic perspectives that allow for the kind of participatory political behavior by the "majority" associated with the classical democratic ideal. Instead, neoliberals

> tend to favour governance by experts and elites. A strong preference exists for governments by executive order and by judicial decision rather than democratic and parliamentary decision making [and] neoliberals prefer to insulate key institutions, such as the central bank, from democratic pressures.[22]

This managed democracy project is perhaps best understood as polyarchy.

NEOLIBERAL DEMOCRACY AS POLYARCHY

Put simply, polyarchy refers to a system in which a small group actually rules, and mass participation in decision making is confined to leadership choice in elections managed by competing elites.[23] It is, in this sense, rule by an elite with "democratic" characteristics, in which democratic participation is limited to the electoral process and the simple act of choosing between elites every few years.[24] More significantly, the polyarchic notion of democracy does not acknowledge the significance of economic equality as integral to democracy. Unlike the "popular" notion of democracy, then, which proposes that political, economic, and ethical outcomes are crucial to a democratic system, the polyarchic approach is concerned only with political and institutional process. It insists that "issues of so-called economic and social democracy be separated from the question of governmental structure." Thus, "economics" (and economic inequality) is theoretically insulated from the "political" (and political critique), and for figures such as Seymour Martin Lipset and others, this notion of democracy refers to "a political system, separate and apart from the economic and social system."[25]

The significance of this radically reduced notion of democracy is clear enough, in that "there is no contradiction between a democratic process and a social order punctuated by sharp social inequalities."[26] Consequently, with its concentration solely on electoral contestation between political elites, the polyarchic definition of democracy deemphasizes the questions of social and economic inequality intrinsic to democracy's classical and early-modern articulations and suggests, instead, that the minority monopolization of wealth and power is in fact consistent with democracy—as long as there are "free and fair elections" at regular intervals.

The logic underlying this perspective derives from Joseph Schumpeter's *Capitalism, Socialism and Democracy* (1942). Schumpeter is particularly interesting in the present context because a half century before figures such as Friedman and Mandelbaum were projecting the irreducible connection between democracy and capitalism as the key to the good modern (neoliberal) society, he was invoking the same connection for (broadly) the same political and intellectual purpose. "History clearly confirms," writes Schumpeter, that "modern democracy is a product of the capitalist process."[27] More precisely, Schumpeter makes clear that the historical narrative of Western development remains intrinsic to the question of democracy. At the core of this narrative, Schumpeter places a particular sector of modern capitalist society—the aspirational bourgeoisie, who from the seventeenth century on sought freedom from traditional constraints in civil society and upon the free market but who remained wary of more radical challenges to the status quo. Thus, in any era, capitalist markets, an entrepreneurial middle class, and educated, conservative elites are the crucial components of an ordered, stable capitalist democracy, one characterized by civic and political freedoms, periodic elections, and constitutional government.

Beyond this is delusion and anarchy, delusion on the part of those who perceive the uneducated, politically disengaged working masses as capable of democratic responsibilities and obligations, and anarchy resulting from the agitation of radical democrats for the "rule of the majority." Accordingly, popular forms of democracy are neither possible nor desirable within an advanced liberal-capitalist world order. Indeed, in practice, and so that the capitalist market has the social and political order it requires to function effectively, the democratic participation of the masses is best reduced to regular elections, an institutional gesture (albeit a public and celebrated one) that helps decide which, among competing elites, gets to rule.

Schumpeter's view was popularized and developed by Robert Dahl in his *Polyarchy* (1972), which followed up his more explicit Schumpeterian viewpoint in *A Preface to Democratic Theory* (1956), where he argued that increased political participation by the masses should not be encouraged in contemporary liberal-capitalist societies. In particular, he suggests, increased political participation by those in the "lower" socioeconomic classes could destabilize the stable pluralism of U.S. democracy.[28] This sense of anxiety about the threat to order from the "uncontrollable" masses is, of course, a theme inherent to the contestation over democracy since its beginning in ancient Greece. In the 1950s and 1960s, it saw a range of scholars protesting that Dahl and his supporters were effectively promoting an old and deeply embedded antidemocratic elite theory in the guise of modern liberal pluralism.[29] More recently, French political philosopher and democratic theorist Jacques Rancière has argued that this "hatred of democracy" has become central to neoliberal politics at the end of the twentieth and beginning of the twenty-first centuries.[30]

Particularly important in this era has been Samuel Huntington, who has consistently advocated the polyarchy position, primarily regarding events in the Third World / global South, where demands for change to the status quo have often resonated with a radical democratic ethos. In the 1960s, for example, Huntington was warning of the perils of the liberal modernization-theory perspective on social progress and, in particular, the proposition that capitalist development will create politically stable democracies around the world. This is not the case, argues Huntington, insisting instead that democratic freedom must be managed if it is not to trigger social and political instability.

For Huntington, the equation is simple—elites must rule if there is to be social stability in any society. The consequences of mass rule are most dire on the global periphery, he argues, where they jeopardize the crucial economic and geostrategic interests of the United States and its Western allies. Any challenge to this rule on behalf of popular democracy, there-fore, must be eliminated or managed—by military force if necessary—if Western access to raw materials and markets is to be assured and a stable environment for investment and business is to prevail. Democratic out-comes must therefore be of a minimalist kind and configured so as to serve the local and global status quo.[31] In the 1970s, Huntington's anxiet-ies about "too much democracy" were again on display in his contribution to the Trilateral Commission's *The Crisis of Democracy* (1976). And this view is expressed in more explicitly polyarchic terms in his 1991 book on the "third wave" of democratic agitation in Latin America, Asia, and Africa, where he endorses, at best, a "minimalist-procedural" form of de-mocracy designed to take the edge off radical demands for change while leaving the socioeconomic status quo intact.[32]

There is little explicit attention paid to economics in the literature on polyarchic democracy. The latter is, after all, considered an exclusively "political" phenomenon. But in the work of Schumpeter, Dahl, and Huntington, and others, a taken-for-granted market logic underpins and directs their musings on the democratic process. At the core of their cen-tral "procedural" definition, for example, is a free-market thematic that assumes all voters to be engaged in an electoral marketplace in which the best candidate will receive most votes. In this sense,

> citizens have "freedom of choice," they can select the candidate who will govern them. This is an economic model for a supposedly democratic process. Voters can be compared to consumers involved in selecting the "product" of their choice. They do not act like citizens who participate in the polity.[33]

This is the severely limited model of polyarchic democracy advocated by Schumpeter, Dahl, and Huntington in the liberal-capitalist world. For Huntington, it is the only practical option for the global system also, if the U.S. and Western political culture is to remain dominant into the twenty-first century. In this regard, the archconservative Huntington sounds remarkably like the arch-neoliberal (Thomas) Friedman when he extols the virtues of an "American creed" as the foundations for a civilized and stable world order, a creed that takes for granted the civilizing role of free-market capitalism as much as it takes for granted the "tyranny of the mob" as the insurmountable problem of participatory democracy.[34]

It is in this regard that the theory and practice of polyarchy intersects most explicitly with the current debates over neoliberal democracy touched on above, because, as David Harvey suggests, for neoliberals,

> governance by majority rule is seen as a potential threat to individual rights and constitutional liberties. [Consequently] democracy is viewed as a luxury, only possible under conditions of relative affluence coupled with a strong middle class presence to guarantee political stability.[35]

This critique of polyarchic democracy has been updated and developed in a provocative way by Sheldon Wolin in *Democracy Inc.* (2008), to which we now turn. Recognizing polyarchic democracy not as a foundational given of the good society in a globalizing world, Wolin describes how it has actually helped to produce a "managed" democracy of the polyarchic kind that has flourished in the neoliberal era as the democratic majority in the United States has become increasingly passive and disengaged politically, with significant consequences for democracy throughout the world.[36]

NEOLIBERALISM AND "MANAGED" DEMOCRACY IN THE UNITED STATES: A CASE OF "INVERTED TOTALITARIANISM"?

Wolin's views on the nature of U.S. democracy are consistent in many ways with those of Schumpeter in the 1940s and Dahl in the 1950s, in that Wolin, too, points to an elite manipulation of power as the defining characteristic of the U.S. political system.[37] Wolin, however, is much less sanguine about this in *Democracy Inc.*, which emphasizes the crucial role played by neoliberal corporate actors and ideas in the resulting "managed" democracy. The implications of this for the American people and for U.S. society are stark, in a system in which antidemocratic elements have become increasingly systemic and neoliberal corporatism has become increasingly powerful. The results in the twenty-first century are everywhere to be seen

> in widening income disparities and class distinctions, polarized educational systems (elite institutions with billion dollar endowments versus struggling public schools and universities), health care denied to millions, national political institutions controlled by wealth and corporate power.[38]

This, for Wolin, and critics of neoliberalism in general, is entirely predictable. A neoliberal democracy, it is argued, governs for a small minority and is much less concerned about the fate of those outside of this privileged category. For Wolin, the particular polyarchic structure evident in the contemporary United States is imbued with the desire of wealthy and powerful minorities to wrench back power, privilege, and prosperity in the wake of New Deal egalitarianism, the political and cultural dissent of the 1960s, and crises in American capitalism and foreign policy since the 1970s. This is a project that is flourishing in the neoliberal era.

The nature of this struggle for American democracy, he argues, can be analogized to the struggles over "enclosure" in sixteenth-century England at the dawn of capitalist modernity. This struggle ensued over the "commons"—those areas of arable land designated during the medieval period as "open" or public land in order that peasant people could use it for food production. As the modern era emerged, however, rich landowners increasingly blocked off the open land with hedges as a means of "privatizing" it and excluding the poor from it. This action, Wolin suggests, is indeed analogous to the attempts of the contemporary rich within the United States, and elsewhere in the neoliberal era, to reverse gains made regarding the "political commons" of the modern era—democratic gains—concerning open and public access to education, health care, and welfare provisions in particular. The major consequence of this for U.S. society, he proposes, is a system of "inverted totalitarianism" at the twenty-first-century core of ostensibly the most prominent democracy in the modern world.

Wolin is at pains to differentiate between classical totalitarian systems, associated with Nazi Germany and the USSR, and life in contemporary America that, he suggests, has inverted a number of totalitarian themes as part of its elite management of democracy. Thus, whereas real totalitarianisms sought to mobilize the masses as a vanguard of often violent and destructive political change, the American inverted variant thrives on the passivity, conservatism, and political demobilization of its citizens. Similarly, while totalitarian regimes were often partly socialist in their orientations and strategies (which helped them control and manipulate the masses), the U.S. inverted system is committed to corporate capitalism and is largely indifferent to the plight of the masses. And whereas, in classical totalitarianism, there was a distinct connection between its theory (i.e., fascism) and practice (i.e., a military culture and expansionism), American inverted totalitarianism speaks in terms of liberal humanism and benign democracy—but it acts in often ruthless power-politics terms—to maintain and expand its global status, either through its market power or via its overwhelming military presence on the global stage.

This "inverted totalitarianism" is operationalized throughout the everyday workings of a managed democracy, in which a government and public-service sector, ostensibly committed to the welfare of the American people, actually operates as a top-down system of elite control wedded to the ideology and logics of a business corporation. Moreover, instead of a commitment to a democratic politics of accountability and social justice, the dominant ideology and logic in twenty-first-century America is that of the capitalist manager and the corporate administrator. And while, at face value, the democratic structures of American society remain firmly in place and the democratic rituals (e.g., elections) are regularly and extravagantly observed, the content of this democracy is depreciated by the power of an increasingly wealthy minority, by rich lobbying interests, and by a corporate media that trivializes and demeans the political process and democratic culture in general. Similarly, instead of focusing its massive resources and energy on the welfare of its people, in regard to health and education and basic infrastructure, successive American democratic governments spend trillions of dollars on planning for, fighting, and recovering from interventionist wars around the world.

In Wolin's view, this systemic scenario developed into its present form after World War II, and it became entrenched in the (post-1970s) era of neoliberalism, particularly in the period between the Reagan and G. W. Bush administrations. In this context, the Democratic Party in power has proved no real alternative, committed as it also is to neoliberal principles and the corporate management of the democratic system. Genuine change, Wolin argues, would require the development of a "popular" democratic culture, which is highly unlikely in a U.S. context where a classical democratic consciousness has never been as deeply embedded as in other regions of the world. Not surprisingly, argues Wolin, this has considerably slowed down democratic advances for those seeking change to the system (e.g., black Americans, women, and trade unions), and it has significantly alienated and pacified millions of Americans in their relationships with the system.

Neoliberalism, per se, did not really emerge until the early 1980s in the United States, during the Reagan era, in particular, as Keynesian corporatism, centered on the compromise between capital, the state, and labor, unraveled, and monetarist perspectives were utilized (somewhat inconsistently) at the base of "Reaganomics" and as part of the reassertion of American global power after Vietnam. But, as Wolin argues, during the 1950s and 1960s, the shift from a Keynesian culture back to a laissez-faire mind-set was already emerging, in the rise of a managerial class that was to transform American business and the social and political landscape as the neoliberal world order developed.

This was the "Mad Men" phenomenon in actuality, a revolution in American capitalism that saw a new breed of corporate managers emerging from business and law schools, imbued with a passion for competition, for high-risk business strategies, and profit-directed management. This became an issue of even greater significance when the business model of the "Mad Men" was transposed upon many other areas of society, including the media and cultural institutions and the education sector through university administrations. The new managerialism in education was thus exemplified when the "president trained at the Harvard business school succeeded the Rhodes scholar president" in U.S. universities.[39]

Just as importantly, the shift from Keynesianism to neoliberalism was advanced by major shifts in the political and ideological realms as a new American conservatism (a neoconservatism) emerged and reconfigured its traditional principles to embrace the free market as the site of Western freedom, liberty, and democracy. Integral to this shift were liberal intellectuals who in the early Cold War years had shifted to the right in line with the zealous anticommunism of the time. During the Vietnam War and the culture wars of the 1960s and 1970s, a further shift took place— away from the liberal mainstream and its perceived association with leftist radicalism and social democracy and toward the Republican Party, now increasingly stimulated by its neoconservative sector.

By the time that Reagan came to power in 1980, a shaky but nevertheless powerful amalgamation of forces was evident that saw the concern for traditional "values" (religion, patriotism, Western cultural pride) combined with a commitment to the free market and to the neoliberal managerialist revolution. For Wolin, "the revelatory moment came [in the 1990s] when the neo-cons joined with the neoliberal managerialists to proclaim the 'New American Century' and lay plans for the expansion of American power."[40] This was crucially significant because "imperial politics represents the conquest of domestic politics and the latter's conversion into a crucial element of inverted totalitarianism." More precisely, and in relation to the fate of contemporary democratic politics, "it makes no sense to ask how the democratic citizen could 'participate' substantively in imperial politics."[41]

By the early twenty-first century, with George W. Bush in the White House and neoconservative influences resonant within the business and foreign-policy communities, an increasingly narrow conception of democracy thus came to dominate in the United States, as its central classical terminology of liberty, equality, freedom, and social justice was either ridiculed as "utopian," imbued with a narrow economistic meaning, and/or used as a rhetoric of war and "regime change." In such a cultural environment, an inverted totalitarianism and contemporary polyarchy have become increasingly evident.[42]

All this, Wolin contends, has led to the current contempt for democracy in which governments routinely and systematically lie to their citizens. Lying, Wolin acknowledges, has always been part of government, but it has a particular salience in democracies, which require a "political culture that values and supports the honest efforts to reach judgments aimed at promoting as far as possible the best interests of the whole society." This is not the case in the age of polyarchic managed democracy, he proposes, where corporate interests prevail and where U.S. governments have become increasingly reliant on deceit to legitimate the ongoing global pursuit of geopolitical and economic hegemony. In this context, "democracy becomes dangerously empty" and increasingly receptive to appeals to "blind patriotism, fear and demagoguery."[43]

The Iraq War and the deceit of the G. W. Bush administration resonate powerfully here, of course, and a number of critics of neoliberal democracy have, in one way or another, invoked this episode as emblematic of its problems and dangers. Some have done so as part of critical engagement with the "democracy promotion" and/or "low intensity" strategy central to U.S. foreign policy since the Reagan era of the 1980s and intrinsic to the war-on-terrorism project of the Bush administration after September 11, 2001.[44]

NEOLIBERALISM AND THE U.S. PROMOTION OF GLOBAL POLYARCHY

In the 1980s, the democracy promotion theme was an intrinsic part of the anti-communist crusade undertaken by Ronald Reagan, particularly in the Third World where the United States sought to counter Soviet influence. It emanated, primarily, from the acknowledgment that supporting capitalist authoritarianism in Latin America, and elsewhere, was creating more problems than it was solving and that there was a popular and perhaps uncontrollable backlash under way by the 1980s. Consequently, and as the tide turned against once-favored oligarchs and their military backers, a reformulated democratic doctrine was constructed in U.S. foreign-policy circles.

At the core of the new democracy-promotion strategy was the invocation of polyarchy as the political mechanism by which radical indigenous forces might be controlled and the drive for social change directed toward market liberalism under the guidance of U.S.-approved elites. This intent is summarized by Robinson in terms of a scenario in which

> the demands, grievances and aspirations of the popular classes tend to become neutralized or redirected less through direct repression than through ideological mechanisms, political co-option and the limits employed by the global economy and the legitimate parameters of polyarchy.[45]

In practice, this has required support for formal democratic structures and a range of social, political, and economic programs designed to introduce, stabilize, and/or buttress the kind of democracy the United States and its neoliberal allies favor around the world—a "low-intensity" democracy for a high-intensity era of globalization. And because it is interested primarily in ideological persuasion, rather than old-fashioned state/military coercion, it has meant more subtle methods of gaining mass support in civil society. Accordingly, much of this interventionism has been aimed at influential groups such as trade unions, the media, women's groups, and political parties, rather than the state apparatus per se.

In the 1980s, institutions such as the State Department's Center for Democratic Governance and the National Endowment for Democracy (NED) under the guidance of the neoconservative Carl Gershwin, began the task of encouraging support for the new "consensus" model of neoliberal democracy. Between 1985 and 1995, another dozen new agencies were created with the specific task of promoting this particular brand of democracy. At least two main categories of state were recognized as crucial for democratic support. The first concerned programs designed to consolidate and stabilize already existing polyarchal-type regimes. In the 1990s, this included most Latin American countries under conservative civilian governments (e.g., Cristiani and Arena in El Salvador, Chamorro and Uno in Nicaragua, Callejas in Honduras, Calderon in Costa Rica, and Serrano in Guatemala) and the ex–Soviet bloc states where oligarchs and elites ruled but where the trappings of democracy (e.g., regular elections) represented a real sense of polyarchal progress. The task here was to bolster elite forces in political and civil society and further "promote" the benefits of a neoliberal economy, locally and globally.

The second major category concerned those societies regarded as in "transition to democracy," either from right-wing dictatorships to elitist civilian rule or from left-wing, socialist, or nationalist regimes to similarly structured polyarchies (e.g., in the 1980s/1990s, the Philippines, Chile, Nicaragua, and Haiti). The immediate task here was to gain influence over the major transition groups and direct their struggles in ways that preempted their radical dimensions and shaped their success toward U.S. geopolitical interests and neoliberal globalization.

The early template of success was the overthrow of the Marcos regime in the Philippines in 1985. Previously, the United States and its Western democratic allies had given Marcos unqualified support as the Philippines became a haven for transnational corporate capital in the 1970s, and, initially at least, they maintained this support when the regime cracked down on leftist forces in the early 1980s.[46] But when the brutality of the regime and the "crony capitalism" of the ruling family saw an alternative, elite-led challenge to the status quo, the U.S. moved to promote its new democratic strategy in favor of the anti-Marcos forces. The more specific task then became one of controlling the popular uprising against Marcos (via a military revolt directed by U.S. advisors and diplomats) and actively supporting the Aquino-led elite into "democratic" office. Importantly, too, the new government immediately launched a major program of neoliberal restructuring under the guidance of the NED and USAID. This paid (literal and political) dividends for those in the business and political elite, ensuring support for the new polyarchic system.[47]

In this period, and since, there have been mixed results for the "low-intensity" approach to democratic politics in the global periphery. This has been particularly so in Chile, where, by the mid-1980s, a popular movement arose against the brutality of the Pinochet regime, and the United States effectively changed sides and began (via NED and USAID) to channel aid and political support to a (mainly) civilian elite committed to the continuation of neoliberal principles and practices. In 1989, an acceptable center-left "coalition of parties for democracy" (the Concertación) took power and maintained it until 2010, when the neoliberal Sebastián Piñera, at the head of a center-right grouping, became president.

In places such as Nicaragua and Haiti, the promotion of polyarchal democracy was a more complex issue. Years of U.S. support for the brutal Somoza regime in Nicaragua could not prevent the coming to power of the leftist Sandinistas (1979), and the U.S.-directed counterrevolutionary strategy under Reagan was unable to change this situation sufficiently by coercive means. It was not until the United States changed the strategic mix (around 1987), increasing the consensual elements and pouring more money (including major bribery projects) into a conservative political elite headed by Violeta Chamorro, that success was achieved in the early 1990s, in what were described as "transparent and democratic" elections.[48] To underscore the volatility of this situation, however, history has effectively repeated itself, with the Sandinistas under Daniel Ortega regaining power in the elections of 2006.

In Haiti, years of political violence and social turmoil during the 1980s and 1990s saw different elite groups vying for power, with the United States seeking to organize and maintain a polyarchal structure of its choice. It supported the conservative Marc Bazin against the liberation theologian Bertrand Aristide in 1990 but couldn't prevent a "leftist" victory in the elections of that year in which Aristide gained 67 percent of the vote. The United States was then implicated (via the CIA) in the military coup that overthrew Aristide only a year later.[49] But in 1994, with Bill Clinton in power (1992–2000), the United States changed its allegiance again, with Clinton intervening in a chaotic Haiti, via Operation Uphold Freedom, to help reinstall Aristide, albeit now in a more tightly controlled and neoliberal-oriented polyarchy. Once again, in terms of a volatile history repeating itself, Aristide was ousted in a coup in 2004, which he alleged had been orchestrated by the United States.

Democracy promotion then has been an integral dimension of U.S. attempts to maintain its hegemonic status in the wake of the Vietnam War, in particular, and while it has not always been as successful as it might have wished, its campaign to install polyarchic democracies remains essential to its leadership of the neoliberal world order. Bill Clinton was an enthusiastic advocate of this particular kind of global democracy in the space after the Cold War. A 1993 speech by Clinton's then deputy national security advisor, Anthony Lake, made clear the central role of democracy promotion in U.S. foreign policy in the post–Cold War era.[50] Above all, stressed Lake, the era of Cold War containment should now give way to a strategy of enlargement—the "enlargement of the world's free community of market democracies." Three ambitions characterized the Clinton globalized perspective in this regard: the first, to "increase our prosperity"; the second, to "update our security arrangements"; and the third, to "promote democracy abroad."

The three were inexorably interwoven, explained Lake, because "the expansion of market-based economics abroad helps expand our exports and create American jobs." Moreover, "the addition of new democracies makes us more secure because democracies tend not to wage war on each other or sponsor terrorism." Developing this theme further, Lake outlined the principles by which this promotion of market democracy should take place, keeping in mind that "democracy and market economics are not everywhere triumphant." In this regard, it was crucial that the United States "should help foster and consolidate new democracies and market economies, where possible, especially in states of special significance and opportunity . . . [and] must counter the aggression—and support the liberalization—of states hostile to democracy and markets."

The question of how market democracy should be promoted in areas where hostility was evident is dealt with by Lake in interesting fashion because as well as giving new democracies "the fullest benefits of integration into foreign markets," the United States, he contends, must utilize other means to enlargement "through an enlarged circle not only of government officials but also of private and non-governmental groups." Private firms, he notes, "are natural allies" when it comes to strengthening market economies, and the United States has a "natural ally" in "labor unions, human rights groups, environmental advocates, chambers of commerce and election monitors" when it comes to democracy promotion in civil society. But, suggests Lake, just as defense relies on force multipliers to prevail in military struggles, so "we should welcome 'diplomacy multipliers' such as the National Endowment for Democracy" in the struggle with those opposed to neoliberal forms of democracy. By the mid-1990s, then, NED and its counterparts throughout the official and nonofficial ranks of "diplomacy multipliers" had become integral to U.S. foreign policy and its globalization strategies.[51]

It is the case also that, unlike the Reagan administration that preceded it and the G. W. Bush presidency that was to follow it, there was in the Clinton era some sensitivity toward diversity in the global order, at least to the extent that it acknowledged that "democracy and markets can come in many legitimate variants. Freedom has many faces."[52] Unacknowledged, however, is the notion that democracy might be possible without fealty to American-style capitalist markets, let alone the notion that the face of freedom might be hostile to a U.S.-led, neoliberal global order. Consequently, as Carothers has noted, while Clinton was in office, he massively increased the clandestine "diplomacy multiplier" effect of the democracy-promotion strategy, increasing funding from $100 million in 1990 to $700 million when Clinton left office in 2000, when the United States was engaged in "low-intensity" interventionism in around one hundred countries around the world.[53]

During the G. W. Bush era of the twenty-first century, the democracy-promotion strategy was further upgraded and made more explicit under the direct influence of neoconservatives in the Pentagon and White House. In particular, after 9/11, Bush invoked it as central to the "War on Terror," proposing that "it is a policy of the United States to seek and support the growth of democratic movements and institutions in every nation and culture, with the ultimate goal of ending tyranny in our world."[54] In the same vein, Condoleezza Rice in 2005 reiterated that the U.S. "mission" under G. W. Bush was to "spread freedom and democracy throughout the world."[55] More precisely, she proposed, the interventions into Afghanistan and Iraq were consistent with "the United States want[ing] to be thought of as liberators," dedicated to "the democratization or the march of freedom in the Muslim world."[56]

The template for the Bush era, of course, was the Iraq War (2003–2011) in which the democracy-promotion theme became a major rationale for U.S. military intervention. The orthodox perspective on this issue is perhaps best represented in the proposition that

> just as the eradication of malaria requires draining the swamps that harbour the mosquitoes that carry the disease, so abolishing or at least controlling terrorism, American officials reasoned, requires ending the conditions that breed terrorists. This meant replacing dictatorships with democracies.[57]

Not everyone is convinced by this particular attempt at mosquito eradication. Instead, what is represented in U.S. foreign-policy circles as a necessary strategy in the struggle to destroy terrorism and install democratic regimes is understood by many as an effective continuation of the Reagan policy—of utilizing democratic rhetoric for hegemonic purposes—albeit this time with the model of a fully blown neoliberal democracy at its core.

What this means in practice was evident enough in the attitudes and practices of the Bush administration as it sought to install a neoliberal democracy in Iraq in 2003. Consequently, in the days following the successful "shock and awe" campaign, the Iraq Coalition Provisional Authority headed by Paul Bremer announced its four priorities for the new democratic Iraq. The first, that all public enterprises were to be immediately privatized; the second, that trade barriers were to be eliminated; the third, that all Iraqi banks, firms, and businesses were to be opened to foreign competition; the fourth, that trade unions were to be banned and the right to strike outlawed for Iraqi workers.[58]

Iraqi members of the Coalition Provisional Authority protested (to no avail) that this was free-market fundamentalism, not democracy. Or, as David Harvey has put it, "the Iraqis were expected to ride their [democratic] horse of freedom straight into the corral of neoliberalism."[59] Democracy was, in this instance, what neoliberalism said it was, and the process of democracy was to be little more than polyarchy—the minimalist process by which the Iraqi people got to "choose" the (U.S.-sanctioned) elite that was to rule them, as Iraq was formally introduced to the neoliberal world order.

THE INSTABILITY OF NEOLIBERAL DEMOCRACY

Since 2003, the "democracy" strategy in Iraq has gone tragically awry. This is partly, of course, due to the arrogance and sheer ignorance of a neoconservative-inspired "regime change" strategy, imposed by the Bush administration upon a complex and inherently volatile political and cultural environment. In this sense, it was always doomed to failure and tragedy, as many warned in 2003. But, the Iraq debacle aside, there is a deeper dimension to the failure of the U.S. democracy-promotion project in many areas of the world, and it has to do with the basic instability of the neoliberal global order as it seeks to represent itself as something it is not, particularly when its misrepresentation of its nature and motivation is couched in democratic terms. In this regard, as neoliberalism's commitment to market forces and corporate profit inclines it toward statist and "crony capitalist" regimes that best serve its interests or, at best, toward a tightly managed polyarchy, it can become a powerful incitement to resistance for those genuinely seeking political freedom and social justice.

This, we suggest, is becoming increasingly evident at the periphery of the neoliberal global order, particularly in Latin America, where radical democratic perspectives have sporadically challenged the Western economic and geopolitical hegemony over many years. In more recent times, however, Latin America has become the site of concerted attempts to confront the dominant global order with alternatives to neoliberal globalization and its particular (polyarchic) variation on the democratic theme. In Venezuela, in particular, this challenge to neoliberalism has resulted in an increasingly influential reconfiguration of the dominant democratic model—as Bolivarian socialism—that explicitly privileges the poor majority and encourages greater and greater levels of social, economic, and political participation by those previously excluded from access to power and prosperity. It is to this, arguably the most radical challenge to neoliberal globalization, that we now turn.

CHAPTER 3

WHAT DOES DEMOCRACY MEAN IN THE NEOLIBERAL ERA?

THE CASE OF VENEZUELA AND "BOLIVARIAN DEMOCRACY"

The death of Hugo Chávez, in March 2013, poses a range of serious questions for Venezuela. In particular, there are questions of social and political stability in the wake of a charismatic but deeply polarizing leader. More specifically, there is the question of whether Chávez's successor, Nicolás Maduro, can hold together the extraordinary but fragile phenomenon known as "Chavismo" in the face of an inflationary economy, major infrastructural and law and order problems, and a deep and relentless hostility emanating from the large landholding oligarchs, the middle classes, and the business community in Venezuela. This hostility is not surprising. It was, after all, Hugo Chávez who, during his fourteen-year domination of Venezuelan politics, most personified the anti-neoliberal sentiment of the post-1990s era and who, via his "Bolivarian Revolution," expressed most fiercely the desire to refashion the theory and practice of democracy in Venezuela and across the Latin American continent. This hardly endeared him to those traditionally in control of the Venezuelan society and economy, who railed at policy programs designed to radically improve the living standards of the poorest in Venezuelan society. In this regard, as a Chávez government minister put it, the traditional ruling classes despised Chávez because he created a society in which "the people who clean their houses are now politically more important than them."[1]

More generally, the death of Chávez raises questions about the whole democracy debate within the pink-tide states in Latin America, which he, more than any other regional leader, encouraged and facilitated. And it was Chávez's concern to harness Venezuela's natural resources (particularly oil) for indigenous democratic purposes that sparked similar responses in many areas of Latin America and a more generalized hostility from a global corporate sector with traditional designs on Latin American markets and profitability. It also created anger and frustration within a U.S. foreign-policy community imbued with its own notions of what global democracy should look like and with traditional expectations of its dominant role in the Latin American region. In spite of continuing U.S. hostility, the end of the Chávez era raises more directly the question of the future prospects of the democratic zeal awakened by Chávez among the majority of poor Venezuelans, those who made up his support base for fourteen years and who are crucial to the continuing political success of his United Socialist Party of Venezuela (PSUV). The question more precisely is whether the structural and ideological legacy of Chávez's Bolivarian Revolution will survive and flourish among the barrio dwellers and previously disenfranchised Venezuelans without his iconic presence.

Structurally, the Chávez legacy is to be seen in the thousands of grassroots institutions—district councils, cooperatives, and local communes—established to facilitate the delivery of new social services for the poor and illiterate, principally health clinics, schools, and subsidized food outlets, and to allow the masses direct access to the levers of power and decision making as the foundation of a genuine participatory democracy. Ideologically, the Chávez legacy is apparent in the ongoing process that sees the "common sense" of the neoliberal era challenged at almost every level by the PSUV and its supporters. In its place, an adapted Bolivarian ethos is proclaimed that emphasizes human capital over its "monetarist" counterpart and that imbues the Venezuelan masses with the sense that they have both the capacity and the right to take democratic power and use it for the benefit of the poorest and the indigenous peoples, in Venezuela and in Latin America as a whole. This Chávez-induced Bolivarianism seeks to emancipate the Venezuelan masses from their poverty and disenfranchisement as the basis of a new democratic order in which an educated, politically engaged Latin American society might free itself more generally. Integral to this process is an inclusive, multifaceted attitude to the democratic process, which represents it as much more than a political or institutional project (as in polyarchy) but argues that "where the calamities of hunger and poverty exist . . . democracy is in doubt and human rights are a fiction."[2] This particular notion of democracy necessarily confronts the neoliberal world order, perceived as the corporatized projection of a global ruling class that, from Chávez's perspective, seeks to exploit Venezuela's crucial resources and undermine the development of democratic desires throughout Latin America.

The question in 2014 is whether the "Chavistas" can sustain and develop the democratic structure and ideology bequeathed by Chávez or whether their great enthusiasm for Bolivarian democracy will dissipate without his powerful presence. There are some positive signs in this regard, at least in terms of the commitment of the Venezuelan voters in the election of October 2012, which saw Chávez reelected by an impressive margin (11 percent) as president of Venezuela following a turnout of over 80 percent of Venezuelan citizens; Chávez thus received 55 percent of the vote, almost the same percentage he obtained in 1998.[3] This was a remarkable result, given that elected presidents invariably suffer an erosion of support, particularly over such a long time period and in the kind of volatile social and political environment such as that in Venezuela.

And while the Western media cried foul and alleged corrupt practices and intimidation on the part of Chávez, other responses emanating from those actually on the ground during the election process concluded otherwise.[4] From the Carter Center, for example, global experts on democratic electoral practices who concluded that the election was scrupulously fair and that, moreover, "of the 92 elections that we've monitored . . . the election process in Venezuela is the best in the world." Moreover, those sent to validate a BBC report that insisted that the intimidation of the state-owned media was the key to Chávez's victory found something else—that only 5 percent of the Venezuelan media is actually state controlled, with the great majority of TV and radio in the hands of the private sector, almost all of it opposed to president Chávez.[5]

Consequently, reported Tamara Pearson, despite the best efforts of the corporate media, inside and outside Venezuela, to denigrate Chávez, "eight million people voted for a man who stands up to U.S. imperialism.

They re-confirmed a passionate desire for a country that prioritizes humanity over profits." Similarly, and contesting the Western media's allegation that Chávez's anti-neoliberal democracy has ruined the Venezuelan economy, and was therefore bound to lose to his free-market opponent, she noted that, since Chávez took power,

> extreme poverty has dropped from nearly a quarter [25 percent] to 8.6 percent last year [2011]; unemployment has halved; and GDP per capita has more than doubled. [And] rather than ruining the economy—as his critics allege—oil exports have surged from $14.4bn to $60bn in 2011, providing revenue to spend on Chavez's ambitious social programs.[6]

In this context, there is no great mystery concerning the reasons why a clear majority of Venezuelans support the Chávez project and why, in the face of considerable odds, they might well continue to do so into the future. There is evidence too that this commitment to democracy was never entirely dependent upon support for Chávez, with the Venezuelan people on at least two occasions willing to use their democratic power against the wishes of their president (e.g., the Constitutional Referendum of 2007 and the University Act of 2009). In short, there are indications that a radical form of democracy has become embedded in Venezuela and that it could be difficult to dislodge it, either structurally or ideologically. Indeed, if Chávez's legacy is as potent as he wished it to be, this democratic radicalism could well become integral to the politics of some of his pink-tide allies in Latin America also and at the very least consolidate the strong antipathy to the neoliberal world order and U.S. leadership of it.

All this indicates that the barely concealed hostility to Chávez, evident within the Western liberal commentary on Venezuela and within the U.S. foreign-policy elite in particular, seems destined to continue. The lowest point in this whole affair was reached when George W. Bush's secretary of defense, Donald Rumsfeld, likened Chávez's Venezuela to the Third Reich, with Chávez "a person elected legally—just as Adolf Hitler was elected legally—and who then consolidated power."[7] A similar insight was offered by the Republican spokesman Connie Mack in 2010, who described the leader of Venezuela, and his counterparts in Ecuador, Bolivia, Nicaragua, and Cuba, as "thugocrats . . . [who] alter their constitutions so they can remain leaders for life."[8] And George W. Bush saw fit to distinguish between his own role in the world, as the chief promoter of "freedom, justice and human dignity," and "that demagogue awash in oil money [who] is undermining democracy and seeking to destabilize the [Latin American] region."[9]

Chávez's contribution to this particular dialogue of vilification was equally crude. He referred to George W. Bush, for example, as a "devil" and "a donkey" and a "drunkard," who dealt with the global community and Latin America in particular "as if he was the owner of the world."[10] Chávez concluded also that after a promising beginning the Obama administration was fundamentally no different (albeit a little more polite) from those that preceded it, representing Hillary Clinton, when she was secretary of state, as little more than a "blonde Condoleezza Rice."[11] Insults aside, Chávez's attitude toward the Obama administration had everything to do with Obama's perpetuation of the democracy-promotion program of the Bush administration. For the most part, nevertheless, the relationship with Obama was relatively civil, at least on the surface. But Chávez was always aware of the enhanced role played beneath the diplomatic surface, by USAID in particular, as Obama ramped up attempts to undermine the Bolivarian Revolution in Venezuela.

We explore this issue in more detail later in this chapter. Its significance here is that it sees a democracy-promotion strategy being used against a fairly elected democracy. Indeed, Venezuela has now witnessed three U.S. presidents (Clinton, Bush, and Obama) using government instrumentalities designed to project democratic values worldwide (e.g., NED, USAID) to undermine an administration that was fairly elected on five occasions and that never resorted to force in order to either retain or maintain its position. It is worth reiterating in this regard that there were fifteen elections or referendums held during Chávez's time in power (one of which he lost), but Venezuela's democracy has never been accepted by the United States. Rather, as the former undersecretary of state for Western Hemisphere affairs Peter Romero insisted, "in Venezuela you do not see a government that rules; only plebiscites, referenda, and more elections."[12] Leaving aside any (polyarchic) irony associated with this statement, it is clear that for the United States, Venezuela's democracy was never considered valid while Hugo Chávez won its elections.

Crude rhetoric aside, the often bitter engagements between the United States and Chávez's Venezuela bring into stark relief the very deep contestation over what "democracy" means in the neoliberal era. This contestation is central to the discussion to follow, which concentrates principally upon the Venezuelan alternative to neoliberal democracy, with its emphasis upon social justice and political egalitarianism as key systemic features of its Bolivarian Revolution. It provides a broad historical and intellectual account of this alternative democracy, it says something more substantial about Venezuelan democracy and its critics, and it touches on some of its implications for Latin American and global political economy more generally in an era dominated by a U.S.-led neoliberalism. It indicates finally what the Venezuela–United States conflict contributes to the question of what democracy means in the early years of the twenty-first century.

CHÁVEZ AND BOLIVARIAN DEMOCRACY: A BRIEF OVERVIEW

During the Punto Fijo era in Venezuela (1958–1998), the country was led by conservative elites who sought in the 1970s to protect important industries from the incursions of foreign capital (e.g., the oil industry). They failed to institute promised programs of social progressivism and political democracy, however, and the plight of Venezuela's poor worsened under the neoliberalism of the 1980s. Consequently, by 1989, under the presidency of Carlos Andrés Pérez, the great social and class divisions in Venezuelan society were starkly evident, with the government now explicitly supportive of its traditionally wealthy and powerful sectors and, increasingly, of international capital seeking control of Venezuela's oil industry. Indeed, within a month of his inauguration in 1989, Pérez announced his *paquete económico* in line with IMF parameters, which saw the installation of neoliberal programs and major cuts in social spending alongside an unequivocal commitment to trade liberalization, deregulation, and privatization.

The poor now faced massive increases in the price of food and transport and an even more precarious situation regarding jobs and health care. The result was the Caracazo (1989), which saw widespread riots and protests against the ruling political parties and the democratic system in general. In the wake of these protests, that saw impoverished barrio dwellers involved in rioting in downtown Caracas and middle-class suburbs, at least 1,000 people were dead and there was open resistance to neoliberalism and its promises of modernity, progress, and democracy.[13] Violent protests continued through the 1990s, reaching a peak in response to the imposition of a second wave of neoliberal austerity measures by Perez's successor, Rafael Caldera, in 1996. By 1998, consequently, 63 percent of people believed "radical change" was necessary to rescue Venezuela from neoliberalism.[14]

Chávez had already sought to intervene in this situation via a failed coup in 1992. But in the 1998 elections, his major weapons were his narrative of the Bolivarian Revolution and his commitment to a "real" popular democracy. The Punto Fijo elites, he argued, were "not defending democracy . . . [but rather] trying to defend their privileges."[15] In contrast, Chávez pledged to defend the (democratic) interests of the poorest and most marginalized in Venezuelan society. In this way, by emancipating the poorest people (*el pueblo*), he would emancipate Venezuela, per se, from its antidemocratic past and from its dependencies upon the United States and its global capitalist allies and create in the Americas a living symbol of "Bolivarian" emancipation and social justice.

There was skepticism, and widespread alarm in some quarters, at the crude populism sometimes apparent during the Chávez era, but it was always something more than just opportunistic populism. The most disadvantaged among *el pueblo* were structurally and ideologically privileged under Chávez, and where once they were ignored and marginalized, they were now given a political voice, and their concerns over housing, food prices, education, employment, sanitation, and health care were prioritized. More precisely, from its beginning, the Chávez administration sought to introduce programs of participatory democracy that involved *el pueblo* in decision-making processes at all levels of society—hence, the increased use of referenda to ask the people for their support, or otherwise, and the initiatives for local organizations in urban and rural areas to become engaged in the processes by which public officials are chosen and by which local and regional concerns can be channeled quickly and effectively to government. Hence, the two additional branches of government, created to democratically complement the traditional divisions of the executive, legislative, and judicial sectors. The first mandates the participation of *el pueblo* in the selection of the judiciary and appointment of the National Electoral Council. The second centers on "citizens power" organizations designed to be independent from the other branches of government. Its members are nominated by civil society and tasked with protecting the interests of the masses from the state. Citizens are given rights to recall elected officials, initiate laws by referendum, and promote social audits of any government activity.

The response to these efforts to increase political participation has been mixed since 1998. Great numbers of previously marginalized people mobilized to support Chávez when his radical restructuring plans were in danger, forming grassroots "Bolivarian Circles" to support his referenda proposals and to demand his return to power after the coup against him in 2002. On the other hand, there was fear and skepticism among *el pueblo* about becoming involved in a formal political system so long dominated by the traditional elites.[16] Chávez nevertheless pushed on with his participatory programs, effectively constructing a parallel governmental structure designed to give direct institutional expression to the everyday needs of *el pueblo*. Central to this process are the Communal Councils, which are tasked with creating committees and working groups to undertake social and structural projects in their neighborhoods.[17] Proposals for the funding of these projects are put to various state agencies, and the funds are deposited into communal banks and administered collectively. The Communal Councils, therefore, allow people to take an active role in planning, financing, administering, and carrying out projects in their own communities. There have been 30,000 of these councils established since 2006.[18]

Another initiative for encouraging grassroots participation in decision making saw the creation of the United Socialist Party of Venezuela (PSUV) in 2006 to provide local groups and individuals the opportunity to develop a political organization from the ground up, in ways that specifically engage the social and political concerns of the poorest citizens. By 2009, the PSUV had 6.7 million members, almost half the registered voters in Venezuela.[19] Moreover, the unparalleled numbers of the previously marginalized who attend rallies, marches, and other forms of political activity in Venezuela indicate that democratic participation has become embedded in the popular consciousness.[20] This was indicated also in a Latinobarómetro poll that showed an extraordinary rise in satisfaction with democracy in Venezuela, from 35 percent in 1998 to 77 percent in 2011.[21] The 81 percent voter turnout in the election of 2012 is perhaps the strongest indicator yet of this deepening democratic consciousness.

Important, too, in this regard are changes in the economic sphere, designed again to democratize Venezuelan society. On this issue, Chávez emphasized the need to confront neoliberalism with a new kind of economics, "based on the principles of social justice, democratization, efficiency, free competition, protection of the environment, productivity, and solidarity."[22] In practice, this has seen a range of economic changes, some emanating from government, some initiated by the broader community with government assistance. Most significantly, crucial sectors of the economy, such as steel, cement, banking, electricity, and communications, have been nationalized, as have a number of smaller companies in food production and agriculture. Many of these companies have been reconfigured into social production enterprises, whose priority now is to "privilege the values of solidarity, cooperation, complementarity, reciprocity, equity and sustainability ahead of the value of profitability."[23] This obliges these companies to dedicate 10 percent of their net revenue to "social labor" programs that benefit the communities where they are located, that give workers the opportunity to make decisions about how the money is allocated in the interests of the local community, and that provide discounted goods and services for the local populations. In this regard, Chávez directly confronted neoliberal logic in refuting the notion that every sector of modern life should be open to market principles, arguing instead that food, health care, education, and social welfare are "public goods" and must be insulated from market forces.[24]

There have been some problems with these programs, with the government deeming it necessary to expropriate companies that fail to live up to their social responsibilities. Many of these expropriations were designed to achieve what Chávez called "food sovereignty." In this regard, there has been significant success, and in 2012, state-owned companies were producing rice, coffee, cooking oil, milk, and other foodstuffs at discounted prices.[25] In a poll taken in September 2012, there was widespread support for this policy initiative and for Chávez, more generally, whose performance as president was deemed "above average" by 62.4 percent of respondents.[26]

Chávez, nevertheless, was consistently under great pressure from the middle classes and business sectors alarmed at the implications of the increasingly democratic changes intrinsic to his Bolivarian Revolution. For example, he encouraged the development of people's cooperatives that are assisted with low-interest loans, tax rebates, and preferential contracts for community-designed projects. Some of the expropriated companies have also been reinscribed as comanagement enterprises, with workers engaged in a consciously democratized workplace dedicated to the collective good rather than to capitalist first principles. After an enthusiastic beginning, with 141,000 people's cooperatives established within the first year, this project has faltered, both because of resistance from anti-Chávez forces and the lack of a consistent "democratic" consciousness on the part of those tasked with carrying out Chávez's Bolivarian restructuring programs.[27]

Central to Chávez's response to this, and other setbacks, was a massive investment in education, both to raise the basic literacy levels of

those who previously had little chance of a formal education and to install alongside the traditional education curriculum an alternative body
of political knowledge aimed at raising the consciousness of democracy
and democratic participation. As Chávez put it in 2007, the alternative
curriculum aimed to create for Venezuelans "our own collective, creative
and diverse ideology," as opposed to the "colonial Eurocentric, ideological
education," which "promotes consumerism and contempt for others."[28] In
2009, he developed this theme, proposing that a "Bolivarian" education
would prioritize the "democratization of knowledge and the promotion
of the school as a space for the formation of citizenship and community
participation, for the reconstruction of the public spirit."[29]

Education then, for Chávez, was the way in which a radical democratic
culture might become embedded in the next generation of Venezuelans,
which is why priority was given to structurally democratizing the whole
education system in recent years. Thus, fees have been abolished in
schools and universities, and free meals, scholarships, and public transport concessions have been provided to assist even the poorest to become
part of the education revolution. The funding of education was increased
from 3.38 percent of GDP in 1998 to 5.43 percent in 2007, with special attention paid to the establishment of education "missions" in poor
neighborhoods.[30] These include Misión Robinson, which has eliminated
illiteracy by teaching over 1.3 million adults to read and write; Misión
Ribas, which provides free secondary education to almost 2 million adult
Venezuelans; and Misión Sucre, which provided tertiary-level education
and was subsequently expanded into a new system of Bolivarian Universities (Universidad Bolivariana de Venezuela, UBV), with campuses across
the country.[31] As a result, participation rates have increased across the
board between 1998 and 2006: from 89.7 to 99.5 percent for primary-
school children, from 27.3 to 41 percent for secondary school, and from
21.8 to 30.2 percent for tertiary education.[32] Most important, there was an
increase in participation from the poorest sectors, especially at the tertiary
level, with the proportion of twenty- to twenty-four-year-olds in higher
education in the bottom four quintiles increasing by 4.4, 7.8, 5.2, and 8.2
percent between 1997 and 2002.[33]

The basic philosophy of education has also undergone reconstruction,
with the perceived capitalist notion of education—as a "commodity" to
be bought by an individual consumer and then sold in the occupational
marketplace for the benefit of that individual—altered, to one that is re-
defined as "a human right and a fundamental social duty," at the service

of society.[34] A new national curriculum was constructed in 2007, which sought to translate this philosophy into everyday practice. It has seen significant changes to the way teaching and learning take place. Less emphasis is placed on a "fragmented" approach to knowledge, designed to prepare students for specialized functions in a capitalist economy, and more on integrated, holistic knowledge designed to allow students a broader, deeper understanding of a complex sociopolitical reality, particularly that experienced on the global economic periphery.[35] Emphasis too has been placed on the need for schools and universities to integrate more closely with their local communities. In 2009, the government sought to move this process forward by encouraging students and other community members to become involved in the management of universities through their Communal Councils. This provoked an outcry about university autonomy, and Chávez backed off.[36]

Interesting initiatives have nevertheless taken place in this context. Most significant perhaps is the introduction of "participatory action" research, which sees a range of students from various disciplines working in and with the poorest communities, in order to advance both their problem-solving skills and their sense of political *praxis*.[37] Outside of the formal education system, Chávez urged *el pueblo* to work hard at their education, to study as individuals and in groups, to read widely, and to decide for themselves what changes they would like to see made in a democratic Venezuela. Shortly after this exhortation to self-education, over 700 study groups (between 10 and 30 members) emerged, from basic literacy collectives to political forums.[38]

The oil economy has been a crucial site of struggle to make an alternative democracy a reality for Venezuela. A central part of Chávez's program has been the strategic use of Venezuela's oil supply, represented now as a resource increasingly for the benefit of the Venezuelan people and less for the national and multinational capitalist sectors that previously controlled it. In Venezuela, oil has been widely viewed as the symbol of modernity and prosperity since the 1920s, always something more than a mere commodity, representing instead the nation's "collective inheritance," its key to a future of national prosperity and the kind of social and political modernity enjoyed by the rich world. But Chávez emphasized that it has been an inheritance squandered by generations of elites who have plundered the nation's wealth and sold out to foreign oil companies.[39]

In an effort to reassert Venezuela's economic sovereignty, and to be in a position to redistribute the national inheritance, Chávez sought to regain control of the oil industry. This meant a constant battle with the management of the state-owned oil company PDVSA, which, during the late Punto Fijo era, committed itself to neoliberal principles and effectively operated as a transnational company, investing in foreign markets and spiriting profits out of the country. The confrontations with PDVSA resulted in management locking out oil workers in 2002 and 2003 and a crisis in Venezuela's primary export industry. But Chávez prevailed and managed to stop the siphoning off of oil profits to foreign subsidiaries, thus increasing government revenue. Revenues were also boosted by the high oil prices in the first decade of the twenty-first century, partially as a result of the Iraq War but also as a consequence of Chávez's efforts to revive OPEC and strengthen its hand in setting prices. Chávez also sought to diversify Venezuela's economic base, by encouraging investment and trade relations with China, in particular, and a range of other states, for example, Iran, Russia, Belarus, and Brazil, and by developing closer trading ties with regional neighbors.

The results have been positive for Venezuela. Between 2003 and 2008, Venezuela's GDP grew by 78.8 percent, or 11.7 percent annually.[40] The economy suffered between 2009 and 2010, due primarily to the Global Financial Crisis (GFC), but it rebounded with 4.2 percent growth in 2011.[41] Unemployment, which reached an alarming high of 19.2 percent during the oil lockout (2002–2003), was down to 6.2 percent in 2011. Meanwhile, the minimum wage was increased from Bs120,000 in 1999 to Bs614,790 in 2007.[42] This was only one dimension of the equation for Chávez, of course, and he used the increased oil revenue specifically to serve the interests of the majority of Venezuelan people, as part of their national and cultural "inheritance." In particular, the government used the increased oil revenue to fund a range of welfare programs and to increase general spending on democratic projects by 300 percent between 1999 and 2006. Indeed, spending in this area continued even after the problems of the GFC in 2008.[43] Most important here have been the "missions" programs (see above) set up in the poorest neighborhoods to provide free health care, education, heavily subsidized food and housing, and other benefits to the most impoverished sections of the population. Poverty rates have thus dropped, from 48.6 percent of the population in 2002, to 27.8 percent in 2010. Infant mortality has declined by 34 percent. Deaths from malnutrition have dropped by more than 50 percent, and while there were just 3.5 million Venezuelans with health coverage in 1998, in 2007, the figure was 20.5 million.[44] In 2008, under Chávez's

Bolivarian democracy, Venezuela had the least unequal distribution of income in Latin America, a status it still retains.[45]

For all this, or perhaps because of it, there was significant resentment and dissent in Venezuela against Chávez's Bolivarian Revolution. Inflation in Venezuela's economy was a problem throughout the Chávez era, and this hurt many of his supporters in the poorest sectors of the economy. This had become less of a problem before his death, with inflation in decline in 2012, but in 2014 it spiked again, effectively cancelling out president Mauro's decision to raise the minimum wage by 30 percent.[46] There was general dissent also from some within the ranks of Chavistas, whose expectations were raised by the early democratic gains of the Chávez era and who became frustrated by the difficulties of the post-GFC era in particular.[47] Overwhelmingly, however, the dissent has come from the middle classes and the business community, many of whom profited from the upsurge in Venezuela's economic fortunes during the Chávez era but who always feared the growing influence of the "mob" under Chávez. Likewise, while Chávez's "twenty-first-century socialism" did not seek to abolish capitalism, both national and international capitalist sectors saw fit to punish him. Following the GFC, for example, domestic capital largely withdrew its cooperation, and in response to Chávez's reassertion of Venezuelan economic sovereignty, the rate of international investment capital significantly slowed.[48] Hostility from the United States and corporate elites also persisted. This is important because the Venezuelan economy remains to a large extent dependent upon its relations with the global economy, particularly concerning oil—a finite resource dominated by price fixers in the neoliberal marketplace. And, as indicated above, in response to Chávez's attempts to construct an alternative democratic model to that preferred by the United States and neoliberalism, there was a constant stream of invective and politico-strategic enmity toward him and his Bolivarian Revolution. This saw an upscaling of the U.S. democracy-promotion programs aimed at undermining Chávez, and we will return to that theme shortly.

For now, however, it is worth returning to the proposition inherent in U.S. critiques of Venezuela under Chávez, which insists that he ruled there by the manipulation of the democratic system and as head of a regime of terror and fear. Even on the basis of the skim across the surface of the Chávez era presented here, this does not appear plausible. On the contrary, there is more plausibility in the notion that, in the most difficult of national and global circumstances, a genuine democratic impulse underlies Chávez's Bolivarian Revolution and that it has had some genuinely democratic outcomes for those most in need of social, political, and economic reform. More specifically, it is hard to see on what basis Chávez's alternative democracy can be considered "thuggish" or likened to the fascist viciousness of Hitler and the Nazis, as major U.S. spokespeople have charged.

A more sensible summation of the Chávez era is to be found in the works of commentators such as Ellner and Hellinger, who proposed in 2004 that "Chávez's record on democracy and the efforts to deepen it were far from uniform or consistent. Undoubtedly, his government scored pluses for some initiatives and minuses for others."[49] Crucially also, as Phil Gunson points out:

> There are no mass executions, death squads, or concentration camps in Venezuela. Civil society has not disappeared, as it did in Cuba after the 1959 revolution. There is no systematic state-sponsored terror leaving scores of *desaparecidos* as in Argentina and Chile in the 1970s. And there is no efficiently repressive and meddlesome bureaucracy a la the Warsaw pact.[50]

Which begs, more precisely, the question of why there is so much hostility from the mainstream of the democratic world to the alternative Bolivarian democracy in Venezuela when, *by any criteria, it is structurally democratic, it is functionally democratic, and it has profoundly democratized the everyday realities of the Venezuelan majority.*

The answer, we suggest, is that the dominant democratic model adopted by partisans of neoliberalism is the polyarchal model touched on in the previous chapter—a model of democracy in which corporate and political elites rule in the interests of neoliberal globalism and a systemic status quo dominated by the major states of the capitalist world. In this context, the Bolivarian democracy in Venezuela perhaps does pose something of a threat, albeit perhaps a rather exaggerated one at times. But as Gramsci suggests, even the most powerful and deeply embedded hegemonies are never entirely secure, never entirely in total control, and are always susceptible to counterhegemonic tendencies. Hugo Chávez has perhaps prompted such tendencies.

A DEMOCRATIC THREAT TO DEMOCRACY? EXPORTING THE BOLIVARIAN MODEL

Above all, Chávez challenged fundamental liberal-capitalist logic, which insists that only markets can create "real" economic prosperity. In so doing, he reasserted the role of a democratic state in the development of the good modern society, particularly for states on the global periphery. The nature of the Bolivarian state is thus important, both structurally and symbolically, in directly challenging the polyarchic democratic model favored by the global hegemon, the United States, seeking to maintain the systemic and conceptual status quo. Ideologically, too, Chávez's "twenty-first-century socialism," inconsistent and incoherent as it might occasionally be, has infused millions of otherwise marginalized people with a sense that they are capable of meaningful intellectual and political participation in the societies in which they live and that they don't "need" to be ruled— either by indigenous elites, powerful foreigners, or global hegemons. This sense of democratic power might not be easily suppressed.

For all this, the threat posed by Venezuela's democracy should not be overstated. It is eminently manageable by the United States and the neoliberal world order as long as it remains contained within the parameters of a still relatively poor Latin American country. The larger danger lies in the proliferation of Venezuelan popular democracy models elsewhere in Latin America and beyond. Chávez understood this and worked both to bolster the confidence of his supporters and to help buttress his vulnerable economy in a hostile neoliberal world, to transport his Bolivarian perspectives far and wide. Hence, his reaching out to China and other "friendly" states for enhanced trade relationships. Hence also, his consistent attempts to influence the broader Latin America region, at the expense of the United States in particular. In this regard, his strengthening of relations with Cuba, via special oil deals, is important, in that it disrupts the U.S. sanctions regime and indicates to others that perhaps the regional hegemon is not quite as powerful as it once was.

This is a message that has resonated powerfully in Latin America in recent years particularly among the so-called pink-tide states, which, following Chávez's lead in 1998, shifted Latin America to the left or, more accurately perhaps, the center-left, during the 2000s, in Argentina (2003), Bolivia (2005), Brazil (2002), Chile (2000), Ecuador (2006), El Salvador (2009), Guatemala (2007), Nicaragua (2006), Paraguay (2008), Peru (2011), and Uruguay (2005). Circumstances have changed in some of these countries (e.g., Paraguay, Chile) since the early successes of the pink tide, and there has been no real equivalent of Bolivarian democracy in any of them.

But Chávez's influence was evident across the region for many years as he agitated for an alternative democratic vision for Latin America, primarily via his *Social Charter of the Americas* introduced in 2001 at the Organization of American States (OAS) general assembly. At the core of the *Social Charter* is the notion of a regional and global democracy characterized, above all, by social justice. Or, as the Venezuelan foreign minister Ali Rodriguez put it in 2005, it represents "an inclusive democracy with equality" as a counterpart to "an elitist democracy, a democracy that is merely electoral." Going further, Rodriguez proposed that democracy "cannot be limited purely to the political realm. It has to be included in the economic, the social, and the cultural . . . [and recognize] social justice as a fundamental component of democracy."[51] In other words, and with the United States firmly in his sights, Rodriguez, on behalf of Chávez, explicitly and publicly condemned polyarchy as a democratic model, with its emphasis on the formal political process and its insistence on the compatibility of free-market economics.

In this regard, in particular, the Venezuelan model has received support from a number of otherwise more moderate actors among the pink-tide states in Latin America. The Bolsa Familia (Brazil without Poverty) program in Brazil and social welfare programs in Argentina have, for example, explicitly acknowledged the "economic" as intrinsic to the political in their movement toward democracy.[52] Constitutional reforms in Ecuador (2008) and Bolivia (2009) also reflect attempts to develop broader democratic participation in their societies.

For all this, the Venezuelan-sponsored *Social Charter of the Americas* was resisted and strongly opposed by the United States, in particular, for many years. The volatility of the debate was evident enough during the 2005 meeting of the OAS, in Miami, when the United States put forward its counter to Chávez's *Social Charter* in the form of the *Declaration of Florida*, which proposed the need to "monitor" the development of democracy in the region, particularly the radical variants of it in places such as Venezuela. This raised the ire of a number of Latin American states who perceived it as, at best, more North American paternalism and, at worst, an updated interventionist strategy for the post–Cold War era. Consequently, there was resistance to the U.S. proposal from a number of OAS members. Brazil's foreign minister, Celso Amorim, responded that democracy cannot be "imposed," and that while Brazil fully supported the strengthening of democracy in the region, "we'd also like to avoid intruding mechanisms." The Mexican spokesman also agreed in principle but warned that "we are not in agreement with any tutelage [about democracy] from anybody."[53] Chávez was, typically, more blunt, insisting that, "if any member government of the OAS needs monitoring, it is the government of the United States . . . a government that supports terrorists and invades other countries, . . . a government that violates human rights around the world, a false democracy."[54] The Venezuelan OAS ambassador Jorge Valero perhaps summed up the concerns best, proposing that there would be "no acceptance in the heart of the Americas for any proposal that means trying to impose a *single model of democracy* [italics added]."[55]

As an indication of the increasing influence of this attitude in the region, Venezuela's *Social Charter* was finally approved at the OAS meeting in Bolivia in June 2012. The approved text now states that in a democratizing region, "the peoples of the Americas have a legitimate aspiration for social justice and their governments the responsibility to promote it." Chávez reflected bitterly upon U.S. intransigence on the *Social Charter* issue over eleven years but made it clear that a range of previously ignored social rights—to health, work, education, basic services, and the political and economic participation of all citizens—must now be integral to democracy in the Americas. If this was not accepted by the United States and its allies, he suggested, the OAS should be "finished with" and greater emphasis placed on the new "geopolitical spaces of unity" being developed in the region.[56]

Chávez was here pointing, in particular, to institutions such as the Community of Latin American and Caribbean States (Comunidad de Estados Latinoamericanos y Caribeños), CELAC, which brings together all the countries in the Western Hemisphere, aside from the United States and Canada, and aims to supersede the U.S.-controlled OAS. Important too is the Union of South American Nations (Unión de Naciones Suramericanas), UNASUR, established in 2008, which has been increasingly concerned to monitor democratic affairs from a Latin American rather than a U.S. perspective. In 2012, UNASUR introduced a "democracy clause" into its constitution aimed at imposing sanctions and bringing other pressures to bear upon those who overthrow democratically elected governments (i.e., in Paraguay, 2012) or seek to disrupt democracy per se (e.g., in Ecuador, 2012).[57] Of great significance for Venezuela also is the Bolivarian Alliance for the Peoples of Our America (Alianza Bolivariana para los Pueblos de Nuestra América), ALBA, which emerged from the trading alliance between Venezuela and Cuba and also includes Antigua, Bolivia, Dominica, Ecuador, and Nicaragua.

These bodies are not without their tensions, but they indicate that Venezuela, in particular, has widespread support in its attempts to confront and modify the neoliberal world order. At the Summit of the Americas in Argentina in 2005, consequently, the U.S.-sponsored Free Trade Area of the Americas (FTAA) plan was rejected in favor of closer economic and political integration programs between the members of CELAC, UNASUR, and ALBA. In December 2010, thus, UNASUR introduced a $13.7 billion ten-year plan for infrastructure projects and energy integration within the Latin American region. Moreover, UNASUR has established a South American Defense Council, to create "a regional defense strategy outside of the tutelage umbrella from the United States."[58] This defense initiative was prompted by suspicions (later proved to be warranted) that a proposed U.S. security agreement with Colombia, ostensibly part of the war on drugs, was actually part of a U.S. plan to get its military closer to "anti-U.S. governments" in Latin America.[59]

Another issue that has indicated a growing sense of unity in the Americas is the response to U.S. attempts to widen divisions within the pink tide and isolate the "bad left" (e.g., Venezuela, Bolivia, and Ecuador) from the "good left" (e.g., Brazil, Uruguay, and Chile).[60] The latter grouping is distinguished effectively by its acceptance of the neoliberal free market as fundamental to its political and economic status in the global order. There has been tension here, nevertheless, and the relationship between the United States and Brazil under Lula and now Dilma Rousseff has been sometimes prickly. But the "moderate" democratization of Brazil in recent years has found favor in the United States, which has applauded and assisted the economic growth and lessening of poverty in that country, often using it as a "good" counterpart to the "bad" Venezuela under Chávez. This "bad left," meanwhile, is distinguished by its animosity toward the neoliberal world order and its unwillingness to acknowledge the leadership and good intent of the global hierarchy led by the United States. This "bad left" is perceived as unconcerned about economic rationality and democracy but intent upon "picking as many fights as possible with Washington and getting as much control as they can over sources of revenue."[61]

In some of the U.S. global-security literature, the alleged irresponsibility and danger of this "bad left" is even more specifically condemned, via the suggestion that its "radical populism" is connected to the Islamic terrorism of al Qaeda and Iran, thus posing a direct threat to the United States.[62] The major target here, unsurprisingly, is Venezuela, deemed the "terrorism hub of South America" by a U.S. House of Representatives report in 2006.[63] This is a theme still constant within sectors of the U.S. political spectrum. Republican senator Marco Rubio, for example, in 2012, invoked the view that

> Hugo Chavez is not only a threat to the Venezuelan people's freedom and democratic aspirations, he has also supported Iran's regime in its attempts to expand its intelligence network throughout the hemisphere, facilitated money laundering activities that finance state sponsors of terrorism and provided a safe haven for FARC narco-terrorists, among many other actions.[64]

The rhetoric has been reined in a little under Obama, but the "two lefts" thesis remains integral to U.S. Latin American policy. Thus, in Brazil in 2010, Hillary Clinton made clear her "deep concern" with the Venezuelan situation, insisting that the solution to the problem was for Venezuela to "look at Brazil and look at Chile and other models of successful countries." Most of Latin America, she proposed, was in a period of economic growth "and sustainable democracy" under the neoliberal world order, "with the notable exceptions" of Venezuela, Bolivia, Cuba, and Nicaragua.[65]

This divide-and-conquer strategy has not been lost on the Latin American states, of course, and while there are obvious benefits in going along with it, this has not always been the response of the pink tide. In 2004, for example, on the eve of an opposition referendum designed to force Chávez out of power, Venezuela was invited to join Mercosur (the Common Market of the South) led by Brazil—a powerful political and symbolic act of unity between "bad" and "good" Latin Americans. Likewise, as indicated above, when the United States introduced its proposed "monitoring" program of Latin American democracies—a strategy aimed squarely at Venezuela—Brazil, Mexico, and others stood just as squarely with their "bad state" colleague. And when Evo Morales was under threat from a U.S.-backed rebellion in Bolivia in 2008, UNASUR stood with Morales and against U.S. interests.

This is not to suggest that the pink tide is becoming a hotbed of Bolivarian-type leftism. There are real differences, for example, between the social democracy in Brazil and the radical version under Chávez. But the resistance against the "two lefts" strategy and the development of major forums for political integration in Latin America does indicate perhaps that Chávez's alternative democracy stance has resonated at all kinds of levels within the Latin American community and is stiffening the resolve against U.S. attempts to destroy the Bolivarian Revolution. However, for all his growing influence in the region, Chávez was always concerned about the democracy-promotion strategies of the United States that are continuing in the Obama era. The belligerence of the G. W. Bush years has largely gone, and the more obvious stylistic continuity now is with the Clinton administration, which also spoke softly while carrying a big stick, albeit a concealed one (via NED, USAID, etc.). And while Obama, like Clinton, shook Chávez's hand and spoke of his desire to help establish prosperity and democracy in the Americas, the nature of that democracy remains effectively beyond discussion.

In an interview in 2011 with the anti-Chávez *El Universal* in Caracas, Obama outlined his carefully worded position on Chávez and Venezuela.[66] He began, as he invariably does, in conciliatory terms, stressing his desire for Latin Americans in general to make their own decisions about how they are governed and reiterating the U.S. attitude to this as one of "equality, shared responsibility, mutual interests and mutual respect." He went on to stress that Venezuela under Chávez has not helped itself with its "anti-American tendencies." Obama absolved the great majority of Venezuelans and Latin Americans from this sentiment, suggesting that they generally support the United States and are opposed to living in the "ideological" past. Obama then connected Chávez's Venezuela directly to that of Cuba and Iran, as anti-American terrorist sympathizers, noting that "here in the Americas, we take Iranian activities, including in Venezuela, very seriously and we will continue to monitor them closely"—not a threat as such but another intimation that the notion of independence for the people of the Americas remains a highly restricted one that must effectively serve the interests of the United States and neoliberalism to be acceptable. Obama subsequently played down the significance of any terrorist threat from Venezuela, but Chávez always responded by insisting that Obama and the United States "leave us alone" and "mind your own business," when it comes to Latin America, reminding Obama that "we are free now and will never again be a colony of yours or anyone else."[67]

At first glance, and primed by years of newspaper and media coverage that represented Chávez as an excitable buffoon, this response was generally perceived as just another overreaction to a polite and respectful U.S. president understandably concerned about terrorism. But, as indicated, Chávez knew something else about Obama's politeness and respect—that it concealed the continuation of a democracy-promotion project that in scale and function, if not in tone, owes as much to George W. Bush as it does to liberals such as Clinton and Obama. Thus, while Obama has made more sensitive noises in his public commentary on Venezuela, he has done so while overseeing a concerted attempt to destroy Chávez's Bolivarian democracy.[68] Central to these efforts has been the U.S. Agency for International Development (USAID), which was created in the J. F. Kennedy era to compete with the USSR for the hearts and minds of peoples in the global periphery, and, since George W. Bush reprioritized it in 2002, has been tasked with "winning" Venezuela for the post–Cold War neoliberal world order.

During its first two years of this program, USAID, and a subsidiary organization, the Office of Transition Initiatives (OTI), had a budget of US$10 million, the majority of which was used to fund approximately 64 opposition groups and programs in Venezuela. More specifically, the USAID funding in the early years of the first decade of the twenty-first century went mainly to anti-Chávez propaganda programs in the Venezuelan media and to the unsuccessful attempt to topple Chávez in the recall election of 2004.[69] The United States has also been on a charm offensive regarding the anti-Chávez opposition. Echoing earlier strategies that saw anticommunists welcomed (whatever their human-rights records) from, among others, Guatemala, El Salvador, and Nicaragua, anti-Chávez groups and the individuals heading them have been privileged, when it comes to U.S. financial and cultural largesse. The quid pro quo here was clear enough during Chávez's presidency, in that, "to receive U.S. financing, the opposition is required to advocate neoliberalism, support U.S. foreign policy and denounce Chávez."[70] Increasing effort has also gone into reformulating Venezuelan civil society, at all levels, with the NED in particular committed to the funding of anti-Chavista elements among workers, teachers, students, journalists, and local government officials. By 2010, under Obama, external funding for these programs had reached more than US$57 million, the majority coming from USAID and the NED. Moreover, from 2006 to 2010, over 34 percent of USAID's budget was used to fund programs for Venezuelan youth in the attempt to turn them away from the "Chavistas."[71]

In this regard Obama has illustrated clearly enough that his respect for democratic diversity is not much more profound than that of Condoleezza Rice, who in 2005 responded to the proposition that there might be room for a diversity of democratic models in Latin America by insisting that

I don't believe that there are different kinds of democracy . . . when people talk about different kinds of democracy, I say let's go back to the basics of democracy . . . I don't think we need a new definition of democracy. We know it when we see it.[72]

In explaining the nature of this singular, universally applicable democracy, that is easy to know and easy to see, Rice emphasized what it decidedly is not, in pointing to "the authoritarian leadership and commodity driven economy" of a state such as Venezuela. And to indicate again the continuity of this view following the George W. Bush era, Obama's first secretary of state, Hillary Clinton, when asked how Venezuela might become a *real* democracy, proposed that above all, it "must restore private property and return to a free-market economy."[73] Democracy, it would seem, can only be "real" if it functions in a capitalist system and if, in the twenty-first century, it works in the interests of neoliberalism.

This, of course, is precisely what any number of groups and individuals have sought to contest in the current era. Indeed, social movements around the world have been contesting the notion of neoliberal democracy for decades, often appealing for the kind of social-justice perspectives and mass participation in the political and economic spheres that Hugo Chávez championed in Venezuela (e.g., the World Social Forum—see chapter 6). Indeed, at the heart of the neoliberal world order are increasing democratic challenges to the contemporary status quo. The Occupy movements in the United States, for example, have explicitly challenged both the inequality of wealth associated with the "winner take all" mentality of free-market logic and the inequality of social and political power that is perceived as integral to a neoliberal (e.g., polyarchic) democratic system. Chapters 5 and 6 return to this "rich world" challenge. The following chapter develops some of the themes introduced here in exploring the ways in which peoples and organizations in very difficult situations around the world have sought to challenge neoliberal democracy on behalf of a more inclusive, more emancipatory variant of it. It does so via three discussions on democracy drawn from three ostensibly very different places—South Africa, India, and Russia.

CHAPTER 4

DEMOCRACY AS A CHALLENGE TO NEOLIBERALISM

HETERODOXY IN SOUTH AFRICA, INDIA, AND RUSSIA

In this chapter, we explore three more sites of neoliberal democracy and a variety of responses to it, in post-apartheid South Africa, in the "shining India" of the post-1990s era, and in post–Cold War Russia. These are, on the surface, very different places with distinct histories, cultures, and contemporary narratives. In the present context, however, it is their similarities that are most prescient. All, for example, have been "liberated" from structural and/or ideological imperialism. All have, in their era of liberation, proclaimed themselves democracies, intent on serving the interests of a previously oppressed and disenfranchised "people." And since the 1990s, all have adopted neoliberalism as the politico-economic ideology most capable of infusing their societies with the attitudes and practices of a modern democratic society. All, subsequently, have experienced the particular neoliberal invocation of (individualist) liberty, (market) freedom, and (narrow) political participation in the democratic system. More specifically, all have experienced the predict-able neoliberal pattern of development—in which the traditionally rich (and a small nouveau entrepreneurial sector) get progressively richer and the poor, poorer, with only the ubiquitous "trickle down" promise on the horizon. Consequently, in all of these societies, there has been growing dissent against the neoliberal status quo and its particular framing of a "managed" democracy. There has been no equivalent of a Bolivarian Revolution in any of these places, but in all of them, there are individuals, groups, organizations, and communities engaged in struggles for a demo-cratic future centered not just on formal electoral processes and elite rule but also on social justice, economic fairness, and genuine participation in the political system. We look briefly at some of the many ways in which people in South Africa, India, and Russia have struggled to achieve these democratic goals in the neoliberal era. We pay special attention to non-mainstream indigenous voices in so doing.

FRAMING THE SOUTH AFRICAN NEOLIBERAL STATE IN THE POST-APARTHEID ERA

The struggles against apartheid in South Africa have an iconic place in the contemporary political imagination, particularly among those concerned more generally with issues of freedom, social justice, and democracy. During the second half of the twentieth century, in particular, the anti-apartheid movements—within South Africa and around the world—were unified in the desire to overturn an often-brutal racist regime and a social system imbued with deeply antiegalitarian and antidemocratic principles. After decades of struggle, the crucial breakthrough came in the early 1990s, with the release of exiled African National Congress (ANC) lead-ers from their many years of incarceration, and the triumphant "long walk to freedom" of Nelson Mandela, which effectively signaled the end of apartheid. In 1994, consequently, an ANC-led government took power following the first democratic elections in South African history. For mil-lions, within South Africa and around the world, this was a moment for celebration and the recalibration of expectation concerning the standards and quality of life of the South Africa masses and their prospects for a democratic future.[1]

Eighteen years on, however, a rather different and troubling scenario is evident in post-apartheid South Africa, one that sees it now acknowledged as the most unequal society on the planet, with one of the highest unemployment rates in the world (33 percent), with more of the black majority now living below the poverty line than under apartheid, and with increasing anger and frustration at the antidemocratic processes and attitudes of the still-ruling ANC.[2]

The plight of the black majority was starkly underlined in a census carried out in 2011. It indicated that in the democratic South Africa of the ANC, black Africans make up 80 percent of the (56 million) population, while less than 9 percent are white. Yet in terms of income, wealth, employment, and education, the differences between the races remain very substantial. The wealthiest (mainly white) sector of the population thus earns 60 percent of its total income, with the bottom (mainly black) 50 percent earning just 8 percent.[3] On average, moreover, white households earn six times more than black households, even though the emerging black middle class is now roughly the same size as its white counterpart and even though black households are invariably larger. At this rate of development, analysts suggest, even if some kind of concerted linear progress takes place, it would take until 2061 before black and white families were potentially earning the same kind of salaries.[4]

On the crucial issue of education, the census showed that while 76 percent of whites graduated from high school, only 35 percent of black Africans did so. The situation for the black majority is particularly acute in this regard, with 8.6 percent of the population having had no education at all.[5] This has obvious implications in relation to employment prospects in an economy shifting from primary production to a service-sector profile. Not surprisingly, thus, while 69 percent of working-age whites are classified as employed, only 35 percent of black people have a job. The impact of the global financial crisis of 2008 has been devastating in this context. It resulted in 650,000 workers losing their jobs, a number that rises to around 1.8 million when one takes into account those so discouraged by the situation that they stopped looking for work.[6] The ANC government has increased social-assistance grants to the poorest, but as a 2012 World Bank Report insists, "social assistance is clearly not enough and needs to be complimented by other initiatives." In particular, a focus on "human capital development," rather than conventional economic development per se.[7]

A diverse range of social movements, workers associations, and local grassroots organizations have been at the forefront of the challenges to the ANC on issues such as these, articulating their concerns with successive governments about the nature and rate of change in a liberated South

Africa. Intrinsic to these challenges has been a common understanding of the primary reason for the perceived failure of the ANC to fulfill the expectations invested in it by the antiapartheid movements—its adherence to neoliberalism and antidemocratic elitism.

The proposition, more specifically, is that in 1994 the incoming ANC government was faced with two choices as to its present and future character. The first was to ride the (anti-neoliberal) democratic wave of the early 1990s, which saw resistance to neoliberalism becoming more explicit around the world—a resistance given radical momentum by the Zapatista movement in Chiapas and by events in Venezuela under Hugo Chávez and the Latin American pink tide. The second was to bind the new "people's democracy" of the post-apartheid era firmly to the neoliberal globalization project led by the United States, at a moment when the downsides of neoliberalism were becoming increasingly evident. The ANC, its critics lament, even with its unique national and global mandate for change, chose the latter option. Thus, when faced with an opportunity to structurally and ideologically reconfigure South Africa in favor of an oppressed, deprived, and excluded majority, rather than the interests of national and global capital, it chose free-market orthodoxy and "Afro-neoliberalism."[8]

In this regard, it chose not just to reconcile with the privileged white minority (which was largely supported) but also to concede the liberated South African state to the vicissitudes of the free market and the (national and global) minority interests it serves. The result, it is argued, is a South Africa in the current era in which the (white) corporate capitalist sector has not been called upon to take responsibility for its complicity with apartheid, in which rich whites still own and control 87 percent of the best agricultural land and most of the wealth; in which endemic corruption and elite greed characterizes ANC governance; in which the black majority are no closer to material security or democracy than under apartheid; and in which a co-opted black middle class acts to legitimate the whole scenario.[9]

Initially, in 1994, under the leadership of Nelson Mandela, there were deeply felt expectations regarding the post-apartheid world, which, via its Freedom Charter (1955), the ANC promised would see South Africa become a nonracial democratic state in which the "the people shall govern" and in which South Africa would belong to all of its people, no matter what their color. There would, it maintained, be work, education, and security for all, and everyone would be equal before the law.

It was never quite as simple as this. Indeed, while the Western media hailed the "Mandela miracle" of national reconciliation, a deal was done that "handed political power to the black majority and left economic power in the hands of whites. There was to be no seizure of white assets." Indeed, Jacob Zuma admitted in 2012 that nothing has been done structurally to change this status quo, acknowledging that "the economic power relations of the apartheid era have in the main remained intact. The ownership of the economy is still primarily in the hands of white males as it has always been."[10]

A balance of sorts was attempted during the presidency of Zuma's predecessor, Thabo Mbeki (1999–2008), who accelerated the commitment to neoliberalism and market democracy. In this period, Mbeki made it clear that his priority was to "create and strengthen a black capitalist class" as the foundation of a post-racist South Africa.[11] The result was the creation of a significantly larger black bourgeoisie, indebted to the ANC and the embracing of a fully blown neoliberal democracy committed to privatization and market forces. One equation above all perhaps illustrates the nature of the problem this has created. It illustrates that, in the wake of the Mbeki era, South Africa can boast 25,000 black millionaires, while more than a quarter of its black population live on less than $2 per day, and their conditions of life are deteriorating.[12]

Thus far, nevertheless, the masses have remained loyal to the ANC in each election since 1994, though there is increasing evidence that a deep disenchantment has set in. As Karon put it in 2012, "When poor South Africans look at the ANC they no longer see a party led by people just like them; instead, they see a party led by a new black elite that has enriched itself by virtue of its access to political power."[13]

There is a certain inevitability about of all this, proposes Vishwas Satgar, to the extent that, as elsewhere in the neoliberal world order, the ANC government has abandoned the poorest to their fate in a world of "winners" and "losers." Just as inevitably, the ANC political elite "have become technocrats: [who] manage 'market democracy' such that the juggernaut of accumulation is not constrained and growth is realized at all costs." In 2009, Jacob Zuma replaced Mbeki with a radical promise to change all this and to ameliorate the impact of neoliberalism in favor of the "people." This was just crude populism, counters Satgar; consequently, under Zuma, "the dream of a people's democracy has been [increasingly] shrunk . . . to a form of weak representational democracy [where] free and fair elections with a voter turnout is adequate to legitimate the rule of capital."[14]

There is much here that is consistent with the concerns of others around the world in the neoliberal era, which has seen small minorities getting richer and more powerful as the majority gets poorer and democratically marginalized. And while the ANC in government has argued, rightly, that it cannot be expected to overturn the social and cultural damage of centuries of white minority rule in two decades, it has been the decision to take the neoliberal road to South Africa's economic and political development that has become central to the burgeoning protests over a democratic deficit in contemporary South Africa.

NEOLIBERALISM IN PRACTICE: THE GEAR PROGRAM (1996–)

There was some evidence of a "redistributive" inclination within Mandela's first post-apartheid administration and its original Reconstruction and Development Program (RDP). But by 1996, under Mbeki, a new policy framework was announced, centered on the GEAR program, of Growth, Employment and Redistribution.[15] This was a fully blown neoliberal project that sought to rapidly integrate South Africa into the mainstream global economy through the New Partnership for Africa's Development (NEPAD). The GEAR program thus followed exemplary neoliberal principles as it simultaneously invoked a "black empowerment" program in the private sector. In the public sector, however, the usual range of important government services was turned over to the market.[16] Indeed, to underscore its enthusiasm for the neoliberal world order, the Mbeki government proposed zero protection for its telecommunications industry, even though the then GATT (now WTO) required tariff protection only to fall to 20 percent. It also opened up a range of other controls over trade and capital movements, and the financial sector swiftly increased to 20 percent of the entire economy, although it employed only 1 percent of the workforce. Crucial, too, was the privatization of essential services—water, housing, electricity, education, and health care—in an economy already racked with poverty, neglect, and disenfranchisement.[17]

In this context, the policy targets of GEAR were founded upon the neoliberal notion that, freed from the yoke of state intervention, the South African economy could be rapidly transformed into a prosperous, entrepreneurially driven economy that, via "trickle down," would benefit all. A GDP growth factor of around 6 percent annually was thus muted, as was a job-creation target of 400,000 jobs per year, an increase in foreign direct investment (FDI) equivalent to 4 percent of GDP, and some more general targets concerning the education of the black masses, the elimination of poverty, and the redistribution of wealth.[18]

The GEAR targets have not been met. South Africa's GDP growth, for example, has averaged 3.26 percent since 1996 and is currently (2012) around 2.6 percent.[19] After an initial surge in FDI activity, there has also been major disappointment in the neoliberal era. In the first half of 2012, while the African continent as a whole saw an increase of 5 percent, the FDI inflow to South Africa fell to $1.7 billion (from $3 billion in 2011).[20] This is very far away from the projected 4 percent of a $450 billion economy. Unemployment rates, too, are far greater now than when GEAR was introduced. At the dawn of South Africa's democracy, unemployment stood at around 13 percent; in late 2012, it stood at close to 40 percent. Around 50 percent of young South Africans, under the age of twenty-four, are out of work.[21]

As indicated earlier, one of the major problems facing the ANC regarding employment concerns the lack of an educated workforce, and the ANC is not entirely to blame for this. But on this issue, too, the record in the neoliberal era is unimpressive. The *Economist* goes further, charging that "education is a disgrace" under the GEAR strategy, with South Africa ranking 132nd out of 144 countries for its primary education, and 143rd in science and mathematics.[22] It is estimated that only 15 percent of children can read and write at the minimally prescribed levels by the age of twelve, with no improvement in sight.[23]

The GEAR targets concerning the elimination of poverty and the redistribution of wealth have met a similar fate, as the figures above indicate. As Oupa Lehulere puts it, "not only does the [neoliberal] strategy fail to eradicate poverty, but it creates poverty. It is the redistribution of wealth from the poor to the rich."[24] Integral to this failure have been the GEAR privatization programs. Consequently, while the electricity and water grid was expanded to poor areas under private ownership, ten million people suffered water and power cutoffs because they couldn't pay the market price.[25] The issue of land redistribution is crucial also if the aim is to assist the black poor in the rural areas. However, in the GEAR era, only 3.3 percent of the promised 30 percent of land transfers have gone ahead, while rural Africans remain the poorest of the poor.[26]

Summing up the GEAR period, Dennis Brutus, an original contributor to the Freedom Charter, suggests that it marks the end of any serious commitment to redistribution and to a genuine democracy in South Africa. Instead, it has installed a system in which "the people [have] become the victims of a new ideology, aimed at satisfying the World Bank, IMF, and the WTO."[27] In the view of one veteran union leader, this has devastating implications for democracy because now "there is a deep and growing mistrust of leaders in our country, and the expanding underclass feels it has no voice through legitimate formal [democratic] structures." Thus, "violence becomes the only viable language."[28]

THE PROTESTS OF THE "POORS"

There has indeed been violence, as the "poors" have sought to have their voices heard outside of the formal democratic processes. The rate of protest has been accelerating in recent years, with commentators in 2012 speaking of a "massive rebellion of the poor" throughout South Africa.[29] For the most part, these protests have been defensive actions on localized issues, but as they have escalated, they have become more explicitly focused on an ideology (neoliberalism) that removes the state from its (democratic) role as the social protector of last resort and provider of fundamental public goods. This acknowledgment has seen widening support for groups such as the Landless People's Movement, the Unemployed People's Movement, the Western Cape Anti-Eviction Campaigners, and many more. And as a range of community groups has mobilized around demands for fairer treatment regarding water and electricity supplies and access to housing and health facilities, an "Anti-Privatisation Forum" has developed to confront neoliberalism on behalf of the democratic rights of the poorest communities. The perspective of the "poors" is perhaps best captured by S'bu Zikode, who proposes that

> during the struggle prior to 1994 there were only two levels, two classes—
> the rich and the poor. Now . . . there are three classes—the poor, the
> middle class and the rich. The poor have been isolated from the middle
> class. We are becoming more poor and the rest are becoming more rich.
> We are on our own. We are completely on our own.[30]

Widespread protests about the conditions in shack settlements have seen the rise to prominence of Zikode's Abahlali baseMjondolo (AbM, Shack Dwellers) movement. It has around 25,000 members in more than sixty shack settlements across the country as part of a Poor People's Alliance.

It has fought against the appropriation of urban land by developers and the government (e.g., before the FIFA World Cup in 2010). It has been successful in preventing forced evictions and has won victories in the courts for a small number of the poorest South Africans effectively abandoned by the ANC and the neoliberal state. It is now, however, much more than a single-issue movement, leading village groups in the construction of childcare facilities, kitchens, and vegetable gardens; working within poor communities against xenophobic attacks on foreigners (e.g., Zimbabweans); organizing seminars to teach the "poors" a range of skills (from computer skills to plumbing to philosophy, via the works of Frantz Fanon in particular); and fighting for equal access to education, even for the poorest children.[31]

The cost, however, has been great and is ongoing. Police violence (and violence by ANC thugs) has been an ever-present danger, and the AbM has been disowned and discredited by others in the broad liberal-left community. This latter problem is perhaps due to the "neurotically democratic" nature of the AbM, which seeks to develop its "politics of the poor" independently of the traditional articulators of emancipatory theory and practice.[32] It insists on its autonomy in this regard, committed to a radical "democracy from below" instead of a neoliberal (polyarchal) democracy it considers corrupt, inept, and malevolent. In this regard, it shares some characteristics with the Zapatistas in Mexico and other social movements around the world seeking democratic autonomy in the neoliberal era. Strategically, this means directly engaging the formal power regime in those spaces and places where it most damages the poor majority. It thus assists the poor and dispossessed in Occupy movements in appropriated properties and on plantations and mining sites and in factories and government buildings. Philosophically, it argues for non-violence in its civil-disobedience engagements with the state and against a vanguardist perspective in its engagement with the people it represents. Vanguardism, it suggests, is precisely what the ANC liberation movement has been reduced to, and any real resistance to it must be founded upon the capacity of people to govern their own affairs and participate in genuinely democratic politics.[33]

This might appear inconsistent with the decision of the AbM (and all the organizations of the Poor People's Alliance) to boycott local and national elections in recent years. It is not, argues Pithouse, and others, because it represents the acknowledgment *that another form of democracy is necessary* if the interests of the great majority are to be taken into account in South Africa,[34] a form of democracy that prioritizes social justice and the living standards of the most downtrodden, rather than a small minority able to take advantage of the structures and attitudes that resonate within a neoliberal social order. In South Africa, however, argues Pithouse,

> the affirmation of democratic principles has seldom translated into a meaningful commitment to democratic practices. Our public sphere has largely understood itself to be a site in which contending elites debate each other. And elites across the political spectrum . . . have often responded to the demand for real inclusion in discussions and decision making by poor people with astonishing paranoia and hostility.[35]

A dramatic and tragic instance of the resort to hostility by the ruling elite was evident in the Marikana mine massacre of October 2012.[36] The protest at the mine, and indeed the ongoing protests of miners and other workers in recent years, might, at first glance, seem to have little in common with the hundreds of small-scale conflicts over basic services touched on above. On the surface, it was about wages and conditions, and it involved a complex internecine struggle between unions. But there is much that binds together the desperate attempts of the underground rock drillers to improve their awful working conditions with the more generalized confrontations with neoliberalism. Most obviously, it pitted some of the poorest (yet hardest working) South Africans against a highly profitable, foreign multinational company supported by the ANC.

More profoundly, it was, at heart, a protest against the abandonment of a vulnerable black workforce by the ANC, by their union body (the National Union of Mineworkers, NUM), by the larger union movement (COASU), and by the SA Communist Party, who, rhetorically at least, support their struggle. All of these groups, however, are integral to the ANC coalition in government and, along with the white corporate sector, supportive of GEAR and global neoliberalism. In this context, the majority of the rock drillers shifted their allegiance to a more radical union (the AMCU), which only increased the risk of major violence. When it came, it was reminiscent of the worst days of apartheid, with the police opening fire on black protesters, leaving thirty-four dead and eighty injured. This time, however, it was black police—representing the party of Nelson Mandela and South African liberation—doing the killing. And in its aftermath there was no remorse, only condemnation of the protest and continuing support for the British platinum company, Lonmin.

In retrospect, the post-apartheid reality of democratic South Africa was starkly evident at Marikana. A neoliberal reality, as Mphutlane wa Bofelo puts it, has made the "losers" in the system increasingly aware that "it does not take a white skin to install or perpetuate a system based on unequal allocation of power and inequitable distribution of wealth and resources."[37]

NEOLIBERALISM, "INDIA SHINING," AND THE DEMOCRATIC ALTERNATIVE OF KERALA

India is often characterized as the world's largest democracy, and it does indeed have over 700 million people eligible to vote in regularly held national and regional elections. Moreover, following its independence from Britain in 1947, the Constitution of India (1950) was founded on the principles of a Western, parliamentary-style federal government. It guarantees periodic elections, it gives executive responsibility to the elected legislature, and it provides for an independent judiciary. More specifically, under its first president, Jawaharlal Nehru (1947–1964), India was perceived, in broadly Keynesian terms, as a modern democracy in which the state would play a dominant role in a "mixed economy" aimed at industrialized capitalist development and political and geostrategic self-reliance. Since independence, it has had two major political parties, the liberal Indian National Congress (Congress Party), which led the struggles against the British and has largely dominated Indian politics since, and the Bharatiya Janata Party (BJP), a Hindu nationalist party of the right that has successfully challenged Congress Party dominance on occasion in recent times. In the general election of 2009, the Congress Party, led by the neoliberal economist Manmohan Singh, won power and currently rules as part of a United Progressive Alliance.[38]

Beyond the structural formality, however, there are very real questions as to the substance of Indian democracy. Since 1991, in particular, as both major parties in government have advanced neoliberalism as the keystone of a modern and prosperous India, this critical questioning has taken on more strident tones. The major issues here, as elsewhere in the neoliberal world order, concern the relationship between winners and losers in the system, the significance of neoliberalism in widening the social and economic gap between them, and the implications this has for an ostensibly democratic system.

Those wedded to neoliberal theory and practice reject the need for such criticism, pointing to the GDP growth in India since the invocation of neoliberalism in 1991, the rise in middle-class wealth and opportunity in the major cities, the sense of Indian national resurgence as one of the designated BRIC economies (alongside Brazil, Russia, and China), and the promise of "trickle down" in the years to come. It was in this context that the BJP utilized the "India Shining" slogan in 2004, to reiterate to critics the optimism of the political and economic elites toward the neoliberal road to prosperity and democracy. As befits the fierce nationalism of the party, the BJP insisted that "'India Shining' is all about pride. It gives us brown-skinned Indians a huge sense of achievement. Look at the middle-class and they tell the story of a resurgent India."[39]

Not only Indian nationalists were enamored of the "India Shining" notion. The high priest of neoliberal globalization, Thomas Friedman, has perhaps done more than anyone to advance a "shining" India theme globally. Indeed, in *The World Is Flat* (2005), Friedman insists that the shape of India's future, and of global neoliberalism in general, is to be gleaned in its purest form in Bangalore in the middle years of the first decade of the twenty-first century. Here, young high-tech entrepreneurs illustrate that globalization, driven by a borderless free market, has flattened the economic and political playing field and that Indians, in particular, are spearheading the revolution in "broadband connectivity" destined to transform Indian society and global geoeconomic reality.[40] In the ensuing period, even Friedman has acknowledged that there has been a slowing of the global economy, but the answers to the problem India faces are still perceived, predictably enough, as more of the same—more privatization, more deregulation, and more "creative destruction" by entrepreneurial innovators.[41]

From this perspective, accordingly, the rise of neoliberal India is understood as another impressive example of the global free market at work. A GDP growth rate of 8–9 percent during the 1990s (down to around 6 percent in 2012) is celebrated as indicative of the power of market forces to rapidly change for the better even the largest and most complex of developing states.[42] The global corporate sector has played its designated role in this neoliberal success story, with foreign direct investment (FDI) rising in India, from less than US$1 billion in 1990 to US$10.4 billion in 2011. An UNCTAD survey in 2012 indicated that India is (after China) the second-most-attractive investment destination for transnational corporations, with the service sector, telecommunications, and the construction and IT industries receiving most FDI attention.[43] In 2012, consequently, India was ranked as the world's tenth richest economy in GDP terms and is projected to become a top-six economy by 2017.[44]

As indicated above, however, there are other ways of evaluating the neoliberal achievements in India since 1991, which place less emphasis on GDP criteria and broadband connectivity and more on human and social development and questions of democratic rights and opportunities.[45] In this regard, some familiar themes have emerged in recent times as the transformative powers of a neoliberal democracy have been addressed in critical terms. In particular, a familiar pattern of wealth distribution has become apparent, which has seen the top 10–15 percent of the Indian population brightly "shining" as they become richer and more privileged, while conditions for the vast multitude of the poor have only marginally improved or have worsened. The Harvard economist Gita Gopinath has outlined the problem in comparative terms, proposing that "each percentage growth in the Indian economy has benefitted negligible proportions of poor people as compared to China or South Korea."[46]

Consequently, while the already rich and powerful in India have, like their counterparts elsewhere in the neoliberal world, enthusiastically surfed the initial waves of enhanced market freedom, and while the ranks of the winners have been swelled, as elsewhere, by young, tertiary educated, tech-savvy urban dwellers, another narrative is evident regarding the neoliberal experiences of the great majority of Indians. Summarizing this situation, Praful Bidwai suggests that "at the end of the two highest-growth decades in recent history, India still has the highest number of dirt-poor people of any country in the world." More specifically, while the neoliberal "winners" engage in a luxury-consumption boom in cities such as Delhi, Bangalore, and Mumbai, it is estimated that over 400 million Indians simultaneously struggle to feed and clothe and educate themselves in conditions of squalor and deprivation.[47] In this context, argues Bidwai, it is sadly predictable that, under neoliberalism, "more Indians have cell-phones than toilets."[48]

This is not for a moment to lose sight of the traditionally poverty-stricken nature of the Indian masses or the great divisions of caste, class, religion, and wealth that have historically beset Indian society. Nor can neoliberalism (or even capitalism per se) be held totally responsible for the seemingly endemic greed, corruption, and nepotism of the Indian social and political landscape or its post-independence democratic system. But as a number of critical commentators have stressed in their evaluations of the period since 1991, neoliberal attitudes and policy practices have made things worse for the great majority of Indians, and neoliberal influences have further eroded any emancipatory dimension in Indian democracy.[49]

Structurally, it is argued, the celebrated GDP growth since 1991 has actually aided the shift away from democracy toward greater inequality and exploitation of the majority. This is because of the profit-induced nature of this growth and its narrow arc of distribution throughout Indian society. There has been investment growth in the stock market, for example, and in the more profitable areas of the country and economy, but in regard to the interests of the majority, the "nongrowth" implications have been devastating for so many. In particular, while the globally connected service sectors now account for 50 percent of India's GDP, the agricultural sector—crucial to the survival of around 70 percent of all Indians—has been reduced to less than 20 percent of GDP.[50]

Under neoliberalism, moreover, there is little likelihood of any state-sponsored support for those left destitute by this particular case of structural adjustment or for the kinds of manufacturing industries capable of absorbing the surplus agricultural labor. As Gopinath explains, "India needs a strong manufacturing base which today [2012] accounts for just 16 percent of the GDP. The progress from agriculture to service economy can't exclude the step of manufacturing. Manufacturing brings money to large sections of the society."[51] This structural omission at the core of the Indian economy has had more than just economic implications, with 200,000 Indian farmers having committed suicide since 1991 and whole villages, communities, and regions left devastated.[52]

The works of Amartya Sen and others, such as Utsa Patnaik, give voice to these disenfranchised people in their investigations of hunger among India's rural poor in the neoliberal age.[53] Patnaik, in particular, focuses on the way in which neoliberal policy choices—for example, to prioritize the development of high-tech service industries in urban areas—have had direct and catastrophic implications for millions of rural dwellers. Accordingly, as urban infrastructure and global connectivity have improved, village and community life has deteriorated, to the extent that chronic hunger still threatens the lives of millions of children.[54] The UNDP Human Development Index adds a dimension to this story in reporting, in 2011, that for all the neoliberal-infused triumphalism over the past two decades, India is placed between 124th and 128th in a ranking of 175 countries on a variety of development indicators, including life expectancy, literacy rates, and infant mortality rates—well behind Venezuela (73rd) and trailing even South Africa (123rd).[55]

This makes absolute sense to Bidwai, who comments that income, wealth, and regional disparities, "always grotesque" in India, have become even more grotesque under neoliberalism. Consequently, after two decades of neoliberalism, there is a "huge cesspool of poverty, social backwardness and acute deprivation, especially in India's [rural] heartland," existing alongside "islands" of high GDP growth and extravagant materialist consumption in the south and west of the country.[56] In any real democracy, argues Bidwai, this issue would be seriously addressed. In India, however, it will not be, he suggests, because India is a democracy in form only, where elections take place, where governments are created and defeated, but where the notion of rule by and on behalf of "the people" is effectively alien to the tiny elite that rules and that has embraced neoliberalism in order to maintain and enhance its status and privilege.

This does not quite add up to the classical polyarchal elitism touched on earlier. It has a more distinct Indian character. The intersections of religion, caste, and neofeudal traditionalism are always complicating factors in this regard and so is the tendency toward rule by family dynasty. Since independence, for example, the Congress Party has been dominated by the Nehru-Gandhi family, and indeed, for 60 percent of this time, a member of this one family has been in office.[57] This is a trait very evident at the state and regional level also, where nepotism and political corruption stifle and undermine democratic instincts and practices.

In the neoliberal era, this undermining of democracy has increased, argue Singh and Murari, who propose, more precisely, that "there has been an unprecedented growth of the weeds of corruption and criminalization of politics since the rise of neoliberalism." An increasingly unregulated financial system has allowed for increased venality in this regard, as has the lack of public regulation on party finances and a lack of internal party democracy. The result has been rampant exploitation of the political system and an "undemocratic nexus between the corporate capitalist sector and political parties, vitiating the electoral and governmental decision-making processes."[58]

There are shades of the ANC and neoliberal South Africa here, of course, and in the Indian context, the corruption themes are similar, with major political figures caught up in corporate scandals and the government in general perceived as a plaything of the extremely rich.

The analysis of Singh and Murari is instructive in this context. It indicates, for example, that, following the 2009 general election, the number of "Crorepatis" (Indians worth 10 million rupees, approximately US$184,000) in the two major parties stood at 71 percent in the Congress Party and 58 percent in the BJP. Around the federal system, the percentages are even higher, in the Punjab and in Delhi rising to 100 percent of all elected officials.[59]

In Western terms, this is perhaps not a great deal of money, but it is estimated that just 1 percent of Indians are Crorepatis,[60] and per capita GDP, even in the "shining" age of Indian neoliberalism, is about US$1,500.[61]Another piece of data is pertinent here too. It illustrates that 22 percent of the (206) Congress Party MPs and 38 percent of their (116) BJP counterparts elected to the Indian parliament in 2009 were facing criminal charges of one kind or another when elected, mostly to do with fraud, corruption, and embezzlement. Extraordinarily, in most smaller parties, the figure for those under some kind of criminal investigation was 100 percent.[62] As Chand explains:

> Criminality and dubious wealth combine to send to parliament men and women who are demonstrably unfit for public office, which is a blot on the respectability of the world's largest democracy. Despite the widespread perception that Indian politicians and bureaucrats are among the most corrupt and incompetent in the world, successive governments have done little to bring about even minimum reforms to the country's political and administrative system.[63]

It is for reasons such as these that Singh, Murari, Chand, and others have concluded that, since 1991, neoliberalism "has increased the hiatus between the two major goals of the Indian constitution, i.e., democracy and social justice" and is placing in jeopardy the capacity of Indian society to reach these goals.[64] It is for similar reasons that a range of scholars and activists in India and around the world have looked at the experiences of Kerala in Southern India as another way of seeking democracy and social justice in the neoliberal era.

THE KERALA EXPERIENCE: RETHINKING INDIAN DEMOCRACY

The distinctiveness of Kerala, in this context, is that it represents for many an alternative to top-down GDP-driven models of democratic development and, instead, emphasizes social justice, economic fairness, and a genuine mass political participation on issues of power and public policy.[65] Kerala has always been a poor state in per capita GDP terms and has lagged behind much of "shining India" in the neoliberal era. But while India generally has seen the living standards of its great majority made more precarious at best (see UNDP figures above), Kerala has seen extraordinarily high quality-of-life indicators on issues of life expectancy, health care, literacy, infant mortality, education, hunger eradication, and political democracy. In the neoliberal era, moreover, as conditions of inequality and political disenfranchisement have been exacerbated throughout the developing world, Kerala, suggests Shirin, "stands out like the moon against the night sky."[66]

Its infant mortality rate is half that of India in general[67] and, according to Stephen Shalom, was lower than that among black Americans in 1999.[68] It has a universal health-care system that is the envy of India generally and many richer countries, a low population growth (about the same as Western Europe and the United States), a 94 percent literacy rate (as against 65 percent nationally), and its rate of female literacy (87 percent— double the national average) is in some ways even more extraordinary in a country such as India.[69] Its life expectancy rate, sixty-eight years for men, seventy-three for women, is again remarkable in a society with UNDP Human Development characteristics outlined above, and in terms of wages and working conditions, nutrition, social-security provisions, anti-caste discrimination, and gender equality, it leads the low-income world and indeed many parts of the "developed" world.[70] In recent times, there have been some potentially significant setbacks to this Kerala narrative, and we will touch on this issue shortly. The larger question that is begged, initially, is how precisely did Kerala come to appear "like an entirely different country"[71] within India, and what does the Kerala experience indicate more generally about neoliberal democracy in India.

There is ongoing contention about the reasons for Kerala's difference in this regard, but three themes are constant in the debate. The first is that Kerala was always a bit "different"—its isolation from much of mainstream India (deep in the southwest corner) saw it developing an open and tolerant social and political culture, as it engaged for centuries in trading relationships with people as diverse as those from China, Egypt, Greece, Portugal, and Holland, among others.[72] Second, it was internally different, in that it was a matrilineal society and had women rulers in the nineteenth century who decreed, remarkably, that the state must fund an education system for the masses, "in order that there might be no backwardness in the spread of enlightenment among them, and that they might become better subjects and public servants."[73]

Others have acknowledged this framing of Kerala's difference while emphasizing a third theme that emphasizes the significance of Kerala as the site of the world's first democratic election of a Communist Party (CPI) government in 1957—and the subsequent commitment to a development model based on egalitarianism and social justice and democracy "from below."[74] Hence, a range of social-justice initiatives has become part of everyday life for Kerala's citizens, including food-distribution systems that provide free rice for the poorest, union protections for agricultural workers, pensions for retired agricultural laborers, and programs designed to provide government employment for low-caste communities.[75]

At least four major public-policy principles have been integral to Kerala society since the 1960s. The first and most radical of these, given its philosophical and practical significance to the capitalist world order, is a commitment to land reform. Long agitated for by peasant groups, the reform act was passed into law in 1957 as a practical and symbolic attack on traditional feudalism in India. It abolished the exploitative tenancy structures of rural life and redistributed landownership to the benefit of millions of peasant families.[76] Important, too, second, has been the continuing policy commitment to education and spreading literacy to all, including women and the lowest castes. By 1991, a literacy rate of 91 percent had been achieved across Kerala, as millions of rural dwellers were taught to read and write by thousands of volunteers using, in particular, the methods of Paulo Freire.[77] This task continues, and between 1998 and 2003, the Kerala government spent US$7.4 million on 3,500 adult continuing-education centers, to keep improving the education standards of the previously illiterate. In 2005, approximately 37 percent of the state's annual budget was being spent on education, and there were 12,271 state schools, and a primary school within three kilometers of every village or community in Kerala.[78]

The third policy principle intrinsic to the Kerala experience is its government-funded health-care program, which can now boast more hospital beds per capita than anywhere else in India and the highest access rates to doctors and nursing care. Moreover, Kerala has the lowest rates of cholera and malaria in India and the highest rates of vaccination for TB, polio, and diphtheria (100 percent by the early 1990s).[79] The fourth and most explicit attempt to construct a genuine democratic environment for its people has seen successive government support for "democratic decentralization" programs, which were introduced in the mid-1990s to give people at the grassroots the opportunity to make the decisions about their everyday social reality.

THE KERALA PEOPLE'S CAMPAIGN
FOR DEMOCRATIC DECENTRALISM

The People's Campaign for Democratic Decentralism after 1996 saw the Kerala state government increasingly transferring power to people at the local-government and village-council (*panchayat*) level while providing resources, training, and infrastructural support for this purpose. Initiatives toward decentralization had been part of the five-year plans introduced by radical Kerala governments since the late 1950s, and while the CPI and other radical-left groups have been in and out of government since this time, popular agitation by increasingly educated and politically engaged movements of peasants, workers, and local communities has forced their centrist counterparts to continue the decentralization programs. Accordingly, when the Congress Party government, and the finance minister of the time (now prime minister), Manmohan Singh, sought, in 1993, to further "liberalize" the responsibilities of the federal state as part of its neoliberal restructuring of the Indian political scene, the people of Kerala used the opportunity to increase their radical anti-neoliberal democracy. The results, from 1996 on, when the "People's Campaign" got under way, have been remarkable, hence the interest and fascination from around the world, particularly from those skeptical of the neoliberal TINA proclamation.[80]

On the basis of their detailed analysis of the early years of these campaigns, Thomas Isaac and Franke conclude that they represent an important case study of an alternative democracy—one that extends "democracy from its representative form to one of participation" and one that has seen participatory democracy "used as a major vehicle for economic growth and development."[81] Thus, in around 1,000 *panchayats* across the state, people with limited education and little experience of budgeting and formal political decision making have been "doing" democracy in a decidedly non-neoliberal way. Responsible, on occasions, for budgets fifty times greater than ever before experienced by village councils, priorities are agreed upon and voted on and work carried out in line with the wishes of the democratic majority. In Panjal *panchayat*, for example, between 1996 and 2000, a veterinary hospital was built, new classrooms were added to the state school, and toilets were constructed at the school and at local market centers. This latter decision was particularly significant in that it saw priority given to separate toilet facilities for women, who traditionally had been forced to find somewhere to relieve themselves, often at the risk of humiliation and physical danger. A full-time doctor was to be hired for the local health clinic; money was allotted to the further provision of safe, piped drinking water and for the construction of sanitary latrines. In the 2000 *panchayat* plan, better roads around the village were a priority, as was the training of women auto-rickshaw drivers and computer training for women from the poorest households.

This is all pretty basic stuff in the grander developmental scheme of things, of course, but as Thomas Isaac and Franke contend, after their experiences of *panchayat* meetings around Kerala, it had major political and ideological significance. In particular,

> it decentralized the functions of government bureaucracy, it decentralized planning while mobilizing the energy of hundreds of thousands of activists and volunteers to go beyond what government funded projects can accomplish, . . . it ensure[d] delivery of project funds to the former untouchable caste, . . . it brought about special projects for women and simultaneously encouraged women elected officials, . . . [and] it has created conditions for eliminating or drastically reducing corruption in several areas of government spending.[82]

For all of its achievements, however, there are some significant and ongoing problems facing the Kerala experiment, as its critics have been quick to point out.[83] Kerala has been described, for all its great social-justice achievements, as "a straggler economy" in the neoliberal era, almost entirely dependent on tourism and the remittances sent back by the two million of its people who live and work abroad, mostly in the Gulf States.[84] There is some validity to this criticism. Kerala has never been productive enough to employ all its working-age citizens or to adequately fund its First-World social-welfare system. Unemployment and underemployment are perennial problems. It was estimated that 16 percent in rural areas and 20 percent in urban areas had no jobs in 2005. The 2008 global financial crisis worsened the situation, particularly in regard to Kerala's tourism industry, which accounts for around 60 percent of state GDP and 66 percent of its employment opportunities. There is, however, evidence of an improvement since then, with rural unemployment in 2012 down to 9 percent and 8.3 percent in the urban areas.[85]

In the context of this chapter, of course, it is worth remembering that in percentage terms this is a much better situation than South Africa's and better, too, currently than developed societies such as Spain or Greece. In absolute terms, nevertheless, in a state of thirty million people, the numbers remain very high. The generous pension scheme (from age fifty-five on) and unemployment benefits compensate to some extent, but youth unemployment in urban areas is a particular concern, as is the rate of alcohol abuse and associated social problems. There was some industrial investment in Kerala in the 1990s, but for the most part, in the neoliberal era, global and Indian capitalism has stayed away, discouraged by powerful trade unions, pro-union courts, and high minimum wages. Kerala, thus, albeit for different reasons, suffers from the lack of a robust manufacturing sector in the same way as does India per se in the neoliberal era.

As indicated above, the combination of a "slow" economy and a strong commitment to a welfare state has also left the state with significant budget deficits. Put simply, Kerala spends more than it earns in taxes and nontax revenues, and because it continues to spend on social justice and welfare provisions for its people (salaries and pensions take up almost 80 percent of its revenues), it accepts these deficits, and the need to borrow to service them, as part of its distributive philosophy.[86] In 2012–2013, the projected deficit was 350 crore (3.5 billion rupees or US$64.3 million), with the Congress Party–led alliance, now in government, promising a more stringent budgetary approach and a new "entrepreneurial" spirit for the state.[87] This, however, needs to be understood in a Kerala context, given that amid previous commitments to stringency, spending on pensions and social-welfare programs was actually increased in the 2011–2012 budget.[88]

Kerala then is radically different from most of India and indeed most of the global community in the neoliberal era, and its difference has been lauded by those increasingly aware of its vulnerabilities in a neoliberal world order. McKibben sums it up this way:

> There is chronic unemployment, a stagnant economy that may have trouble coping with world markets, and a budget deficit that is often described as out of control. But these are the kinds of problems you find in France. [On the other hand], Kerala utterly lacks the squalid drama of the Third

World—the beggars reaching through the car window, the children with distended bellies, the baby girls left to die.[89]

The debate continues about the Kerala experience. Neoliberals and some of those otherwise supportive of its social objectives point to the unsustainability of an economic system operating against the logics and interests of both domestic and global capitalism. Conversely, those more optimistic about the prospects of alternatives to neoliberal hegemony in the twenty-first century suggest that the social and political impulses set free in Kerala will ultimately sustain its democratic experiment, despite its economic malaise. There is growth, it is argued, albeit slower than in many other parts of India, and its deficit-budgeting strategy is hardly unheard of in the capitalist world. Indeed, as Amartya Sen argued in January 2013, Kerala's standard of living looks relatively good if one compares its median per capita income (9,987 Rs, about US$185) with those of the new "entrepreneurial" states (Gujarat, Himachal Pradesh, and Tamil Nadu), and on quality-of-life criteria it remains way out in front of India generally.[90]

From this perspective, Kerala's economic malaise is considered an ideological exaggeration, which rings increasingly hollow in terms of both a not-so-shining India and a global environment in which the sheen has also very definitely come off neoliberal theory and practice. Kerala, consequently, is acknowledged as a far from a perfect "people's democracy" but as a striking example of a society engaged in a process that seriously problematizes neoliberal reality and the TINA principle, a process that seeks to create and redistribute wealth and social goods as it simultaneously seeks to democratize and emancipate its people.

We wish Kerala well in this enterprise while acknowledging that major problems face it on a daily basis and while accepting that too many of its people still live in conditions of poverty and social hardship for there to be any sense of triumphalism about its alternative to neoliberal democracy.

POST-SOVIET RUSSIA AND NEOLIBERALISM: A STORY OF "SHOCK THERAPY" AND "MANAGED DEMOCRACY"

The issue of neoliberal democracy in post-Soviet Russia is inexorably bound up with events surrounding the end of the Cold War, the initial "democratization" of the Soviet superpower under Mikhail Gorbachev, and the extraordinary and controversial leadership of his successors, Boris Yeltsin (1990–2000) and Vladimir Putin (2000–2008, 2012–). In this regard, Russia represents the site of a crude and mostly destructive application of the free-market doctrines of Hayek and Friedman, in a situation which, to a greater extent even than South Africa and India, lacked the institutional and cultural capacity to absorb it or curb its excesses. The most damaging feature of the neoliberal experiment was its "shock therapy" strategy encouraged by Yeltsin between 1991 and 1998, which saw social and political catastrophe and endemic political corruption, and "seven years of economic devastation unseen anywhere else in peacetime in this [twentieth] century."[91]

Under Putin's rule, the free-market frenzy has been moderated somewhat in favor of significant state involvement in the Russian economy, and there has been an upturn in economic fortune for millions of Russians, albeit as part of a more explicitly authoritarian approach to government and society. Through all of this, the democratic dimension of the post-Soviet era has been paid lip service to but effectively ignored in practical terms. Since 1990, consequently, Russia has been a democracy in name only. In reality, it has seen rule by one variant or another of a tiny, corrupt, and often ruthless elite, infused with either implicit or explicit contempt for notions of popular sovereignty and/or the genuine political participation of the majority. Russians have shown their anger and frustration with this state of affairs, albeit with little success. In the Putin era, in particular, a more cohesive protest movement has emerged to challenge the current era of "managed democracy." We touch on these protests toward the end of the chapter. Our initial and major concentration here is the period of neoliberal dominance (1991–1998), its impact upon the prospects for democracy in post-Soviet Russia, and its legacy in the Putin era.

YELTSIN AND THE "SHOCK THERAPY" DISASTER (1991–1998)

Mikhail Gorbachev's attempts to open up and resuscitate a corrupt and dysfunctional Soviet system provoked, instead, the extraordinary stampede of people, states, and cultures away from the USSR. Within its Russian heartland, too, the Gorbachev reforms exposed a profound rejection of the Soviet command economy, its "socialist" values, and its rigid authoritarian political structures. In particular, in Moscow and other major Russian cities, liberals, intellectuals, students, and Westernized youth

movements were at the forefront of the demands for a more radical liberalization and democratization of Russian society.[92]

What they got was Boris Yeltsin and his enthusiasm for a free-market
solution to the many problems faced by a distressed nuclear superpower
seemingly in economic and social free fall by the early 1990s. Yeltsin thus
installed a new government dominated by professional economists who,
while they lived and studied in the Soviet Union, had become devoted followers of Western neoliberalism and the U.S.-led Washington Consensus.
Indeed, the Russian press designated them the new "Chicago Boys," ob-
serving that "for the first time Russia will get in its government a team of
liberals who consider themselves followers of Friedrich Hayek and Milton
Friedman." Their influence was underlined in Yeltsin's choice of Yegor
Gaidar as his deputy and Anatoly Chubais as minister for privatization.[93]

Yeltsin also reached out to the G7 and the IMF for large sums of financial aid for Russia, a request that was supported by the coterie of foreign
neoliberal economists invited to Russia to do for the newest member of
the capitalist world order what they had recently done for Poland in its
post-Soviet transition, with their "shock therapy." Led by figures such as
Jeffrey Sachs and Anders Åslund, the team of foreign neoliberal technocrats joined forces with the Russian "Chicago Boys" to effectively reinvent
a global superpower in their own (Friedmanite) image.[94]

From this perspective, a swift and unequivocal "therapy" was necessary for ailing economies, which shifted their structure and focus from
a public (state) to private (market) enterprise. It had to be done rapidly
in order to take advantage of "extraordinary conditions" and so that the
"pain" it caused might be better endured.[95] More precisely, Sachs insisted
that (1) all price controls must be lifted, (2) all subsidies must be eliminated and the economy thrown open to global trade, (3) there must be
an abrupt tightening of the money supply, (4) there must be immediate
and major cuts in government borrowing and spending, (5) there must
be privatization of all major industries, (6) and there must be massive
amounts of foreign aid to stabilize the economy during the initial "dislocation" period.[96] This, it was argued, would create the conditions for a
booming capitalist market, greater prosperity for Russia's people, and the
kinds of social and political freedoms associated with the rise to global
prominence of the liberal-democratic West.

For some, at least, there was much greater prosperity, and some sectors of the new Russian economy did "boom," albeit before a disastrous
"bust" in 1998. In particular, the Russian financial markets "boomed,"

becoming the new focus of corporate investors and global-commodity speculators, drawn to Russia by extraordinary profit margins and wide-open deregulation and privatization provisions. And for the winners in the new market economy, the rewards were quite fantastic, with profits of US$2 billion being shipped offshore each month, as Russia was asset stripped at an equally fantastic rate.[97]

But the predictable neoliberal wealth bonanza was somewhat different in Russia, to the extent that while transnational corporations and global speculators gained their usual rewards from the opening up of a vulnerable society, a small group of homegrown oligarchs gained control of the real "gems of the Soviet inheritance"—the oil and gas industries, the energy and banking sectors, the Cold War munitions industry, and the huge Soviet-era media apparatus.[98] Before the neoliberal era, there were no millionaires in Russia—by 2003, there were seventeen billionaires, mostly within the ranks of the oligarchs,[99] some of whom "ended up controlling a vast slice of national wealth, most of the media and much of the Duma."[100]

Their wealth and privilege is related directly to decisions made by Yeltsin and his neoliberal inner circle at the end of 1991. Gavriil Popov suggests that the decision ultimately came down to that between the "democratic approach" (divide the property and power of the state among all members of society) and the "nomenklatura/apparatchik approach" (keep it within the ruling elite).[101] Yeltsin and the Russian "Chicago Boys" chose the second option, even while surveys in 1992 indicated that 67 percent of Russians were opposed to this elite reconfiguration.[102]

A shock-therapy strategy was, nevertheless, introduced in January 1992. It paid little heed to democratic concerns but paid great dividends to a small elite (literally and figuratively) and had devastating social and economic consequences for the great majority of Russians. The sudden abolition of price controls on major goods and services was carried out by presidential decree, and amid increasing disquiet, Gaidar announced a radical plan to slash government spending that called for the total elimination of the huge budget deficit within four months.[103]

There were immediate and drastic implications for ordinary Russians. The prices of essential goods rose dramatically in an unregulated free market (on average, in 1992–1993, by 350 percent). The buying power of average real wages fell by 50 percent, and people's savings, accumulated during the difficult days of the Soviet era, were wiped out overnight. City dwellers living in subsidized apartments could not afford free-market rents and were rendered homeless, and while bread lines disappeared, as the neoliberals promised, bread prices soon climbed higher than wages. In fact, with the rapid rise in prices, the end of government subsidies, and sudden trade liberalization, Russia's 225,000 previously state-owned businesses could no longer guarantee wages to their workers nor tax payments to the government. The shortfall in state revenues meant, in turn, that wages to state-sector workers and pensions to retirees could also not be paid on time or at all.[104]

Chubais's initial privatization initiative was designed to sweeten the pill a little. The plan involved every man, woman, and child receiving a voucher for 10,000 rubles for the purchase of shares in newly privatized companies. It didn't work. Most people were incapable of working out the true value of businesses put up for sale and lost their money. Many, hungry and without wages, simply sold their vouchers on the black market, again at a loss. This created further antagonism within the Duma with anti-Yeltsin forces demanding that Gaidar be demoted and his "genocidal economics" be modified.[105] Simultaneously, in the streets of Moscow, in particular, otherwise fragmented political movements joined in condemnation of the neoliberal experiment in much the same terms.

By 1993, food and fuel were scarce, the public health services had collapsed, and violent crime (often involving inter-oligarchic feuds) was making life even more unbearable for all but a privileged few. Demonstrations increased in Moscow and around the country, and the opposition to neoliberalism grew inside the parliament. At this point, the Clinton administration and the IMF became more explicitly involved, as they sought to bolster the position of Yeltsin and the "Chicago Boys." Treasury undersecretary Lawrence Summers made it clear that unless the neoliberal reforms were carried out quickly, and completely, U.S. and Western support could be rescinded. The IMF went further, threatening to withhold a US$1.5 billion loan if the (elected) parliament continued to hinder the progress of the shock-therapy program.[106]

A crisis point was reached in late September 1993, with anti-Yeltsin demonstrators clashing violently with government-sponsored paramilitaries and supporters of the parliament barricading themselves in the Russian White House, to protest Yeltsin's "genocidal economics." Yeltsin bolstered his support with the oligarchs and Western leaders (particularly Bill Clinton) before responding with extreme violence, unleashing tanks and helicopter gunships upon anti-neoliberal resisters in the parliamentary building. According to "official" figures, 187 people were killed and 437 wounded in the ensuing ten-day siege.[107]

In its aftermath, Yeltsin received congratulations (and increased aid) from a doting West ("victory seen for democracy," announced the *Washington Post*).[108] Buoyed by this, Yeltsin announced and duly won an election and simultaneous referendum vote in December 1993, which provided the president with sweeping (undemocratic) powers.[109] This was to be a structure much to the liking of Vladimir Putin when he became president in 2000, but after the elections of 1993, even Yeltsin's (fading) personal popularity could not disguise the general opposition to his neoliberal economics. Candidates and parties associated with neoliberalism were soundly beaten, and a survey sponsored by the EU indicated that just 30.7 percent of Russians supported a "free market" economy, while 53.2 percent opposed it.[110]

Yeltsin responded by sponsoring a second and more frantic phase of shock therapy, and his popularity plummeted in consequence. In December 1994, therefore, he acted as desperate leaders often do and started a war (in Chechnya). But even this manufactured patriotism could not stave off the problems associated with a second round of privatization initiatives in 1995. It saw the government effectively auctioning off the ex-Soviet "commanding heights" to rich oligarchs for knockdown prices. Even Jeffrey Sachs, the hero of the Russian "Chicago Boys," was aghast at the scale of this privatization corruption, acknowledging (at least in retrospect) that "the arrangements were blatantly corrupt from the start." Its motivation was clear enough, too, he explains, in that

> the hyper-corruption surrounding the massive giveaways of the oil and gas sectors was linked to the campaign financing for President Yeltsin's reelection [in 1996]. Tens of billions of dollars of natural resource assets were given away, and hundreds of millions were collected in return as campaign contributions.[111]

The political payoff for Yeltsin, and the neoliberals, did indeed center on the elections of 1996, primarily via US$100 million of financial donations—thirty-three times the legal limit. Added to this was an electoral process "widely seen in Russia (though not in the West) as neither free nor fair."[112] Ultimately, Yeltsin was declared the winner, but the deep suspicion surrounding the 1996 election has never really gone away, and in 2012, Dmitri Medvedev, president of Russia between 2008 and 2012, conceded that the 1996 election was in fact rigged, and Yeltsin actually lost it on the popular vote.[113] Whatever else this particular piece of chicanery indicates, it underscores a truism about the neoliberal era in Russia—that it was integral to a deeply corrupt and antidemocratic system. For Georgi Arbatov, a disillusioned advisor to Yeltsin, this was only to be expected because a neoliberal "policy that breeds poverty and crime . . . can survive only if democracy is suppressed."[114]

There was plenty of poverty and crime. Between 1991 and 1998, more than 80 percent of Russia's farms had gone bankrupt, and around 70,000 factories had closed, spilling millions into penury and unemployment. In 1989, before the neoliberal era, 2 million Russians lived in poverty, on US$4 a day. By the mid-1990s, the World Bank reported that 74 million Russians were poverty stricken. And while the Soviet era was hard on most Russians, there was at least (subsidized) housing. After 1991, in free-market conditions, there was widespread homelessness. A UNICEF report in 1994 spoke of 3.5 million homeless children. Moreover, by the mid-1990s, violent crime in Russia had risen 400 percent from the rate in the pre-neoliberal era.[115] By 2000, male life expectancy in Russia was fifty-eight years, below that of Pakistan.[116] Between 1993 and 2003, the Russian population fell by more than five million.[117]

As for the economic miracle promised by the "Chicago Boys" and their Western mentors, there was, instead, economic disaster. Russia's GDP fell 50 percent between 1991 and 1998, taxes went uncollected, investment in new plants and equipment fell by 75 percent, and Russia was importing 40 percent of its food. The neoliberal monetary policy made money so scarce in Russian society that 70–80 percent of transactions were conducted by barter, and "what had been a diversified industrial economy had been transformed into a raw materials exporting appendage of Western capitalism."[118] By 1999, Yeltsin's approval rating was down to 6 percent. Miners went on strike over unpaid wages (Russian workers by now were owed US$12.5 billion). What was left of the middle class was stunned by the closure of major banks and the loss of life savings. Chubais was sacked for corrupt practices, Yeltsin had a series of heart attacks and fired two prime ministers and a number of his "Chicago Boys," the "financial" oligarchs began to turn on the government, and the impact of the Asian financial crisis only made things worse. The markets, by now, were in panic mode. Russian stock, bond, and currency markets collapsed, and Russia defaulted on its domestic debt and froze its debt repayments to foreign creditors. All this, argue Reddaway and Glinski, was due to a crude neoliberal strategy that resulted in the widespread "plundering of the country, the destruction of its industrial capabilities, a decline in production, the widespread impoverishment of the Russian people and the extreme stratification of wealth [alongside] the debasement of government authority."[119]

Just when it looked as if things could get no more miserable for Russians, they did. Thus, in August and September 1999, apartment buildings and a shopping center were blown up in Moscow, killing hundreds. The official response was that this was a case of "blowback"—a revenge attack by Chechen terrorists aimed at the heart of Russian society. There is ongoing suspicion that it was the work of groups in the FSB/KGB seeking a national crisis to finally impose some order and stability on a chaotic situation.[120] Whatever the case, this incident propelled Vladimir Putin to the national consciousness, and it was Putin (ex–lieutenant colonel in the KGB and ex-head of FSB) who took charge, ordering air strikes on Chechnya and promising bloody vengeance for the "terrorist" outrage.

THE PUTIN YEARS: BRINGING THE STATE BACK IN, STILL LEAVING DEMOCRACY OUT

Putin was anointed by an ailing Yeltsin in late 1999 (on a promise of immunity from any future prosecution). He subsequently saw off the challenges of moderate democrats and won the elections of 2000 and 2004. After eight years in power, Putin (formally) stepped down and became prime minister for a second time, with his protégé, Dmitri Medvedev, as president. Controversially, in 2012, after changing the law to make it possible, Putin won back the presidency, this time for an extended six-year term.

Outside of Russia, there is considerable fascination with the enduring popularity of Putin, who is variously described as a "taciturn little man," "chilling," "steely," and "vaguely sinister."[121] But in Putin's case, there are some relatively straightforward reasons for this popularity, and they are intrinsic to the issues touched above. In short, since Putin has been in power, the standard and quality of life of average Russians has improved considerably. He has restored a significant measure of order to the chaos of the Yeltsin years, rekindled a sense of national pride in the Russian people, taken on and tamed the feared and despised oligarchs, and reclaimed some of the most important elements of the Russian "commanding heights" (e.g., the oil and gas industries) for the state. His critics are many, nevertheless, drawn primarily from the ranks of those who still believe that capitalist economics and social order are not incommensurable with democratic politics.

This clearly is a point of departure with Putin, who, suggests Boris Nemtsov, "believes that Russia needs a healthy market economy [but] unfortunately doesn't believe that Russia needs a democracy too." It is difficult, explains Nemtsov, "to explain to someone with a KGB background that there is a connection between democracy and competitive markets."[122] For all this, the great majority of Russians have appreciated the sense of stability and (relative) composure of the Putin years and appear less concerned with any damage done to the democratic process along the way. And Russians have appreciated Putin's passionate defense of the Russian state after the shock-therapy years, acknowledging that

> the days when the IMF dictated budgets, and the Foreign Ministry acted as little more than an American consulate, are over. Gone are the campaign managers for reelection of the president, jetting in from California. Freed from foreign debt and diplomatic supervision, Russia is an independent state once again.[123]

Above all, it has been the changes in the Russian economy in the Putin years that have most endeared him to the Russian masses. Here, he got lucky, in that he came to power in 2000 and rode the first wave of a twenty-first-century global commodity boom, particularly in regard to oil and gas prices. As the world's largest producer of gas, and a major global oil producer, Russia was suddenly in a prime position to strengthen its domestic and global situation, and Putin has taken advantage of this, regaining control of substantial parts of the oil and gas sectors and using the massive and growing revenues to pay off Russia's debts and invest in the depressed public sector.[124] In his first eight years, consequently, Russian GDP rose by 6–7 percent a year. There was industrial growth of 75 percent, and foreign and local investment increased by 125 percent. Between 2000 and 2008, the average wage increased from 2,200 rubles per month (US$90) to 12,500 rubles (US$500), and the average pension, from 823 rubles (US$33) to 3,500 rubles (US$140).[125] Importantly too, for the first time since the end of the Cold War, workers got their wages and pensioners got their pensions, on time and in full. Unsurprisingly, and in the wake of the shock-therapy disaster, Putin was rewarded in the middle years of the first decade of the twenty-first century with a 72 percent approval rating for a range of sensible and (relatively) humane policy decisions.[126]

By 2012, however, amid the controversy surrounding his third term in office, there was a drop in support for Putin (to 63.6 percent), particularly among the educated middle classes in the major cities. But in the industrial heartland of Russia, which suffered grievously at the height of the neoliberal era, his support was rock solid. Putin the politician is thus well aware that Russia is not just Moscow or St. Petersburg and that to a large extent "the old feudal order still exists in the countryside. It's just put on a democratic coat."[127]

Most important, the majority of Russians have warmed to Putin's "mixed economy" pragmatism on the question of the free market and his acknowledgment of the need for a strong state involvement in economic affairs after the era of a fully blown neoliberalism. The giant Gazprom company, for example, accounts for about 23 percent of global gas supplies, and Putin has used the state's controlling share in the company as something of a signifier of Russia's new assertive place in the global economy. He has also pressured Gazprom to sell its gas to Russians at less than the global market price.[128] Putin, in short, accepts that Russia is now a capitalist state, but when the workings of the "free" market threaten the sovereignty or stability of the Russian state, his primary commitment is clear enough.

This commitment has driven his confrontation with some of the most powerful oligarchs, particularly those in the energy fields. He has prevented them from playing major roles in Russian politics, and through fair means and foul (on issues of tax avoidance, fraud, corrupt practices, etc.), he has "tamed" them and, to some extent at least, has tamed the corrupt and violent behavior that saw them so despised by ordinary Russians.[129] Thus, "the age of the Jurassic oligarchs is now passing. Russia under Putin is retreating from anarchy, and there will be no return to the years when a hundred executives in the aluminum industry alone were murdered."[130] And while no one suggests that Russia is completely free of the corruption and violence that poisoned the Yeltsin years, it is more controlled under Putin and, importantly for his popularity, there is a general feeling among Russia's masses that his regime is not as corrupt as that which preceded it.

As indicated above, however, while Russia has moved into a moderated phase of its capitalist development under Putin, there is no longer even the neoliberal pretense concerning support for democratic politics. In this regard, Russia has much in common with China, in its concern to "liberalize" the economy without any corresponding reform of the political sphere. Putin believes that he has mass support in this regard, proposing, like a previous KGB officer (Andropov) in power, that "first we'll make enough sausages, and then we won't have any dissidents."[131]

In an economically recovering Russia, therefore, Putin is happy enough to have "democratic" elections at local, federal, and national levels, as long as he continues to have control over the electoral process at all these levels.

This, it appears he has, via his party, United Russia, and its dominance in the Duma and via the appointment of powerful figures, infamous *siloviki* ("men of force"—trusted former KGB/FSB officers), in crucial institutional roles, throughout the regional governments and in Moscow's business and political communities.[132] Under Gorbachev, people of this background made up 5 percent of federal officials. Under Putin, they comprise around 58 percent. As Ascherson puts it, "democratic self-confidence does not grow well in their shadow."[133] For those still considered enemies of the new Russian state, consequently, there is relentless and sometimes murderous pursuit, particularly for dissenters in the media and government service.[134]

To further ensure his control over any democratic challenge, Putin has reformulated the parliamentary structure to locate even more power in the presidency. In short, he has restructured the constitution to suit himself, taking advantage of its (Yeltsin-induced) loopholes to effectively rule by presidential decree, without disturbing the rubber-stamp Duma. The result is a managed democracy centered on a dominant presidency, weak legislative institutions, and a "system geared to reward loyalty to the Kremlin above anything else [with] accountability to the actual population neither here nor there."[135]

Dmitry Furman has perhaps summed up the nature of this system best, suggesting that Russia under Putin is a "managed" democracy in the sense that

> elections are held, but the results are known in advance; courts hear cases but give decisions that coincide with the interests of the authorities; the press is plural, yet with few exceptions dependent on the government. [It is] a system of "uncontested power," increasingly similar to the Soviet state, but without any ideological foundation.[136]

This might, as some suggest, be simply a case of history and culture repeating itself as Russians once again accept their need for strong, authoritarian rule from above. On the other hand, it might have less to do with any deeply embedded antidemocratic tendency in Russian culture per se, but more to do with recent experience of its neoliberal variety. This certainly has been one of the tensions in twenty-first-century Russia, played out in confrontations between protesters and the state in recent years.

THE DEMOCRATIC PROTEST MOVEMENTS:
RADICAL CHANGE OR JUST RADICAL CHIC?

There has always been dissent against the ruling powers in Russia, even during the Cold War when it was a central actor in the Soviet empire. Under Stalin, the gulags and mental wards were full of people who couldn't see the error of their ways concerning the correct road to socialist freedom. In the post–Cold War era, under Yeltsin, there was at least (relative) freedom to protest. This was not due to any genuine concern for democratic sensibilities on Yeltsin's part; it was more an understanding that (until 1998–1999) it couldn't hurt him, and it impressed his financial sponsors in the Western world. Those arraigned against him, for the most part unemployed and unpaid workers, pensioners, old-guard communists, and some nationalists irked by the influence of foreign ideologues, could be "managed," at least while the wealthy middle class, the oligarchs, and the liberal intelligentsia (and the army) stayed loyal. This, and the self-interested behavior of most of his political opponents inside the parliament, ensured the general impotence of democratic protest "from below."

During 1998 and 1999, however, in conditions of extreme chaos and massive disillusionment with the whole neoliberal experience, Yeltsin's supportive hard core deserted him. In particular, the young, well-educated, Westernized urban dwellers who had profited significantly from the free-market era became disappointed and angry at the incapacity of Yeltsin and the "Chicago Boys" to maintain the kind of social and economic order in which markets work most efficiently. There was thus a good deal of relief (alongside the trepidation) on the part of many erstwhile Yelstin supporters at the (largely peaceful) changeover to the more austere and ordered rule of Putin.

Under Putin, the numbers of protests dropped significantly, particularly in his first term when more than just a tiny elite was able to enjoy the material benefits of Russia's economic upturn. The protests increased in his second term, as Putin's authoritarian tendencies became more evident. Consistent with these tendencies was his mobilization of state power to intimidate the protesters—for example, by increased fines, draconian public-order laws, or by the feared Nashi.[137] This state-sponsored backlash saw thousands of Putin supporters involved in counterprotests, against those represented as the middle-class stooges of the liberal-democratic West—and of neoliberal globalization—in short, those primarily responsible for the disasters of the Yeltsin years.

The movements of dissent continued to grow nevertheless, particularly in response to Putin's September 2011 announcement that he was standing again for the presidency and that the elected president would now have a six-year mandate. This dissent increased following the highly dubious election process associated with the general parliamentary elections of December 4, 2011, and became more widespread as Putin became president again in March 2012. In Moscow, consequently, an estimated 60,000 turned out to condemn the fraudulent Duma election on December 10, 2011. Simultaneously, in St. Petersburg, 5,000 marched, as they did in smaller numbers across the country. Two weeks later, a larger crowd gathered in Moscow (estimated 80,000), where Gorbachev spoke, alongside opposition politicians, intellectuals, and artists, condemning Putin and his "party of crooks and thieves" in the Kremlin. The momentum increased in February 2012, with large numbers rallying in Moscow and in 113 towns and cities.

A diversity of groups was drawn to these marches, and their increased organization and cohesion has rarely been seen in Russia—a cohesion reflected in the naming of the protests as "For Honest Elections." Under this umbrella was a spectrum of contemporary Russian dissent. It included liberal political organizations such as Yabloko and Solidarity, leftist groups such as the Russian Socialist Movement and Left Front, "moderate" nationalist groups such as the DPNI, and some old monarchists. Alongside them marched TV personalities and other celebrities, social groups protesting the destruction of the Khimki Forest, groups upset by overly aggressive traffic police, and members of the Russian "pirate party."[138]

The protests continued into 2012 as the presidential elections drew nearer, but the Putin forces were by now increasingly muddying the waters. Alongside the "For Honest Elections" protesters thus were a range of aggressive pro-Putin groups (including Nashi thugs), condemning the growth of "orange" revolutionary zeal in the crowds (i.e., as in the Ukraine).[139] On the day before Putin's inauguration, on May 6, 2012, this harassment reached a peak during a protest of 20,000 in Moscow, which saw enhanced levels of violence and the arrests of prominent protesters. In the wake of this event, organizers and opposition figures had their homes raided, human-rights activists were arrested, and a new level of intimidation was established. The point of it all, as an anticorruption advocate notes, was to "scare off the educated middle class professionals" who make up the core of the protest movement and "radicalize" the remainder so as to legitimate an even stronger crackdown in the future.[140]

It seems to have worked. The protests have diminished in size and intensity since early 2012, although they go on sporadically, albeit as large social gatherings complete with music and face-painted children. This is not to trivialize the courage or commitment of the thousands who still defy the intimidation, but it does beg the question of who, in the main, the protesters are and what is likely to be the outcome of their protests.

There has been a good deal said on this issue. The *New York Times*, for example, spoke of "debonair demonstrators in mink coats and designer jeans" marching for democracy in Putin's Russia.[141] Another image is that of a "flighty elite," reveling in their radical activities before quickly "retreating into their lavish apartments, Jeeps, and Land Cruisers, departing on shopping trips to London and Paris."[142] There is a small, more confrontational element to the protests, but the representation of them as radical chic, it seems, has empirical validity. Confirming this, Tony Wood cites a Levada Center study suggesting that "the protesters are on the whole members of the intelligentsia."[143] Paul Starobin, meanwhile, notes that, within the protest environment, to be "anti-Putin" is seen "as a badge of sophistication and good taste."[144]

Susanne Sternthal's firsthand report of the protest on June 12, 2012, in Moscow, is particularly illuminating in this regard. It took place in the face of direct intimidation and harassment, but approximately 20,000 people took part. Most prominent among them, reports Sternthal, was the Russian nouveaux riches, the "dapperly-dressed men and tanned women in high-heeled sandals, laughing," alongside the "students, professors and professionals." A poll taken of the protesters illustrated that "the majority have a university degree or are in the process of getting one." They were, nevertheless, well organized, to the extent that leftists and communists walked on one side of Pushkin Square, with rightists and nationalists on the other side. There were orange flags and blue flags for "democratic elections," and communist red flags. There were green balloons for "save the forest" protesters and the white ribbons of the "liberal" opposition parties. It was, therefore, colorful, diverse, and courageous, but, as Sternthal concludes, "the absence of a compelling, realistic and specific plan for changing the government" effectively played into the hands of the "national stability" theme of the Putin regime.[145]

Dmitri Travin adds an interesting dimension to this issue, suggesting that increasingly there are real doubts among liberals that the protests have seriously challenged Putin. The protest numbers have dwindled since 2012, and according to the Public Opinion Foundation, Putin's popularity is actually on the rise again. The overarching problem, suggests Travin, is that the urban liberals at the core of the protest movements simply presumed that their concerns about Putin and democracy are shared by the rest of Russia. They are not, he argues, nor is there evidence that they will be any time soon. Rather, the great majority of Russians are enjoying a material prosperity under Putin that no "liberal" perspective has ever afforded them, and they are quite willing to forgo the "Western" experience so treasured by their more-educated fellow citizens.[146]

Another conclusion in this vein comes from Anatol Lieven, who suggests that ultimately the protest movements simply do not reflect the broader reality of Russia during the Putin era. This is not just because the great majority of ordinary Russians support Putin but because large sectors of the urban liberal population do also. Here, the legacy of the neoliberal era in Russia continues to cast a large shadow over prospects for its democratic future because, as Lieven suggests, many within the liberal intelligentsia are still haunted by the "awful memories" of the neoliberal era they helped create. They recognize, more precisely, that "no Russian group identified unconditionally with Western economic and political ideas can possibly gain majority support" in today's Russia. More pragmatically, many also see Putin as the best hope for administering Russian capitalism effectively. In short, concludes Lieven, "Putin's administration is not going to fall. The only way that could happen is in the context of a disastrous collapse of the world economy, dragging Russia down with it—something which is hardly to be desired from any point of view."[147]

This does not mean that the protests of the middle class are irrelevant to current Russian politics or that a democratic outcome might not emerge from their efforts at some future time. After all, the whole history of democratic change is punctuated with instances of small groups of educated liberals spearheading radical social change in unlikely circumstances. Unsurprisingly, Thomas Friedman has emphasized this theme, proposing that the anti-Putin protests are, in fact, Russia's "Arab Spring."[148] Others, such as Graeme Robertson, have warned against wishful thinking in this regard, and Robertson's detailed study of protest in Russia is particularly valuable in framing democratic expectation in the current Russian context.[149]

Russia, he proposes, has never been quite as passive as Western scholars have characterized it, but it has never had the open, organized, social-movement culture long established in Western societies. Nor does it have much of a residue of this culture, as it exists in post-imperialist states such as

South Africa and India. Rather, in authoritarian settings such as Russia's, be it under tsarist or Soviet rule, public protest has, as Charles Tilly describes it, been "rare, dangerous, and often violent, . . . [typically] direct in nature rather than symbolic, geographically and politically isolated, spontaneous, and largely without the coordination of organized social movements."[150]

It has not been quite this stark in post–Cold War Russia, but for a range of reasons outlined above, the struggles for "bottom up" democracy under Yeltsin were unsuccessful, and the current "top down" protests under Putin have been largely thwarted. This is no reason to trivialize or sneer at the current protest movements as merely "radical chic." There might be fur coats and PhDs aplenty in the crowd, but there is also courage and persistence and, for some at least, a commitment to the kind of democratic openness and freedom largely unknown in Russia but worth struggling for nevertheless. On the other hand, the cultural memory of the shock-therapy years would seem to rule out mass support for any variant of neoliberalism in the foreseeable future, and the highly compromised position of the liberal intelligentsia in those years will presumably continue to undermine their appeals to the larger democratic audience, even if it finds Putin sometimes a little too authoritarian for twenty-first-century Russia.

POSTSCRIPT: WHY DID NEOLIBERALISM FAIL?

In this chapter, we have touched upon some elements of the post-Soviet era in Russia, commenting most critically on the period in which neoliberal theory and practice dominated (1990–2000). In so doing, we acknowledge the (retrospective) views of those involved in the "shock therapy" experiment, or committed to its ideological framing, who have resolutely defended their positions, effectively by blaming all and sundry for the disasters attributed to it. It was thus the tardiness of the IMF that fatally undermined its "stabilization" phase,[151] or it was old-guard corruption that slowed down and thwarted the dynamism of it,[152] or (mimicking the old socialist line about the USSR) neoliberal market reform didn't fail because it was never really tried in Russia, due to the lack of an appropriate institutional and cultural milieu for its application.[153]

There is a measure of plausibility in all of these arguments. On the other hand, there were plenty of analysts arguing, from the beginning, for a slower, more sensitive installation of market ideology in a space as alien to it as the former capital of the USSR. But, as Desai suggests, the neoliberals simply "neglected the inadequate institutional underpinning under which the Soviet command economy was to be transformed into a market system."[154] Sergei Rogov indicates why, proposing that "the so-called Yeltsin liberals went for the right-wing conservative ideology of the US as an alternative to the Communist planned economy. They exchanged Marxism-Leninism for Friedmanism."[155] The former ambassador to the USSR Jack Matlock articulates it differently, expressing amazement at the fact that a free-market shock-therapy strategy was imposed on 1990s Russia, "ignoring the fact that there was no legitimate capital in the country."[156] This decision has been likened to building a house with no plumbing. This is a good analogy, not least because of an image it creates—of a shonky builder pursuing a fast buck without concern for those living in the house.

But this, we maintain, is not the primary reason for the devastation wrought by neoliberalism in Russia or for the stillbirth of the democracy associated with it. Rather, it resides in the nature of the beast itself, as represented not just in Russia but also in the other places and spaces we have explored in chapters 3 and 4. Indeed, wherever neoliberalism has been invoked as the basis of prosperity and democracy, the same fundamental patterns have emerged to provoke economic dislocation and political dissent: (1) huge sectoral imbalances in the economy favoring the "financial" sectors (stock, bonds, and currency markets, banking, corporate investment, speculative capital) over the "real economy"; (2) an increasing disparity between a rich minority and a poor majority; (3) attacks on public services and worker organizations and a lack of concern for social welfare; (4) increased corruption, often associated with privatization schemes that sell off (at a pittance) major industries built with public wealth; and (5) encouragement of, and accommodation with, a "managed democracy" of one form or another (e.g., polyarchy in the United States, wealthy nepotism in India, ANC hegemony in South Africa) that effectively thwarts meaningful democratic intent and participation.

Ultimately, though, neoliberalism's failure, in its own terms, is about ideological delusion and arrogance—in the Russian context, the delusion, for example, of a figure such as Harvard economist Lawrence Summers, Bill Clinton's undersecretary of state, who insisted that "the laws of economics are like the laws of engineering. One set of laws works everywhere."[157] This, plus the arrogance of figures such as Sachs and Åslund and Gaidar, and the other free-market zealots, saw this alleged "law" imposed crudely and insensitively upon an already devastated Russian society, in a manner entirely consistent with the hegemonic age of neoliberalism.

CHAPTER 5

GLOBALIZATION AND THE DESTABILIZATION OF DEMOCRACY

In the late twentieth and early twenty-first centuries, democratic political projects, including neoliberalism, have had to negotiate the destabilization of the nation-state consequent of the uneven processes of globalization. In this chapter, we turn more directly to this process of democratic negotiation and we look, in particular, at some of the complex global processes that are destabilizing the traditional territorialized nation-state. This, we reiterate, does not imply the end of the modern state system. It means that globalization—understood as a set of powerful social, economic, and technological processes—is destabilizing that multilayered ensemble of factors that created liberal democracy and that has given dominant meaning to the modern world of states since the seventeenth century.

APPROACHING GLOBALIZATION DEMOCRATICALLY

Globalization does not have a single logic and does not comprise a singular, tight-fitting material or ideational infrastructure. Neoliberals—Thomas Friedman is exemplary in this respect[1]—overstate the logical coherence and material unity of globalization. They see the economic integration of capitalism across the globe as globalization's definitive and determinant logic from which new forms of social life and a potential new humanism of the planet will emerge based on the "economic man" of Western capitalist lore. This neo-deterministic preference for a "one world" order chafes against a democratic ethos, especially as neoliberals like Friedman argue that it is inevitable and those like Mandelbaum argue it is necessary to freedom. For this vision, constraints on the possible choices and paths of development are limited, cultural differences submerge beneath an overarching logic of commodification and economic exchange, and political differences harden into seemingly irreducible oppositions of "us" and "them" (the liberal and illiberal democracies of Fareed Zakaria, for example,[2] or in Huntington's apocalyptic "clash of civilizations"), leaving little room for democratic negotiations of the flows and movements of globalization.

This narrow and audacious neoliberal vision, however, betrays the complexity and disjunctive nature of the assemblages of the transnational and deterritorialized flows that comprise twenty-first-century globalization. As the territorial nation-state loosens its hold on the democratic political imagination, new conditions emerge, and new opportunities take hold for democratic "world-making." Some of the same technologies, material and informational processes, and knowledge and ideational flows that have brought into being tighter forms of social and political management, and even made technocratic institutions based on neoliberal logics appear benign or even necessary, have at the same time rekindled more radical political drives and imaginaries of democratic participation and organization. New conditions emerge in globalization, viewed from a democratic perspective, not from the inevitable or necessary triumph of the Western narrative of modernity but from the historically contingent freeing up of collective imaginaries from the narrative structures and tropes of the nation-state and the Westphalian states-system.

Consequently, democracy in globalization may take the form of reimagined nation-states, of new regional and federalist constitutionalisms such as are emerging in human-rights courts in Europe and elsewhere, in social-justice movements in civil societies in and around the world, or in local experiments with participatory self-government that draw solidarity and resources from connection to global networks. From the perspective of neoliberal polyarchy, these alternatives appear as overloads of rational decision-making capacities or as irrational demands of immature publics or as idealistic and unrealistic although well-meaning attempts to make the world more just than is possible. From a perspective of a democratic ethos that values a deeper popular participation and that sees in new technologies and global mobilities conditions of possibility for democracy rather than new necessities and tighter constraints, these alternatives embolden action and activate the creative impulses of democratic world making.

This world-making process often involves a significant deterritorialization of social life with many democratic possibilities. Several sociologists have attempted to capture the nature of this deterritorialization process. Manuel Castells, in perhaps the most well-known characterization of this theme, speaks of a "networked society," which is "made up of networks of production, power and experience, which construct a culture of virtuality in the global flows that transcend time and space."[3] John Urry describes this phenomenon as one that requires the rethinking of the global environment in terms of a new "mobilities paradigm." In his view, these mobilities confront people in the twenty-first century faster and more directly than ever before. He says: "Physical changes appear to be 'de-materializing' connections, as people, machines, images, information, power, money, ideas and dangers are 'on the move,' making and remaking connections at often rapid speed around the world."[4] Anthropologist Arjun Appadurai has described these rapid global flows as occurring "*in and through the growing disjunctures between ethnoscapes, technoscapes, finanscapes, mediascapes and ideoscapes* [italics in original]."[5] This implies that the temporality of modernity that inheres in the interactions between different spatial frames (the state, global capitalism, imperial and colonial systems, communications networks, diasporas, etc.) has been constantly taking new forms rather than having conformed to the essentially linear explanations of time and space to be found in traditional modernity narratives.

The point is that the logics that define these networks of relations are now changing, and new ones are emerging that are not confined or related to the logic of territorial states in ways they have been over the last 300 or so years. As Saskia Sassen has recently emphasized, globalization is taking place not just across but also "inside" states, establishing new logics, constraints, and governmental practices for managing not just information flows but also flows of people, identities, physical commodities, violence, and more.[6] Moreover, more and more aspects of governance are dependent on information flows that transverse and transform the physical nature of territorial borders. Neoliberals often recognize this process but tend to overstate the way in which a territorialized world order is being superseded under conditions of deterritorialization. We stress here, following Sassen's insight, that this process of change is more subtle and nuanced, that relations between territoriality and deterritorialization in modern democratic states have always been complex and contested, and that that logic is now being tested and transformed into new ensembles of democratic politics, reinforcing some aspects of liberal democracy, challenging others, and opening up new possibilities for democratic association and action.

In this context, some contemporary democratic theorists have echoed the ancient concerns of Aristotle (see introduction) concerning the acceleration of the deterritorialized age and the negative impact this has on the time left for democratic decision making.[7] Seyla Benhabib, for example, stresses the problem of fast-track trade legislation that leaves little room for extended debate and discussion over policies and limits legislative oversight of, for example, neoliberal trade practices.[8] There are, likewise, the challenges to democratic accountability associated with the increased speed by which new financial instruments are created and are mutating to take advantage of rapidly changing economic conditions (derivatives and other complex financial securities, for example, that are made possible by computerized information networks). This allows little time for democratic contestation over the logics of financial instruments and seems to limit regulation to "after the fact" legislation. The general concern, as Sheldon Wolin has put it, is that democratic politics requires a "leisurely pace" to ensure genuine accountability and participation, which is increasingly at odds with the current culture of globalization and a speeded up capitalist, consumer culture.[9]

Other democratic theorists, such as William E. Connolly, are also concerned by the rapidity of globalized life for democratic politics but stress some positive implications of an accelerated world of trade, ideas, and communications.[10] In particular, suggests Connolly, there is an increasing ability in the current era for groups and individuals to coordinate effective democratic action through the immediacy of social media and the Internet, as we have seen in the Arab Spring and the various Occupy movements. Another positive factor in this regard concerns the capacity to proliferate real-time information about democratic struggles speedily around the world, creating solidarities across great distances. This has numerous effects that, we suggest, may be creating new democratic political subjectivities, helping to develop ethical-political understandings and enhanced practices of "self-making" that are deepening democratic commitments simultaneously across borders and in local places. In this context, it becomes possible for progressive people to not only support distant democratic movements with money and supplies but also to help create an ethos that folds global commitments to justice and equality into local understandings of democracy. We look at some of these new democratic subjectivities in the final chapter of the book.

Finally, the accelerated pace of air travel has enhanced the importance of diasporic groups around the world and is changing the relation between national and ethnic communities and their home states.[11] For example, note the increased importance of Dominicans living in the United States in the recent presidential election there. In June 2011, a new law allotted seven congressional seats in the Dominican congress to Dominicans living abroad, most of whom live in and around New York City. Polling stations were set up in Dominican neighborhoods, and reports suggest that the vote in the United States was crucial to Danilo Medina's victory in the May 2012 election. Such extraterritorial voting is becoming more and more common. This is also an issue we will touch on shortly as part of a discussion over renegotiated forms of democratic citizenship under globalization.

Suffice it to say, for now, that the new infrastructure of globalization has multiple effects on democracy, operating on multiple registers at once. It affects democracy inside states, and it makes possible new democratic attachments across state borders as established democracies try to adapt to new time signatures of global flows and as the acceleration of contacts creates new conditions for democratic transformation and possibility. It also contains some ironic possibilities for change. For example, the same communication technologies that enhance state surveillance and provide the means for deep repression of democratic movements also enable those movements to organize and communicate, hampering such surveillance and repression and enabling greater democratic interaction. This was evident enough in the way that the Indian peasants of Chiapas in Mexico were able to reach out to the world with their desires for democratic assistance in 1994, as it was to the activists associated with the WikiLeaks affair more recently.

Taken together, these characteristics of contemporary globalization produce several sets of problems and possibilities for democracy. In the remainder of this chapter, we touch on three of these in more detail: (1) the democratic security dilemma in neoliberal globalization, (2) the issue of the "democratic deficit," and (3) the question of a "globalized" democratic citizenship. We do not argue that these problematics can be traced exclusively to neoliberal ideology and policy but that ways that neoliberalism has influenced dominant policies cannot be ignored as helping to frame the ways they have been understood.

DEMOCRATIC NEGOTIATIONS OF SECURITY (1): THE NEOLIBERAL WAY OF WAR

After the Cold War, a "peace dividend" of reduced military spending invoked by the Clinton administration promised to alleviate a contradiction that had emerged in the neoliberal American state. This contradiction resided in the combination of a democracy-promotion strategy that required large state expenditure and an expansive military security presence around the world, with neoliberal deregulation and privatization policies that became manifest in the huge budget deficits during the administrations of Ronald Reagan and G. W. Bush. However, the peace dividend never materialized, and to the extent that the Obama administration has largely adopted a neoliberal economic agenda, this contradiction is not likely to go away any time soon.[12]

After the attacks of September 11, 2001, the contradiction of the neoliberal security policy deepened as the financial pressures of the War on Terror further expanded the U.S. military commitments abroad with the opportunistic invasion of Iraq and Afghanistan. Military spending spiraled upward[13] as the logistics of the wars in the cities of Iraq and the mountains of Afghanistan, together with those of policing the non-state "terrorist" organizations, such as Al-Qaida, furthered the promotion of precision-guided weapons systems and all the complex paraphernalia of modern warfare designed for lethal force and reduced risk to American soldiers.

In this context, neoliberals have sought to turn the inherent contradiction of the post–Cold War era to their advantage, developing what we might call a neoliberal way of war. In the process, they have created a variety of problems and possibilities for democratic theory and practice. This was very evident in the attempts of George W. Bush in Iraq to combine the doctrine of preemptive war with a neoliberal strategy of democracy promotion. Initially, the Bush administration naively assumed that after the war a liberal-democratic government would easily emerge. Expatriate Iraqi leaders were brought back from exile in the West to lead the new democratic Iraq. Market forces were promulgated as the new economic doctrine, the oil fields were to be opened up to foreign investment, labor rights were to be restricted as was the formation of labor unions, and government officials associated with the former regime were arrested or otherwise disqualified from serving in the new democracy. When a liberal-democratic government didn't emerge, and in the ensuring chaos that did, the United States came to worry that a popularly elected democracy might in fact be a problematic outcome leading to a Shiite-led government with strong ties to Iran. Officials in the United States thus entertained and even encouraged de facto divisions of Iraq into Kurdish, Shiite, and Sunni regions that deepened religious and ethnic tensions and conflicts.

In Iraq, Afghanistan, and in the War on Terrorism, neoliberals have pioneered new deployments of forces that can frame warfare as not only legitimate but also as cost effective in the new global battlefields that liberal democracies now face. These deployments rely on mobile weapons rich in computer technologies, utilizing global communications and satellites. War planning creates synergies with the civilian economy, enlisting the scientific, software, and engineering communities through the Defense Advanced Research Projects Agency, or DARPA. Automated weapons systems, from cruise missiles to modern drones, promise limited casualties and more effective strikes, increasingly using satellite communications and new mapping technologies to hone their targeting. Increasing technological sophistication along with a faith in the effectiveness of advanced technologies added to the acceptability of the new form of war. It created the representation of the new warfare as limited and "surgical," a metaphor that draws on legitimations of medical expertise and creates the impression that our violence is careful, discriminate, rationally planned, and respectful of the "patient," against the indiscriminate, unsophisticated, and irrational violence of the enemy who causes the disease that needs to be fought.

While the battlefield has clearly changed, the liberal drive to control war has persisted and intensified, both to use it as a rational tool of policy (now in the name of national interest defined in terms of establishing and policing a normative, democratic world system) and to use more and more advanced weaponry to control violence on the "battlefield." The new warfare perpetuates the neoliberal contradiction between expansive military spending and reduced state resources, further justifying neoliberal cuts to social programs. In the case of contemporary technologically intensive warfare, costs are bound to rise (note how nearly all advanced weapons systems have come in substantially over budget) given "Moore's law," named for one of the cofounders of Intel that states that the pace of technological change in the computer age is exponential, doubling every two years. This means that new, more advanced technologies will need to be acquired almost constantly, putting enormous, continual pressure on the ability of states to fund social and civilian programs even as troop deployments are reduced.

Traditional liberal, democratic, constitutional, and legislative remedies for resort to war, by making it accountable to a democratic public, were of little help. Constitutional provisions designed to ensure civilian control of the military proved no match for the new form of expansive military deployments. The U.S. War Powers Act, for example, that required Congressional approval for foreign deployments of troops beyond ninety days, failed in the case of Iraq and the War on Terrorism, as the Bush administration easily deployed the tropes of patriotism and rhetoric of ever-present threats and dangers that had a chilling effect and short-circuited criticisms and garnered blanket endorsement in Congress for the war along with vast restrictions on civil rights.

Nevertheless, the Bush administration and the Obama administration have had difficulty framing this new form of warfare in order to generate and sustain public support for the longer-term interventions and continual deployments of military forces and spending on weapons that are needed. This is not for lack of effort. The interventions in Iraq and Afghanistan still involved large deployments of troops, and the contradictory nature of neoliberal globalist war between cutting state expenditures while engaging in interventionist wars posed considerable problems for the Bush administration. Tours of duty for soldiers had to be extended, sometimes to several years at a time with little time off, and National Guard troops were called up in order to supplement the all-volunteer forces. This exacerbated the social inequalities generated by neoliberal economic policies as the volunteer force drew disproportionately from poor and lower-middle-class men and women, many of whom saw the military as a way to avoid unemployment and to get job training. The result has been that while physical casualties, although still high, may have been kept to politically acceptable levels, the psychological and personal costs to soldiers and their families, as well as on the social fabric of U.S. society, have been enormous through the problems of veteran homelessness and psychological problems. In neoliberal fashion, the Bush administration cut resources for Veterans Affairs, even as the costs of treatment for physical and psychological effects of the war increased. For example, in 2012, there were 349 reported suicides by active-duty personnel in the United States, against 311 deaths in war zones.[14] Moreover, the tools utilized to frame the new form of warfare as legitimate and cost effective raise serious questions about the effects on democracy.

In order to limit public criticism, during the Iraq War, information made available to the public was carefully scripted by the military, so much so that some argued that the media presentation was itself part of the war.[15] Initial video of massive explosions and news commentary from reporters filmed on their hotel balconies with the bombs bursting in the background created the impression of a controlled battlefield that projected U.S. and NATO power. The surgical nature of the firepower was confirmed in daily, heavily scripted news conferences from the military. Reports of Iraqi casualties and destruction were limited and censored by the military, hiding from the U.S. public the real destructiveness of the war.

The new global media is intensifying the question of democracy and publicity in war. Judith Butler has emphasized the significance of framing the new techno-warfare in particular ways, arguing that the language and discourses through which war is given meaning have become a crucial element of war fighting in the globalization era and of the way in which local and global communities understand and respond to what they see. She proposes that this framing process "does not simply exhibit reality, but actively participates in a strategy that selectively produces and enforces what will count as reality." This is crucial, she suggests, to the success of the contemporary wars of globalization, and she poses this question regarding this "success":

> Can there be the continuation of war or, indeed, the escalation of war, as we are now witnessing in Afghanistan, without first preparing and structuring the public understanding of what war is, and by attempting to suppress any visual, audible, or narrative accounts of war that might help to break open a popular resistance to war?[16]

Hence the extreme attempts to control the imagery and information about the Iraq War by the Bush administration. Nevertheless, as Butler stresses, the visual presentation of war and violence that works in many ways to undermine democracy and strengthen the (neoliberal) status quo is ultimately susceptible to a variety of reactions, including those that prompt resistance to the new modes of warfare. As we will see in the next chapter, more and more democratic movements in globalization are incorporating principled and strategic nonviolence against a neoliberal way of war that promises to bring high-technology violence selectively to anywhere on the planet that recalcitrant (rogue) states and non-state movements threaten to take hold. Increasingly, an antiwar program is becoming part of progressive democratic ideologies.

Viewed from a democratic point of view, the neoliberal way of war poses moral difficulties. Some are consonant with the nuclear age and with the age of machine warfare more generally.[17] One problem is the moral asymmetry that tends to accompany advanced weapons. One of the earliest examples was the machine gun, considered immoral to use by Europeans against one another but perfectly acceptable in Africa and in colonial wars.[18] Another is the way the war theater has been an experimental proving ground for testing and developing innovative weapons that both enhanced the destructiveness of warfare and furthered industrial and technological progress in the liberal states.[19]

Moral questions arise as the violence of war is mediated by machines that distance the soldier from the violence they perpetrate and that have the capacity, and often the aim, of replacing human judgment with split-second decisions. Antiwar liberals have organized against such weapons in the past, often invoking a humanist cosmopolitanism in which killing anonymously and at a distance undermines the human capacity for moral judgment.[20] Current campaigns against drones may in fact be having some effect in this regard, as the Obama administration has recently announced a strategy for their more careful and restricted use. If democracy requires citizens who take responsibility for the moral consequences of their actions, and for the actions of their collective publics, which would seem to be implied by claims to act in the public good, many of the weapons of choice and the strategies of distanced, networked warfare—drones, for example—would not only seem to violate democratic principles but to actively undermine the production of democratic selves.

One critic, Paul Virilio, has described the new warfare as no longer driven by control of territory but by control of speed; he calls it war as "chronopolitics."[21] He worries that this means that war is taken out of the hands of human beings and given over to machines, as decisions have to be made instantaneously. Others, including many in the military, also worry about the ethical and political implications of the merger of man and machine in increasingly automated battlefields and in cyber-warfare. More and more new weapons systems involve bio-enhancement machinery, from night-vision goggles to computerized mapping screens attached to helmets that relay real-time, GPS-guided information to soldiers in the field to drugs that enhance a soldier's senses.[22]

The rhetoric of the Obama administration has reflected these criticisms, even if his practice has not followed through, and he has softened the rhetoric of a permanent state of emergency. Indeed, Obama came to office on the promise of bringing the war system back under democratic control. He promised to close the prison at Guantanamo Bay, citing its inhumanity and violation of international law, and he promised to end the permanent warfare in Iraq and Afghanistan. While he failed to accomplish these in his first term in office, his 2014 State of the Union speech reaffirmed his commitments in this regard.

A softened and more multilateralist vision of democracy promotion pervades the Obama administration's National Security Strategy (2010), which describes the U.S. national interest as "to shape an international system that can meet the challenges of our time." In this context, the current (2013) United States National Security Strategy is worth quoting at length:

> This strategy recognizes *the fundamental connection between our national security, our national competitiveness, resilience, and moral example.* And it reaffirms America's commitment to pursue our interests through an international system *in which all nations have certain rights and responsibilities.* This will allow America *to leverage our engagement abroad on behalf of a world in which individuals enjoy more freedom and opportunity,* and *nations have incentives to act responsibly, while facing consequences when they do not* [emphasis added].[23]

This liberal globalism echoes a core precept of liberal modernity that many neoliberals share—the compatibility and mutual reinforcement of capitalism with a peaceful world order.

The association of liberal capitalism and democracy with a peaceful world order has a long history. In the eighteenth century, Montesquieu and Adam Smith both associated liberal trade with peaceful competition.

They both made fundamentally moral arguments for the connection between liberalism and peace. Free economic competition would channel hostilities and differences of interests into more peaceful pursuits and away from political intrigues. And, perhaps most important, both argued that the individuals who would be inclined to free-market competition were incompatible with non-republican regimes, especially those in which the rule of law was not absolute. Free markets, they believed, required political and religious toleration, representation of the capitalist classes in government (those who used their wealth for investment rather than the conspicuous consumption of the nobility), and, most important, the rule of law.[24] For Smith, although not necessarily for Montesquieu, the aim of government was to provide a framework of rules and institutions in which "economic man" could flourish. For Montesquieu, the primary justification of commerce was to create moral possibilities by constraining human passions, not the reorganization of government in order to make competitive action in the market possible as it was for Smith or to actively promote the development of markets as for contemporary neoliberals. The culmination of the eighteenth-century arguments was Immanuel Kant's *Perpetual Peace*, in which he argues that only a federation of republican states in which all accepted the rule of law could produce a world order in which war would be undertaken only for defense and in cooperation with other republican states. He argues that because elites would most likely benefit from war and the majority of the people would most pay the costs, the more influence the people have the less likely governments would be to resort to war.[25] We should remember that for Kant people's influence is not democratic—that is, through participation in governing—but through a liberal public sphere of a free press and free speech.

A more behavioralist version of the Kantian argument has been revived in recent "democratic peace theory" that clearly resonates with the Obama national security strategy. As one of the advocates of the democratic peace theory, Bruce Russett, puts it: "By this reasoning, the more democracies there are in the world, the fewer potential adversaries we have and other democracies will have and the wider the zone of peace."[26] Michael W. Doyle, more attentive to the ways "aggression by the liberal state has also characterized a large number of wars" outside the liberal-democratic "zone of peace," has been a critic within the democratic peace theory camp of the attempts at forced democratic state building undertaken by the United States in Iraq and Afghanistan. He recognizes the slippery slope along which the best intentions to create democratic states from the outside veer off into authoritarian reaction and renewed cycles of violence. Both in his writings and as an adviser to former secretary general Kofi Annan at the United Nations he has promoted a more multilateralist and soft-power approach to creating a federation of liberal-democratic states as a way to promote peace.[27]

On the one hand, the behavioral argument is not surprising. Eliminating difference reduces occasions of conflict, even as it generates new ones as new differences emerge. As the differences that have difficulty being negotiated in the global world manifest themselves less as differences between states, it stands to reason that state-to-state warfare would recede, as has been the case. This point is actually reinforced by Doyle's finding that as wars between like polyarchal states receded liberals found themselves confronting and engaging in colonial wars and interventions in order to secure raw materials and markets. However, this suggests that rather than supporting a peaceful world, capitalism generates conflicts "beneath" the level of the state that problematize state and human security.

This latter is an insight developed in securitization theory.

DEMOCRATIC NEGOTIATIONS OF SECURITY (2): NEGOTIATING GLOBAL SECURITY

The problematic for democratic security would seem, then, both to contest new modes of warfare that undermine democratic processes and subjectivities and to address, democratically, the challenges of living in a global world in which social relations cut across and through state boundaries and that threaten to unravel social life more generally. The Obama administration's rhetoric seems to recognize this, although framing it within a narrative that is quite sanguine about the compatibility of neoliberal capitalism, democracy, and peace and of a singular, worldwide disciplinary moral order of states. The security rhetoric of the Obama administration cited above suggests this in his references to "*the fundamental connection between our national security, our national competitiveness, resilience, and moral example*," and in his insistence that "*nations have incentives to act responsibly, while facing consequences when they do not.*"

Securitization theory, however, provides an alternative narrative of a problematic of global security. Securitization theory initially developed as a critical discourse against traditional realist ideas of national security as exclusively military. It is associated with the Copenhagen School of Security Studies, named for the Copenhagen Peace Research Institute, which pioneered work on broader understandings of security in a globalized world. Securitization theory seeks to broaden the understanding of security to include threats and dangers in a globalized world beyond the normal military field associated with the Cold War and the Westphalian order of nation-states. For example, one influential text seeks to distinguish and integrate five fields into security studies: military, political, economic, environmental, and societal.[28] Securitization theory is constructivist and critical. It aims to not take threats and dangers as given, but to examine how elements of disorder in the world come to be promoted as security threats and dangers.

Securitization theory appropriates insights well known to subaltern scholars and peoples in the global South, that security depends upon reducing or eliminating poverty, enhancing education, providing health care, ensuring stable environmental conditions that can sustain local ways of life, and ensuring social justice that can inform the work of the Economic and Social Council of the UN General Assembly as well as other UN-affiliated agencies. It refashions these insights into a Western social-science idiom, as problems to be solved. By formalizing social and environmental problematics generated in globalization as an operationalizable field of knowledge, "security," securitization theory provides this insight with an epistemic structure within which a range of fundamental issues in globalization become objects of sustained action. Securitization theory opens up a potential field of political interventions, but at the same time, its insights can be appropriated to limit democratic politics within them.

Securitization theory can be useful for democratizing global problematics, so long as it makes room for alternative perspectives and enters a dialogue democratically with alternative agencies of those concerned with and affected most by the issues that have been "securitized." "Securitizing" a problematic—that is, framing it as a security issue—makes the problem simultaneously susceptible to technical solutions and to potential political participation by broader publics, enabling participation and input by lay persons (i.e., nonsocial scientists, nonscientists, and nongovernmental experts).[29] Global social movements, social justice, and environmental NGOs, as well as local political mobilizations fighting poverty, homelessness, and so forth, have been able to take advantage of these openings, some even gaining observer status at the UN and in other multilateral forums and treaty negotiations. The difficulty is that neoliberalism exploits securitization of social and environmental problematics by stressing market solutions that insulate security from democratic politics and participation and legitimates leaving them to be dealt with by experts within international organizations within which neoliberalism has predominant influence and can therefore control much of the debate.

For neoliberalism, the solution to these problems—of poverty, pollution, ecological damage, human trafficking, and so forth—is the market and economic growth. For neoliberals, the key to a democratic world order is fostering economic growth and the security of the market. Indeed, regulating and managing the flows and externalities of global markets—such as ecological damage, poverty, health risks, and the like—creates new opportunities for furthering the creation of a neoliberal global order through such governmental techniques as ceding state regulatory authority that is more susceptible to democratic political pressures within parliamentary states to international organizations controlled by experts heavily influenced by neoliberal forms of knowledge. It also allows the dominant neoliberal states to dictate, based on economic logics, solutions to global problematics. Thus, for example, the United States was able to weaken and scuttle the Kyoto Protocols on climate change, appealing to the neoliberal mantra of undermining competitiveness and economic growth. The neoliberal problematic in the broader security field can also be furthered by market solutions to creating global institutions to manage social problems, such as empowering private philanthropic and granting agencies such as the Gates Foundation to influence and structure health care and education and relying on voluntary-service NGOs working in conjunction with international organizations and often bypassing state delivery of services. We will turn shortly to how the neoliberal strategies have created a "democratic deficit" and in response generated new arguments for democratizing international organizations by making them accountable to some form of public.

Indeed, securitized social problematics can be objictified in positivistic discourses that constitute them as problems to be solved. One democratic potential of securitization theory, the focus on the ways in which problematics come to be framed and constructed as security issues, is to critique the positivistic attempts to reinforce expert solutions that reinforce polyarchy and the passivity of publics. Global security can be reframed more critically as ongoing political problematics that arise from living in a globally connected world that require continual attentions of multiple subjects coming to the issue fields from different perspectives. The latter can connect to the strategy of Michel Callon and his collaborators in calling for the formation of "hybrid forums" to enable the incorporation of multiple publics in devising strategies to confront technical problems, such as nuclear waste, drawing on actor-network-theory.[30] They cite, for example, processes in which lay persons in France were trained and educated for several weeks in the technical and scientific issues of nuclear-waste disposal and then participated on equal terms with political decision makers and scientific experts. Significantly, these lay participants, drawn from the general affected publics, were empowered to propose and construct solutions and programs, not just to verify or agree or disagree with experts. Participatory forums within the International Coffee Organization, in which small farmers, fair-trade organizations, unions representing coffee workers, economists, and decision makers are included have also been used to propose solutions to fluctuations in coffee prices and the domination of markets by large corporations. One important element of a global democratic politics, then, is the contestation over the framing of securitized problematics. From this point of view, the challenge is to create new forms of democratic forums and organizations within which participation by multiple publics can emerge.

Securitization can, however, also be used to deepen the neoliberal globalist project by promoting solutions that rely primarily on market logics and limit or eliminate democratic inputs. For example, we can cite the promotion of pollution-trading schemes for corporations or the economy of voluntary carbon offsets that make individual agents responsible for policing their own contributions to environmental damage as dominant modes of environmental security that justify resistance to more robust and political climate-control and pollution-control treaties. We can also cite the emerging system of global health care in which research and delivery of health care are privatized and depoliticized through a combination of public/private partnerships in universities and reliance on NGOs and international organizations, such as the World Health Organization, funded primarily through private donations and large foundations, such as the Gates Foundation. As we saw in the last section, even military security is being brought under the neoliberal market, both in staffing that relies on all-volunteer militaries, which absorb excess unemployment and structure the military as job-training organizations for the broader economy and military operations, and on private military contractors and deployments of weapons based on cost-benefit calculations, both in terms of costs and lives lost and put at risk.

Debates over global governance, especially about authority and accountability, echo the democratic problem of globalization.

GLOBALIZATION AND THE QUESTION
OF THE "DEMOCRATIC DEFICIT"

With the Bretton Woods settlement after the Second World War, an international state apparatus began to take shape. While there were disputes at the resort in New Hampshire where the International Monetary Fund (IMF), the World Bank, and the General Agreement on Tariffs and Trade (GATT) were negotiated, there was general consensus that capitalism required more international regulation and management in order to avoid repetition of the Great Depression and the subsequent collapse of world trade. The economy came to be embedded in a liberal, social democratic political project that sanctioned compromises between labor and capital (legalizing trade unions and collective bargaining), with national states willing to use fiscal and monetary policies to achieve full employment and to smooth out business cycles and ameliorate their effects. Social democrats realized that this required coordination with an international order that approached the world economy as a singular whole that required technical, expert management at the international level.

Significantly, in the postwar settlement, the political legitimation of the order would remain within territorial nation-states. No representative system emerged along with the Bretton Woods settlement on a global level, and the legal systems that structured and regulated the capitalist economy remained primarily national. This disjuncture has become an ever-widening gap, from the point of view of social democrats, between the institutionalization of economic power and regulation, which was increasingly transnational, and democratic legitimations of the capitalist state. Over time, the disjuncture deepened as transnational and global corporations grew in power, as finance took advantage of digital communication networks that superseded national control over financial flows, and as a body of international commercial law developed that gave multinational corporations rights against and above states that supposedly were charged with regulating them.[31] The result, many social democrats argue, is a "democratic deficit."

In 1944, Karl Polanyi argued that "normally, the economic order is merely a function of the social, in which it is contained."[32] He argues that, in the nineteenth century, the market economy arose that reversed this condition: the society became "embedded" in the market, and politics came to be understood as separate from, and subordinate to, the economic. In other words, authority and society came to be structured in the service of the market, and "the role of the state became to institute and safeguard the self-regulating market."[33] Polanyi goes on to argue that society rebelled against its colonization by the market, producing reactions by labor and leading to state regulation of the market but not until after the ravages of depression and world war.

Against the embedding of capitalism in a social democratic project of the postwar order, neoliberals, as discussed in chapter 2, seek to separate and insulate the economy from the political and to subordinate the government to the economic logic of the market. Ideologically, neoliberals reject the social democratic idea that a democratic society requires the political regulation of the economy by democratically accountable agencies. In spite of their ideology, however, neoliberals have not dismantled the international state apparatus but have sought to mold it to their aims to produce neoliberal globalism. They created a body of private commercial law enforceable by neoliberal institutions, such as the World Trade Organization and regional trade organizations such as NAFTA, through which transnational corporations can sue states in order to force them to deregulate. They have also promoted market solutions through international organizations to problems as diverse as poverty, health care, and the environment, as we discussed in the previous section.

Many social democrats and democratic theorists also acknowledge that the postwar age of "embedded liberalism" has become untenable. Nevertheless, many social democrats have held firm to social democratic ideals and have sought to broaden and globalize them. They seek new ways to legitimate the global capitalist economy politically by re-embedding the economy in a global liberal-democratic order. Only now, these social democrats argue, the liberal-democratic order needs to be deterritorialized, detached from the territorial state and re-lodged directly in global democratic institutions and practices. Furthermore, the growth over especially the last three decades of an infrastructure of human-rights law and a "global civil society" has made a rethinking of political community necessary, these globalist social democrats argue, for democratic theory. Key claims in defense of this approach are (1) that since people are increasingly affected by global decisions and institutions directly *as individuals* and not as members of a territorially based community, humanity as a whole, rather than the national community, should be considered the source of popular sovereignty (the "all-inclusive principle"); and (2) that democratic legitimacy requires that all affected by decisions should have a say in making them (the "all-affected principle"). Social-democratic theorizing about global democracy, then, points to a gap between the old—the Westphalian system of territorial state sovereignty—and the new—a reimagined deterritorialized global *demos* or some system of *demoi* that inform systems of global governance, which has yet to form.[34]

In neoliberal global capitalism, power has come to be lodged in unaccountable and unrepresentative institutions and practices—transnational corporations, financial firms and networks, transnational class formations manifest in informal networks and organized nongovernmental organizations, and technocratic international organizations. These have become detached from state regulatory structures and have fostered increasingly undemocratic effects: deepening and persistent inequality both within and across state borders; the degrading of labor, including increasing use of forced labor and human trafficking; destruction of the environment and global commons; and the immunity of corporations from local and national tax, environmental, and labor laws. In response, and sometimes in collusion with transnational powers, democratic states have ceded aspects of sovereign control over their economies and societies to undemocratic international organizations such as the World Bank, the IMF, and treaty organizations such as NAFTA. Moreover, states either lack the tools or the political will to control the vast and rapid-fire economic and social networks and flows that comprise global capitalism.[35]

Therefore, the globalist social democrats argue, the Westphalian system of autochthonous and sovereign territorial states no longer provides a secure scaffolding for democracy, manifest in the weakening of liberal-democratic accountability and representation as set out in national constitutions and representative institutions.[36] Jan Aart Scholte describes the problem as one of accountability:

> Little democratic accountability has operated in respect of contemporary global governance arrangements. The past 150 years have seen an unprecedented proliferation and growth of suprastate laws and institutions with transplanetary coverage. However, these regulatory instruments have included only weak, if any, formal accountability mechanisms. The leaderships of the organizations have not been subject to direct popular election. Nor has any global governance institution had a democratically appointed legislative arm. Citizens have in most cases been unable to take global authorities to court for redress.[37]

In somewhat different although complementary fashion, David Held views the problem of democratic legitimacy as one of the consent of those affected by decisions. For Held, the problem is that, in the context of globalization, "communities of fate" stretch beyond the territorial borders of states:

> But the very idea of consent through elections, and the particular notion that the relevant constituencies of voluntary agreement are the communities of a bounded territory or a state, become open to question as soon as the issue of national, regional and global interconnectedness is considered and the nature of a so-called "relevant community" is contested.[38]

This reading of the democratic deficit has yielded three primary, often overlapping, strategies: making the institutions of global governance more accountable and representative, insuring a democratic constitutionalism and juridical architecture of some sort based on the concept of human rights and cosmopolitan norms, and reimagining civil society as a global public sphere.

Many focus on democratizing the institutions and practices of global governance to overcome the "democratic deficit."[39] To overcome the "democratic deficit," democratic theorists such as Held argue that priority must be given to increasingly democratizing the major existing institutions in which global governance now proceeds—the UN, the World Trade Organization, regional legislatures such as the European Parliament, and more informal regulatory agencies such as those that regulate Internet protocols and domains. Others propose creating some new legal architecture that interconnects local, national, international, and global systems of law as best able to further develop and enforce human rights.[40]

Held and other global democrats also put their trust in a double reconstitution of civil society. First, civil society becomes global, now comprised of a wide and growing array of nongovernmental organizations, many of which operate inside many nations and have various kinds of status within the United Nations and in other formal international organizations. Second, civil society is transformed in globalization from the sphere of voluntary, non-state associations and the sphere of bourgeois property and contract into a global public sphere in which a form of popular sovereignty is globalized:

> This new global civil society is not only inhabited by multinationals and transnationals, whether public or private, but also by citizens, movement activists and constituents of various kinds.[41]

Social democratic arguments for democratizing global governance through a global civil society / public sphere most often draw on recent "deliberative democratic theory" inspired by the work of Jürgen Habermas.[42] If these forums are sufficiently open and rational, the argument goes, they can amount to a form of democratic consent, so long as decisions remain open to continual reflection and contestation. This means that the liberal principles of a free press and free speech need to become universally accepted and a plurality of forums, open to all organized interests, must proliferate in global decision-making structures.[43]

Global democrats, then, seek to reengage with a democratic political sovereignty, against the economic sovereignty of neoliberalism that erodes the idea of democratic citizenship as anything other than a formal shell. Through democratizing global-governance institutions and the emboldening of a global civil society dedicated to furthering the norms of human rights, global democrats seek to return some measure of accountability and political authority to the people. This social democratic liberalism does not guarantee overturning of neoliberal policies but seems to suggest creating institutions through which these will be continually contested by globally organized popular movements. By and large, these arguments put their faith in extending principles developed in the context of state-centered liberal democracies to the global sphere.[44]

It is, however, as David Held stresses, unclear who comprises the relevant "people" in a globalized age, raising the all important question of citizenship.[45] Seyla Benhabib has proposed one new formulation of citizenship:

> We are moving away from citizenship understood as national membership increasingly towards *a citizenship of residency* which strengthens the multiple ties to locality, to the region, and to transnational institutions.[46]

As the nation-state comes more and more into question as a secure foundation of a democratic community, as both neoliberals and globalist social democrats realize, citizenship becomes a crucial problematic and is increasingly absorbing the attentions of democratic theorists, state policy makers, and citizens themselves.

NEGOTIATIONS OF DEMOCRATIC CITIZENSHIP IN THE NEW GLOBAL AGE

Within democratic theory, citizenship draws boundaries between the democratic community and others. It delineates and distributes rights, privileges, and duties, grounding them in affective attachments to a distinct political community. Citizenship has been a space of conflict, as multiple principles have vied to define its parameters in modernity. Perhaps most important, the liberal principle of universal inclusion based on human individuality and human rights has combined uneasily with the national to form modern citizenship. Add to these the democratic notion that citizens must be active participants in government, and the modern notion of democratic citizenship appears as complex and perennially unstable, its boundaries continually shifting as historical circumstances change.

In social democracies, citizenship came to involve not only principles of political membership and political and civil rights but also a basket of "social rights."[47] That is, citizenship in liberal-democratic states came to mean entitlement to social protections and access to social rights, most notably to health care, to education, to a basic standard of living, and to a job or support while looking for work. These resulted from the labor compromises of the Fordist capitalism that aimed to manage citizenship by reducing class antagonisms through collective bargaining, corporatist collaborations of workers and management, and public policy, such as welfare, unemployment, and government-provided health care. Citizens came to expect the state to provide both political protection and social security. Significantly, this conception of citizenship informed the development of human rights and is embedded in the UN Charter wherein economic rights are prominent, thereby stretching citizenship beyond the territorial nation-state.

Globalization is destabilizing modern citizenship in significant ways. Modern democracies have managed the population movements that have characterized global modernity in the past and in the present through a combination of formal laws of citizenship, immigration, and foreign residency along with informal social and cultural means—prejudices, tropes of national identity, racial identifications, class affiliation, and others. The principle of sovereign territoriality in the Westphalian state-system has been a powerful tool for managing citizenship in modern states. The formal recognition of the right to organize life within the territory of the state enabled the creation of administrative tools of governing by tracking population movements, differentiating them according to criteria of income, race, ethnicity, religion, and so forth, in a national census that made administering government programs easier and allowed targeting of the different needs of different groups. The census was especially important in managing citizenship in colonial states and became a crucial tool of empire and managing the flows of people prompted by colonialism and later globalization. The idea and institution of state sovereignty also helped to empower states to enact laws to regulate population movements, including the forced labor of slavery, and to foster narratives of national identity that created norms of assimilation that admitted some to full citizenship while limiting the assimilation of others (often based on race and class). It also allowed for the management of immigrant populations. Immigration laws, creating legal categories of immigrants, not only limited or increased population flows as needed for cheap labor but also made tracking them easier. In globalization, and especially within the context of neoliberal globalization, especially with the pressures to open borders to the free flow of capital, finance, and labor and the increasing inequalities and subsequently life-chances for people in the various sectors and divisions of the world economy, these systems of immigration law and administration have come under serious strain.

Of course, the tensions in managing modern citizenship are not new. As scholars of nationalism have pointed out, "nation" and "state" in the Westphalian world have never mapped cleanly on each other. Modern nation-states have never been inclusive of all those living within their borders. Nor have all members of the nation been citizens of the nation-state that bears its identity, creating ambiguous ties across borders. This ambiguity is increasing under globalization as notions of citizenship are stretched beyond the nation-state. People are forming "transnational" communities in diasporas (see chapter 4 on Kerala), and with globalization, the host nation-state is for many no longer the sole or even primary organizing principle of belonging, citizenship, or political subjectivity.

Indian anthropologist Arjun Appadurai has made the point well, proposing that

> the idea of a sovereign and stable territory, the idea of a containable and countable population, the idea of a reliable census, and the idea of stable and transparent categories—have come unglued in the era of globalization. . . . Above all, the certainty that distinctive and singular peoples grow out of and control well-defined national territories has been decisively unsettled by the global fluidity of wealth, arms, people, and images.[48]

Thus, while national citizenship remains for most the basis of democratic rights, political organization, and activity, this is no longer exclusively the case. Indeed, many democrats now argue that for democratic citizenship to be realized, it needs to be both dispersed in local communities below the level of the state—as manifest in demands for cultural recognition by minority cultures[49] and their distinctive practices and in some cases for regional and cultural autonomy, as with the "original nations" in Canada[50]—and stretched to transnational and even global associations beyond the state, manifest for example in the ability of citizens to make legal claims in international human-rights courts.

The destabilization of the spatial frame of citizenship has made citizenship an intense site of democratic contestation, manifest in both the rise of anti-immigrant political parties and increasing violence against immigrants. A major part of contemporary democratic politics centers on attempts to prevent minorities within a democracy—electoral minorities, minority cultures, races and ethnicities, or marginalized ways of being (sexual, familial, social)—from being hardened into "others" (groups that cannot or should not be assimilated or accepted by the majority). In heightening the uncertainty about who "we" are (who properly belongs to the nation and political community and therefore is entitled to the rights and protections of citizenship), globalization exacerbates the incentives, as Appadurai suggests, to turn "minorities" into "others," thereby sanctioning violence against "them" in the name of purifying "us." The hardening of attitudes in the rich world (from the United States, to Western Europe, to Australia) toward "migrants" seeking sanctuary from poverty and trauma is only the most obvious manifestation of the "them/us" response in recent times. The numerous fundamentalisms, religious, racial, and ethnic, that plague so many societies in the neoliberal global order (often strengthened if not created by the upheavals, inequalities, and political strategies of corporations and wealthy elites seeking to open up markets and heightening ethnic divisions in order to control populations), both rich and poor, are more examples, as Appadurai's book discusses.

None of this is entirely new, of course. The mix of the old and the new is captured nicely by sociologist John Urry, who is worth quoting at some length. Urry says:

> Multiple mobilities have been central to much historical development and are not simply "new." Thus, over many centuries there were complex trading and travel routes that constituted what we now call the Mediterranean world. The ships, sea routes, and interconnectivity of the slave and post-slave trade engendered what Gilroy terms the "Black Atlantic." And the complex mobilities of diasporas and transnational migrants are key

to examining many contemporary post-colonial relationships. There is a "diasporization" of communities in the contemporary era.

But although these are not new the mobile character of such processes is now much more evident. Analyses of migration, diasporas and more fluid citizenships are central to critiques of the bounded and static categories of nation, ethnicity and state present in much social science. Various works theorize the multiple, overlapping and turbulent processes of migration, dislocation, displacement, disjuncture, and dialogism. These massive contemporary migrations, often with oscillatory flows between unexpected locations, have been described as a series of turbulent waves, with a hierarchy of eddies and vortices, with globalism being a virus that stimulates resistance, and with the migration system's "cascading" moves away from any state of equilibrium.[51]

In the neoliberal era, consequently, globalization is updating and intensifying contestation over the boundaries of citizenship, as the transformations of the state and the state-system, together with neoliberalism, generate new forms of "multicultural citizenship" as migrants and host societies learn to live with hybridity and multiple social identities. This, of course, is the everyday experience of millions of migrants living in multiple worlds who seek to contribute as fully fledged citizens in more than one "homeland." Many recent immigrants, in particular, retain significant ties to their home nations and opt for dual citizenship—thereby limiting total assimilation in their host society. This kind of diaspora experience is becoming more commonplace, and diaspora communities are becoming more active and organized, significantly influencing both their original home politics (often through repatriations of money) and the politics and culture of their adopted homes. In Europe and elsewhere, large nomadic populations, refugees, and economic migrants are moving in and out of states, as people in the age of neoliberal globalization become less attached to their nation-state and more comfortable with hybridity as part of their personal and collective identity.[52]

NEGOTIATING CITIZENSHIP IN THE EUROPEAN UNION

These are themes at the forefront of the debates over citizenship in the European Union, which is an exemplary site of contestation and adaptation concerning the shifting boundaries of democratic inclusion/exclusion in modern societies. European citizenship is first mentioned explicitly in the

Treaty of Europe (Maastricht Treaty) in 1992, the document that transformed the European Economic Community into the European Union. Its aim was not to replace national citizenship per se but to complement it with a basket of legal rights that individuals could claim on the basis of citizenship in one of the states of the EU. These included: the freedom of movement and residency, the right to vote and run for the European Parliament, diplomatic and consular protection by member states of the union, and the right to petition the European Parliament. Above all, this legislation was designed primarily to ensure the free movement of those engaged in "economic activity" in their attempts to increase EU penetration of global markets, especially the U.S. market. In spite of its primarily economic motivation, the treaty set the stage for the enhancement of the democratic character of the EU, something undertaken in the Treaty of Lisbon, which went into effect in 2009.

The Treaty of Lisbon extended the legislative capacity and jurisdiction of the European Parliament, previously subordinate to the Council of the EU, which represented states rather than individuals. The treaty also proclaimed the "Citizens' Initiative," reaffirmed in 2011, that allows citizens of member states to bring forward new policy proposals to the European Parliament (petitions require one million citizens from a number of member states). The Charter of Fundamental Rights, originally established in 2000, further codified the basic rights of European citizens to dignity, civil and economic freedoms, equality, and nondiscrimination based on race, ethnicity, religion, age, or gender. It also ensured the rights to a fair trial and the presumption of innocence.

Many critics, however, see these provisions as not going very far to creating real democratic institutions that have legitimacy among European citizens. Nor, critics say, are the provisions for free movement and resettlement throughout the union creating a substantial sense of European citizenship. The EU remains, in the eyes of many of its citizens, primarily an elite economic institution that does not reflect or respond to the democratic will of the people. In the current economic crisis, for example, the EU seems unwilling or unable to challenge the neoliberal imposition of austerity policies in spite of considerable democratic protests. Betraying its origins as an economic union concerned to make European capitalism more globally competitive, the EU has thus adopted a thin concept of citizenship, calling for little direct citizen participation and giving little incentive or opportunity for citizens of Europe to participate in meaningful ways in European institutions and decision making.

Nevertheless, some argue that the EU, especially after the Lisbon Treaty, is creating a dynamic that makes a more substantial democratic citizenship possible. Dora Kostakopoulou, for example, has argued that recent acts of the European Court of Justice are enhancing the prospects for a thicker idea of European democratic citizenship,[53] while Polina Tambakaki argues that increased democratic possibilities are arising as the EU provides a space in which citizens, as Europeans, can develop the affective attachments to a European *demos*.[54] Tambakaki's important insight is that if Europe is to become more democratic it will be the result of the reorientation of democratic struggles to encompass multiple levels and sites of contestation in which the solidarities and rights of democratic citizenship are nurtured and given life to confront and contest the undemocratic implications of globalization. In short, Tambakaki argues, it is necessary to go beyond legalistic frameworks and to recognize the EU as a site of democratic contestation and mobilization.

The democratic negotiations of citizenship in Europe are most profound for those on the periphery of Europe. Étienne Balibar insists that understanding the future of democracy and citizenship in Europe requires looking at the millions of migrants subsisting on the periphery of Europe, perched ambiguously inside and outside of the continent and its "thin" democratic principles.[55]

The "periphery" of Europe here refers to those countries at the boundaries of Europe, both physically and temporally (including those countries that by virtue of the breakup of the USSR have been incorporated into the new Europe and which the European community considers to be of special concern, in the Balkans and Eastern Europe). But due to the expansive population movements and the changing scope of economic activity characteristic of globalization, the periphery is now "inside" Europe, concentrated in the poor areas of its major cities, where the various peoples of Europe's borderlands, and its post-colonial subjects, have come seeking work, freedom, and asylum. Less fully integrated into the formal and informal rituals of national citizenship, less able to participate in the performances that would create them as full citizens of the state, these new immigrants maintain (and form) transnational and global ties to diasporas and global networks in which national, cultural, religious, and other collective attachments are formed.

The prolonged financial crisis has heightened the negotiations over citizenship and immigration in Europe. Granting asylum or legitimate immigration status to new immigrants remains largely in the hands of individual European states. In 2011, for example, the European Union rejected a proposal by Italy to allow freer movement of refugees from North Africa in Europe. According to the *New York Times*, "the rejection raised the possibility of tightened intra-European border controls for the first time since visa-free travel was introduced in the 1990s."[56] The success of right-wing, anti-immigrant political parties in many states in Europe has continued, such as the Front National in France, the Independence Party in the UK, the Danish People's Party in Denmark, the Sweden Democrats in Sweden, the True Finns in Finland, and the Freedom Party in the Netherlands. All have recently gained seats in their national parliaments.

The struggle for citizenship by the "peripheral" peoples of Europe is transforming the conditions, subjects, and meaning of democratic citizenship in the modern world and might become a model for transformations elsewhere where the nation-state is under pressure from globalization and democratic citizenship can be affirmed through transnational political and legal actions. When one pays attention, as Balibar does, to the concrete conditions of the "citizens of Europe," it becomes possible to envision a more robust democratic European citizenship in the future. As Balibar puts it:

> Surely freedom of movement is a basic claim that must be incorporated within the citizenship of all people (and not only for representatives of the "powerful nations," for whom this is largely a given). . . . Given the above, the right to full citizenship is indissolubly linked to freedom of movement. "Migrants" are not an undifferentiated floating mass. They are precisely travelers (forced, free, discriminated against) who create relationships between communities that are foreign to each other (and therefore work objectively, not to abolish these communities, but rather to soften their isolation). They also create relationships between distant or neighboring territories (working to short-circuit those distances and construct a human counterpart against the universalization of communication and economic difference.[57]

Democratic citizenship needs to incorporate a sense of plurality and to become more flexible and nuanced. This more nuanced and multispatial plurality in current negotiations of democratic citizenship in neoliberal globalization is evident in transnational justice movements as well as in local democratic experiments and organizations in poorer parts of the world. We turn to these in the next chapter.

CHAPTER 6

NEW DEMOCRATIC SUBJECTS IN NEOLIBERAL GLOBALIZATION

In the previous chapter, we touched on the variety of ways in which contemporary globalization has destabilized the traditional association of democracy with the nation-state that has prevailed for around 250 years. We looked at some of the ways that this destabilizing process has been understood and debated by contemporary democratic theorists and touched on some of its practical manifestations—in the new forms of citizenship, cosmopolitanism, and constitutionalism. In this final chapter, we look at other manifestations of the emerging democratic subjectivities of the neoliberal era that has seen many of the social and political elements of the modern state becoming globalized, albeit at uneven rates and in different ways. Neoliberalism has sought to provide a new totalizing logic to its global order, including a particular form of (elite) democracy, but this logic has not eliminated the disjunctures and fissures that mark the global as contingent, unpredictable, unsettled, and contestable. Indeed, we suggest, for all the certainty and predictability associated with neoliberal articulations of its globalizing project (and the suppression of the participatory democratic instincts), there is much unpredictability, contingency, and potential for democratic change in the current era.

The state remains significant to many current democratic projects. The Arab Spring that inspired democratic movements around the world—most notably the Occupy movements in the United States against deepening inequality, the arrogance of neoliberal economic elites, and the unresponsiveness of governments under the increasing influence of corporate money—has, in many ways, set the tone for a wide range of democratic movements. This is not the first time that a rebellion against an oppressive regime in the colonial and post-colonial world has inspired counterhegemonic movements for greater democracy in the rich core of the world (note the influence of the Haitian slave revolution on the French Revolution[1]), but the developing specter of grassroots democratic movements is widening and deepening in current globalization.

Often noted, in this regard, is the fluidity of tactics that are increasingly apparent and are conditioning many democratic movements and events.[2] Spontaneous mobilizations of democratic protesters, for example, have used cell phones and social networking to bring vast numbers into the streets, generating new populist ways of coming together. These events have been transferred to the global consciousness using this technology, helping to embolden and enhance movements with real-time information and virtual participation. Importantly too, these protests are rarely based on top-down organizations or calls from traditional party leaders but, more often, from the ground up, often beginning in small, spontaneous, and thinly planned actions and growing quickly into mass actions that spawn new ways of being democratic. And ideologies, rather than dictating demands and strategies, remain possible furrows to be plowed in the course of becoming a democratic movement.

It would, nevertheless, be analytically wrong to subsume all of the democratic movements in globalization under a single tactical type or logic. For example, as Jean-François Bayart points out, the Indonesian student movement of 1998 practiced and endorsed norms and values that do not comport easily if at all with those of the World Social Forum.[3] But what all these projects seem to have in common is that they combine the local and global, combining grievances against neoliberal globalization at the general level with more specific calls for political freedoms and reforms of corrupt and oppressive regimes. The differences between them concern the uneven and disparate ways that neoliberal policies and structures have affected different locales, some focusing on the corruption of dictatorial regimes exploiting neoliberal globalism, as in Mubarak's Egypt, or, quite differently, the way the Zapatistas in Mexico formed initially and explicitly in resistance to neoliberal globalization (particularly as a response to NAFTA), developed an ideology that assimilated the European Marxist tradition, via Gramsci, along with Mesoamerican Indian traditions, and created a global audience and far-reaching support using social networking and the global Internet.

Thus, although it is premature to characterize the new global spread of democracy projects with any precision, we speculate here that these are seeing a plurality of heterodox ways of being democratic in the age of neoliberal globalization. In this chapter, consequently, rather than attempting to create a more or less comprehensive typology of recent projects, we focus instead on a diversity of instances in which new kinds of democratic subjects are forming and seeking to re-form the worlds in which they live. This will hopefully enable a better understanding of the breadth and scope of democratic possibilities in twenty-first-century globalization.

THE IDEA OF A DEMOCRATIC "SUBJECT"

The term "subject," as we use it here, refers to an active social and political agency (be it individually or organizationally expressed) framed by a larger system of relations that does not have complete "freedom to choose" how to act and "be" in society but, equally, is not fully determined by the relations and rules within which such agency exists. An analogy with the "subject" in a sentence might explain this better. The subject of a sentence is the active protagonist but does not exist as such outside of its relation to other parts of speech and the overall rules of grammar and syntax that give the subject its meaning and sense. In short, the "subject" never simply refers to an independent object outside of the sentence. And while words can mean different things in different sentences and take on different nuances in meaning, subjects are always located within a particular set of "framing" relationships. Democratic subjects within contemporary globalization are no different. In short, one does not simply exist as a "subject"; one becomes a subject, and how one does so depends on the webs of social and ideational relations in which one finds oneself. Subjectivation thus involves social learning in the process of creating the social, political, and ethical life of the community. Jean-François Bayart's description is helpful:

Contemporary globalization shapes "human types" who are bearers of "conducts of life," with which one can identify in accordance with one's condition, one's activity, norms, imaginary world and the constraints of one's family or other environment.[4]

We contend that forms of popular democratic politics constitute some of these new subjects.

One of the most far-reaching attempts to characterize the new political subjects in general terms in the neoliberal global order is the influential work of Michael Hardt and Antonio Negri. The new sovereign political subject they call "Empire," and the new democratic subject is the "multitude." Empire is "a *decentered* and *deterritorializing* apparatus of rule that progressively incorporates the entire global realm within its open, expanding frontiers."[5] The "multitude" is that "set of all the exploited and the subjugated, a multitude that is directly opposed to Empire, with no mediation between them."[6]

Hardt and Negri propose that we live at a time in which networks of corporate power dominate globally, creating "social worlds" that work primarily for the benefit of global capital and the political organizations that facilitate global capitalism. No one nation-state now fully dominates this new Empire of deterritorialized power centers and globalized networks and institutions, not even the United States, whose ideas set many of its terms and even though it benefits most from this global structure. Adapting Foucault, they argue that power in this the postmodern Empire is not just about managing fundamental economic contradictions and conflicts, for example between capital and labor, but also about the creation of "social worlds" that stretch transversally, no longer determined by logics of place but by far-flung networks of relations made possible by the global organization and movements of capital and labor.

The new logic of sovereignty and domination involves managing the vast flows of people, necessary for the appropriation of the labor necessary for global capitalism, that are creating new spaces and ways of life. Empire seeks to embed the new ways of life within a neoliberal order by progressively absorbing all of humanity into its networks. Flows of people and labor, they argue, can no longer be managed by the traditional means of physical borders but by more direct management of labor markets and capital markets, which can only be done through transversal structures and organizations, that is, through the vast apparatus of international organizations, global corporations that organize networks of data and digital coordination, informal cooperation of elites from all over, and by forms of commodification that turn cultural differences into marketable commodities. But these flows of people and labor overflow the networks of containment, generating the multitude.

This global multitude, argue Hardt and Negri, is no longer determined by their national location or designation or indeed by traditional categories (class, ethnicity, citizenship). What increasingly determines them are their shared experiences of the "social worlds" created by neoliberal corporatism, the shared experiences we have touched on in this work—in South and North America, Africa, subcontinental India, and Russia. "Is it possible to imagine U.S. agriculture and service industries," they ask, "without Mexican migrant labor, or Arab oil without Palestinians and Pakistanis?"[7] The communities of necessary yet "illegal" labor reappropriate the social and political spaces they come to inhabit and that cost them so much suffering. But in their movements, these migrants produce more than the profit of the corporations they work for; they produce themselves as positive political subjects. They exploit the potential of their numbers and of global communication technologies to create new ways of life, including new ways of being political. They engage in forms of autonomous organization, they organize to make claims of rights and for justice against their states and localities, they create solidarities within their new local communities and across them in diasporas, and they participate in transversal coalitions with multiple groups. Hardt and Negri usefully point to the fact that the political organization of those who lose and suffer while reproducing the neoliberal capitalist order does not limit itself or even primarily take the form of participation in the limited sense of legitimating established polyarchal institutions and practices.

To become a political subject, Hardt and Negri argue, requires that the multitude focus on the global arena. Only by confronting the neoliberal global apparatus as such—targeting international organizations, such as the IMF and World Trade Organization, and global corporations—can the multitude take control of their lives and become a political subject. Their account seems to privilege a form of global citizen action that is emerging in the World Social Forum and the Occupy movements. We will turn to them as one form of democratic subjectivity in the next section. While these incorporate local actions, the central focus of their political action, Hardt and Negri argue, needs to be on the global forces if they are to control their own destiny and their own movements in a global order that rules by constraining and managing those movements.[8]

It remains a question if Hardt and Negri's multitude in general can be given sufficient specificity as such to constitute a global democratic community. It seeks to describe a global democratic citizenship based on the idea of "Humankind" as a unity and identity. As we saw in the previous chapter, the discursive democratic theories also raise the conceptual and theoretical difficulty of the collective democratic subject that replaces the national citizenry or "the people" in globalization. But this underplays the positivity of the diversity and distinctiveness of democratic subjects and projects that are forming within neoliberal globalization.[9] Therefore, after turning to the subjectivity of global activism in the next section, we turn to two other forms of democratic subjectivity emerging in neoliberal globalization that engender new ways of being democratic but which do not directly seek to overturn a totalizing neoliberal global order. We describe several examples under the headings of "Intentional Economies," following the lead of J. K. Gibson-Graham, and "Deep Democracy" and "Political Society," following the lead of Arjun Appadurai and Partha Chatterjee.

TRANSVERSAL DEMOCRATIC ACTIVISM

At least two major examples of transversal democratic activism have become significant in recent times, that associated with the Occupy movements, which forced their way into the global consciousness in 2011, and that related to the World Social Forums, which have presented alternative ways of thinking and being to neoliberalism since the early 1990s. While maintaining local diversity, these aim, as Hardt and Negri suggest, at a direct confrontation with neoliberal forms of global power.

THE NEW YORK OCCUPY MOVEMENT

On September 17, 2011, several hundred protesters entered Zuccotti Park, a privately owned but public park on Broadway, a few blocks from the New York Stock Exchange on Wall Street in Lower Manhattan. They were responding to a call from Adbusters, a Canadian magazine and website, to protest corporate influence in government and to highlight inequality. Soon, several hundred had set up tents, and the protest became an occupation, which lasted for two months before New York City mayor Bloomberg ordered its disbandment, citing health and safety concerns.[10] Protests eventually erupted in over 500 cities in the United States and around the world, culminating on October 15 with occupations and protests in 951 cities in 82 countries under the general heading of "United for Global Change."[11]

Inspired by the Arab Spring, the occupation published a set of Principles of Solidarity, whose main democratic orientation in contrast to neoliberalism is encapsulated in the following excerpt:

> As one people, united, we acknowledge the reality: that the future of the human race requires the cooperation of its members; that our system must protect our rights, and upon corruption of that system, it is up to the individuals to protect their own rights, and those of their neighbors; that a democratic government derives its just power from the people, but corporations do not seek consent to extract wealth from the people and the Earth; and that no true democracy is attainable when the process is determined by economic power.[12]

Thus began a potent movement for participatory democracy, equality, and social justice that linked the local and the global. In New York, it attracted a diverse group of activists who found its slogan "We are the 99 percent" an appropriate encapsulation of the influence, greed, and corruption of the 1 percent who, they argued, under neoliberalism, own between 30 and 40 percent of all the wealth in the United States.[13] (See also chapter 2.) The general purpose and meaning of the protest was best summed up in the following statement, also from Occupy Wall Street's Principles of Solidarity:

> People from all across the United States of America and the world came to protest the blatant injustices of our times perpetuated by the economic and political elites. On the 17th we as individuals rose up against political disenfranchisement and social and economic injustice. We spoke out, resisted, and successfully occupied Wall Street. Today, we proudly remain in Liberty Square constituting ourselves as autonomous political beings engaged in non-violent civil disobedience and building solidarity based on mutual respect, acceptance, and love. It is from these reclaimed grounds that we say to all Americans and to the world, Enough! How many crises does it take? *We are the 99 percent* and we have moved to reclaim our mortgaged future. Through a direct democratic process, we have come together as individuals and crafted these principles of solidarity.[14]

The occupation opened itself to a diversity of issues, refusing to focus narrowly on a set of specific demands and policy prescriptions, a point that led to much criticism not just from conservatives but also from the progressivist mainstream.[15] To those assembled in their sites of protest, however, the mobilization of the protesters was their most important achievement and represented in itself a democratic value. In important respects, this is entirely consistent with a much longer tradition of democratic populism in the United States, echoing the American progressive era in its attacks on the corruption of the political system by big capital since the late nineteenth century.[16] However, for the Occupy movement of the twenty-first century, the traditional democratic institutions of liberal states, now beholden to neoliberal theory and practice, are considered thoroughly corrupted by global corporate power and influence, requiring a more radical and non-statist response underpinned by direct participatory democracy to regenerate the democratic values of political and civil rights, equality and social justice, in the United States and worldwide. This has seen various "occupations" establishing direct democracy principles wherever they appear, as part of their transformation from a set of motley encampments to a transversal activist network. After the occupation disbanded its physical encampment, it began a new life, one it had already begun to cultivate while in Zuccotti Park, as a loose, leaderless organization, generating imaginative and novel organizational practices to realize participatory democracy.

The New York occupation of Zuccotti Park became a template for rethinking a decentralized participatory democratic organization. It saw the establishment of a general assembly as the authoritative legislative forum on both policy and organizational matters, with membership and participatory rights open to all. This general assembly gave priority to marginalized groups; decisions were made by discussion and consensus and, when full consensus could not be reached, by the highest percentage of those assembled. The assembly articulated policies and principles recommended by multiple working groups that carried out discussions and the everyday work of the occupation. The emerging political subjectivity of the movement and its individual members is perhaps best appreciated in terms of the statement of principles, cited above, that emerged from the initial occupation in 2011, which states:

> Today, we proudly remain in Liberty Square constituting ourselves as autonomous political beings engaged in non-violent civil disobedience and building solidarity based on mutual respect, acceptance, and love. . . . Through a direct democratic process, we have come together as individuals.

These "principles" contain a strong emphasis on the individual exercising "personal responsibility," an emphasis that repudiates the atomistic individualism of the neoliberal world order in favor of a political subjectivity embedded in collectivist precepts and commitments. The "self" in this sense becomes a "political being" socialized in and by the processes of participatory decision making and the deliberations of the democratic working groups.

This idea invokes elements of the tradition of "developmental democracy" associated with the theories of Rousseau, Tocqueville, and John Stuart Mill and more recently with C. B. Macpherson.[17] They are more in tune with Rousseau, for whom the subject is created less through formal education and more through forms of social learning and interaction that cultivate mutual respect and acceptance of difference. The process of subjectivation counters the individualist, competitive spirit of neoliberal entrepreneurialism. The key idea here is that democratic citizens become such only through participation in forums of genuine democratic deliberation and decision making, in which liberal toleration has become more than a set of rules and more an internalized ethos. From this perspective, no one is naturally a democratic citizen simply by virtue of living in a democratic society, although everyone has the capacity to cultivate the democratic ethos as they participate along with diverse others.

Democratic politics, thus, is a form of "self-making" for the Occupy movement, an attempt to create new processes of subjectivation against the institutions and practices of the neoliberal world order. Political engagement for the developing democratic subject is thus focused both on immediate policy issues (for example, the political economy of neoliberalism, the corruption of the American banking sector, the fate of the "99 percent") and on the creation of a democratic culture that reimagines the social world through political participation. Democratic citizens, from this perspective, are "made" (and remade) through education, political deliberation, and the performance of democracy as an act of solidarity and as a shared "being-in-common."

This begs the question of who or what is the "collective" that creates this sense of common purpose for new democratic subjects of the Occupy movements. The answer, for the activists of Zuccotti Park, is to be found in the "Declaration of the Occupation of New York City," which suggests that the "collective" focus and commitment is both local and global. Thus, echoing Hardt and Negri: "We write so that all people who feel wronged

by the corporate forces of the world can know that we are your allies."
The "people" then are not just those in New York and the United States
suffering under the corrupting influences of Wall Street and the American
corporate sector but also the global 99 percent under social, economic,
and political pressure in the neoliberal age of global corporatism. The
"people" is defined in non-statist terms. For the Occupy movements, thus,
"the people" represents both the concrete unity of citizens as a collective
body, wherever they happen to live, and the abstract whole that grounds
legitimate authority in a popular democracy.

THE WORLD SOCIAL FORUM

The Occupy movement is not the only exemplar of global grassroots
democratic activism that directly confronts the neoliberal global organization of power. The World Social Forum has been doing precisely this
since the beginning of the twenty-first century, as part of a concerted
effort to provide an alternative conceptual and practical image of the
global order to that derived from neoliberalism. The catalyst for this democratized response to market logic and practice was a meeting in Porto
Alegre, Brazil, in late January 2001, that saw a group of intellectuals, aca-
demics, and activists, together with the Brazilian Workers' Party, organizing a radical counterpart to the meeting of the World Economic Forum
(the annual conclave of business leaders, neoliberal governments, and
global investors) taking place, simultaneously, in the wealthy resort town
of Davos, Switzerland. Holding their meeting in the poor and depressed
Brazilian city, the organizers aimed to continue the energy and spectacle
of protests against neoliberalism, most notably in the "Battle of Seattle"
that shut down downtown Seattle and forced the premature cancellation
of the meeting there of the World Trade Organization in November 1999.
Many other protests against neoliberal globalism had taken place from
the 1970s against the IMF's "structural adjustment" programs.[18] The protests in Seattle became significant both for the size of the protest (more
than 50,000 and perhaps as many as 100,000, according to estimates)
and for the remarkable diversity of groups that participated. Perhaps the
most famous images flashed across television screens and on the Internet
were of ecological protesters (dressed as turtles) marching shoulder to
shoulder with old-line trade unionists. The determination of these protesters, their diversity, and their carnivalesque performance of grassroots

democracy generated significant energy to what has come to be called the alter-globalization movement.[19]

The World Social Forum in part meant to capitalize on and to focus the energy that Seattle generated and came to symbolize for a growing number of grassroots activists. It succeeded, at least in the short term. Planning a relatively small meeting of protests, workshops, speeches, and panels, the organizers found themselves with nearly 5,000 delegates from 132 countries, with a total number of demonstrators estimated at more than 15,000 in Porto Alegre. The energy generated by the combination of utopianism—the slogan of the World Social Forum was "Another World Is Possible"—with the call to action and engagement was enormous. Indeed, since 2001, the World Social Forum has convened in different places, building upon the initial Porto Alegre meeting and the anti-neoliberal sentiments articulated there. The meeting in Dakar, Senegal, in 2011, had upward of 75,000 attendees. The World Social Forum is now coordinated by an international council comprised of a whole range of member organizations, a council that seeks to harness the energy and make coherent the radicalism of member organizations, without diluting the diversity of the many groups and individuals committed to its anticorporate, democratic principles.

Faced with the prospect of a large and serious movement, the World Social Forum set up an organization of activists in order to move forward and capture the spirit of solidarity and engagement that swelled up in Porto Alegre. The main problem was to harness the energy and to coordinate the multiplicity of activist organizations without diluting, or worse, destroying, the diversity that, to many, gave the World Social Forum its democratic character.

The Charter of Principles that emerged at the end of the meetings at Porto Alegre declared that going forward, the World Social Forum (WSF) would become "a permanent process" that "brings together and interlinks only organizations and movements of civil society from all the countries of the world, but does not intend to be a body representing world civil society."[20] It is

> an open meeting place for reflective thinking, democratic debate of ideas, formulation of proposals, free exchange of experiences and interlinking for effective action, by groups and movements of civil society that are opposed to neoliberalism and to domination of the world by capital and any

form of imperialism, and are committed to building a planetary society directed towards fruitful relationships among Humankind and between it and the Earth.

The aim is to produce a "network of networks" in which "the future can be imagined and objectively realized through "'prefigurative politics'—or the enactment of the world we envision. . . . Social forum events are attempts to create miniworlds, models the forum process hopes to export around the globe."[21] Finally, it is nonviolent in its philosophy and "radical" conduct, drawing its inspiration from Gandhi and Martin Luther King. In this context, it posits militarism as antidemocratic and seeks through the disciplined performance of nonviolent resistance to create democratic subjects capable of thinking and acting beyond traditional parameters in their engagements with opponents and detractors.

In short, the new democratic subject envisaged by the World Social Forum and the Occupy movements is a politically progressive cosmopolitan agent of the neoliberal age, able to move fluidly among various sites of power and resistance, from the national to the regional, the local and the global. It seeks the flows of people, ideas, organizational capacities, and information in global networks to facilitate the emergence of a democratic ethos that holds together contentious differences while unifying against the neoliberal order. The democratic subject is formed in the space between local confrontation and global techniques of organization and consciousness raising. The image it envisages of this cosmopolitan citizenship does not seek to eliminate or even transcend national political subjectivities but to add wider commitments to traditional identities in the search for a broader and more fluid global community committed to democratic thought and practices. In this sense, it seeks what Deleuze and Guattari describe as a "rhizomatic" culture for future human development that, instead of fixed, hierarchical structures and frames of reference, favors a more contingent, more spontaneous attitude toward life and decision making and an articulation of "humankind" based on more fluid and hybrid criteria.[22] In organizational terms, this rhizomatic tendency is to be found in the diversity and autonomy of the groups, individuals, and movements that have sprouted up from the common democratic core of the World Social Organization.

The World Social Forum and the Occupy movements draw attention toward the direct confrontation with neoliberalism as such. However, other democratic projects are emerging, creating alternative democratic subjectivities, that are not focused on directly overturning the neoliberal global order but that address it in more local, although globally structured and connected, terms. In the next section, we turn to two examples of what J. K. Gibson-Graham (Julie Graham and Katherine Gibson) call "intentional economies."[23]

ALTERNATIVE DEMOCRATIC "INTENTIONAL ECONOMIES"

Neoliberal globalism presumes a single world economy, totalizing the market form for all economies. As we discussed in chapter 2, neoliberals proclaim that globalization is inevitable, and therefore, all economic life must be absorbed into the single global market. Hardt and Negri also proclaim that globalization is "irresistible and irreversible," and therefore, transformational politics must focus on the macro level, the "big picture."[24] Both perspectives assume that the logics of all democratic projects can be subsumed within the logic of the global market or conversely the multitude and, therefore, have little to say about the logics of the plurality of specific democratic projects in globalization that do not directly confront the totality of neoliberal globalization. In this section, we discuss two such projects, focusing on the democratic subjectivities they produce, that presume the possibility of multiple economies rooted in the formation of ethical and democratic communities.

THE MONDRAGON COOPERATIVE

In 1956, a Catholic priest, Father Arizmendiarrieta, began a small cooperative at Mondragón in the Basque region of Spain to produce paraffin lamps.[25] From this modest beginning, the Mondragon Cooperative created a network of cooperatives in a range of goods: consumer electronics, tool and dye manufacturing, retail businesses and services, including a bank, insurance firms, and education facilities. In 1991, it became the Mondragon Cooperative Corporation (MCC) and has grown to an association of more than 140 cooperatives, operating in 41 countries with sales in 150 sites worldwide. It is the tenth-largest business organization in Spain, employing more than 83,000 workers globally.[26] The Mondragon Cooperative remains an inspiration for many seeking ways to fold an ethics of social justice and a democratic ethos into everyday life of their economy. Mondragon, in this sense, is a practical model of alternative democratic subjectivity or what J. K. Gibson-Graham call an "intentional economy," which treats the economy not as a site of individualist competitions and self-aggrandizement but as "a political and ethical space of [democratic] decision making."[27] And there has been important institutional inspiration too, with the UN declaring 2012 the "International Year of the Cooperative." This, in turn, acknowledges the increasing significance of the International Cooperative Alliance, begun in 1895, that opened its head office headquarters in Geneva in 1982 and its first regional office in San José, Costa Rica, in 1990. It now has regional headquarters in Africa, the Americas, Asia, the Pacific, and Europe.

The modern idea of worker-owned producer cooperatives was not born in Spain in the 1950s, of course. It dates from at least the first half of the nineteenth century and the utopian socialism of Robert Owen and others. Against the extraordinary backdrop of the industrial revolution, Owen formed community-based economies based on the principles of worker ownership, democratic participation in decision-making, and commitment to social transformation. He believed, contrary to Marx, that alternative community-based modern economies could be formed against the extremes of capitalist domination—without replacing capitalism. Instead, his "utopian socialism" proposed that active ownership and participation in productive life would create new kinds of modern capitalist subjects—ethical beings who would build new societies and ways of life in which social justice, equality, and cooperation would become second nature. This general theme has continued to inspire radicals and democrats around the world to the present day who, like Father Arizmendiarrieta, see, in local democratic workers cooperatives, a means of contesting the neoliberal approach to globalization while enhancing an everyday lived reality in which economies are structured around social justice, democratic decision making, and participation.

The members of the cooperative are "worker-members." They operate as members of the co-op on several registers: in their jobs as workers, as participants in democratic management, as voters and constituents of representative policy-making and oversight bodies, as bearers and performers of an ethos of social justice and cooperation. The economic, the political, and the social all come together in the ethos of the subject through a democratic organization of the cooperative, the emphasis on cooperative self-management and participation on the part of workers, and in the practices of education and self-development of the workers and solidarity with the larger social world, regional, national, and international. The

MCC is based on a set of democratic political principles and social commitments that promote self-management, equity, social responsibility,
and a democratic organization meant to encourage participation by co-op
members. As Gibson-Graham put it:

> Commitment to [these principles] is part of a practice of subjectiva-
> tion, the cultivation of a distinctive economic way of being. Working
> to realize and concretize them is an ethical practice that simultaneously
> constitutes the cooperators as communal subjects and as members of the
> Mondragón community.[28]

The political structure of the cooperative is centered on strict principles of representative democracy. The preeminent policy-making body
is the General Assembly, consisting of 650 co-op members. It approves
policies and oversees the company's everyday management, including
appointing and, when warranted, removing members of the Governing
Council—a body elected by all members of the General Assembly for
four-year terms that oversees the everyday management of the co-op.
The whole enterprise is guided by the principle that capital is to be
subordinated to labor, echoing Owen's notion that dignified labor is the
main factor in transforming nature, society, and humankind to a more
ethical state of being. Crucial too is the principle concerning the distribution of wealth in the cooperatives, where the divide between the lowest laborer and the highest professionals is one to six. Unlike neoliberal
capitalist corporations that are beholden to financial stockholders, the
cooperative does not seek short-term profit at the expense of the working conditions and the quality of work produced by workers. In this
sense, they create economies—spaces of calculation and materiality—in
which democratic political subjects can form and operate. Thus, the du-
alisms that create subjects in the neoliberal order—between the political
and the economic, between the market and the state, between personal
and collective responsibility, between labor and capital, between ethics
and accumulation—become democratic intersections and sites of negotiating difference rather than subsuming all differences into market
equivalences as in neoliberal capitalism.

In Mondragon the economy is politicized and socialized, contrary to
neoliberalism's efforts to isolate the economy as the dominant and domineering master logic of social relations. The cooperative makes the economy into a site for the production of democratic subjects for whom being-

in-common with others is folded into economic relations. The economic becomes a space in which co-op members develop the skills to make decisions in common with the others with whom they share the economic enterprise. Economic decisions—setting of wages, investment decisions, assignments of tasks including management—become simultaneously political decisions subject to the development of skills for economic and political cooperation. This is why education is so important to the cooperative and why it insists on continual education for its member-workers.

The production of democratic subjectivity within alternative community economies is not limited to the large-scale industrial cooperative. One example of a rural democratic cooperative developed on the Mondragon model is the Mararikulam Experiment, a network of over 1,500 women-owned cooperatives in Kerala, India (see also chapter 4), formed in the late 1990s as a means of combating poverty. As part of the larger democratic experiment in Kerala, these cooperatives bind together the economic, the political, and the social as part of their democratic response to the TINA principle. Important in this context is the emphasis on economic and political self-management, developing programs of literacy and self-development at the community level and building solidarity with workers in the outside world.

We can also cite some community-based tourism in which the economy becomes a site of the formation of democratic subjects. For example, we can cite the Stibrawpa Association, a women's cooperative of handicraft production in Yorkin, a Bribri people's village in the southeast corner of Costa Rica. "Stibrawpa" (Women Who Make Handcrafts) was formed after many of the men of the village returned ill from working on the banana and pineapple plantations of large U.S. multinationals in Costa Rica and elsewhere in Latin America. In 1996, it became the "Stibrawpa Women's House Association" managed by an all-women board from the village. It has since become part of a broader village and Bribri indigenous people's economy that infuses sustainable agriculture, ecotourism, and handicraft production. It was formed to create a community alternative to the reliance on wage labor in the corporate estates of large agribusiness. As one of the prominent members of the board describes the aim of the association:

> In the past, our men had to leave for months to work on banana planta-
> tions, and over time we started noticing that as they aged, their health
> deteriorated. They [often] died young, and, we believe, from exposure to

the chemicals. We wanted to create a local source of income for them to stay here with their families, and live a healthier lifestyle.[29]

Stibrawpa and the Yorkin collective work together with ACTUAR (Costa Rican Community-Based Rural Tourism Association), which was formed in 2001 through the United Nations' Small Grants Program. The aim was to help to foster sustainable rural economies, especially for indigenous peoples, by creating alternative, democratically organized local economies in which the economy became a site of interweaving organic agriculture, cultural preservation, and exchange through community-based and controlled tourism and democratic political decision-making as an alternative to corporate globalization. ACTUAR principles are:

- We believe it is possible to preserve the natural resources and generate sustainable life styles for men and women that run community-based rural tourism initiatives
- We value the cultural identity interchange [with tourists]
- We value the democratic participation and equity of the community in the sustainable use of the natural resources

They instantiate what Gibson-Graham describe as the "community economy" against the neoliberal idea of the economy as a separate, domineering, and totalizing logic and against its TINA principle:

> Resocializing (and repoliticizing) the economy involves making explicit the sociality that is always present, and thus constituting the various forms and practices of interdependence as matters for reflection, discussion, negotiation, and action.[30]

In order to create this alternative community economy and to create the economy as an ethical community under the direction of its members, the village had to become adept at negotiating multiple registers of social relations, such as state agencies, Costa Rican political parties, transnational trade and development NGOs, foreign-aid donors and construction companies (they convinced a company in Oregon to supply the co-op with solar panels for its school, lodge, and workshop), ecotourism companies, the UN, several universities in Costa Rica and abroad, and several fair-trade organizations. It now combines organic farming, handicraft production, and an ecotourist lodge and has been able to create a revived alternative economy to the prevailing corporate agricultural economy. Much of the resultant profits has been channeled back into the community, providing funding for local schools and the revival of the local Bribri language and culture.

Community economies as sites of democratic subjectivation in response to neoliberal globalization share much with more urban spaces. They have similarly become adept at negotiating, as a community, on multiple spatial registers—local, city, regional, national, transnational, and global—with a variety of agents that seek to govern them in order to create themselves as ethical communities infusing democratic politics. We turn to these now.

DEEP DEMOCRACY AND POLITICAL SOCIETY

Throughout this book, we have stressed the need for more participatory and activist forms of democracy in the age of neoliberal globalization. This idea informed the historical vignettes in chapter 1 and led us to stress Sheldon Wolin's critique of the passivity and "inverted totalitarianism" of neoliberalism and polyarchal democracy in chapter 2. In chapters 3 and 4, we examined how neoliberal globalization is limiting participation in its various articulations with states in various parts of the world, and in chapter 5, we discussed how the stretching of democratic norms into forms of global governance and cosmopolitan democracy, while promising in some respects, seems to us too ambiguous and limited in the space it opens for democratic participation. In chapter 6, we have turned to the ways that more participatory forms of democratic subjectivity are emerging in various sites around the world. Perhaps it is ironic that having begun with a discourse of democracy that was largely rooted in Western traditions, we conclude with examples of how templates for participatory democracy are emerging not from advanced states but from the poor struggling in the interstices of neoliberal globalization.

In his 2002 essay, "Deep Democracy: Urban Governmentality and the Horizon of Politics," Arjun Appadurai describes "an urban activist movement with global links" that combines "local activism with horizontal global networking."[31] In 1987, a housing-advocacy partnership called the "Alliance" was formed in Mumbai, India, bringing together three groups: the National Slum Dwellers' Federation (NSDF), a community-based grassroots organization; the Society for the Protection of Area Resource Centers (SPARC), an organization of professional social workers in Mumbai; and Mahila Milan, an organization and network of poor women focused on fostering a savings culture among poor women as a way to combat poverty. The Alliance presents us with an exemplar of a new form of democratic subjectivity that mobilizes the poor to better their lives by forming democratic collectivities that are local and participatory, that develop the capacities to exploit the governmental regulatory regimes of states, and that constitute global linkages to other like communities, thereby creating networks within which a democratic ethos and culture might thrive.

Against the neoliberal claim that free markets produce democracy, the Alliance politicizes and socializes the economy through democratic empowerment and organization.

> Instead of relying on the model of an outside organizer who teaches local communities how to hold the state to its normative obligations to the poor, the Alliance is committed to methods of organization, mobilization, teaching, and learning that build on what poor persons already know and understand. The first principle of this approach is that no one knows more about how to survive poverty than the poor themselves.[32]

At the core of these democratic principles "is the idea of individuals and families as self-organizing members of a political collective who pool resources, organize lobbying, provide mutual risk-management devices, and confront opponents, when necessary." Above all, this principle "serves to remind all members . . . that the power of the Alliance lies not in its donors, its technical expertise, or its administration, but in the will to federate among poor families and communities."[33]

The poor create the meaning of citizenship as they participate in creating their own conditions, their own social world. Appadurai makes clear the functioning of the Alliance as a form of subjectivation, that democratic subjects are created. It aims to create new people, a new ethos and moral life of its members that makes them agents in the creation of their own world:

> As with all serious movements concerned with consciousness-changing and self-mobilization, there is a conscious effort to inculcate protocols of speech, style, and organizational form within the Alliance. The coalition cultivates a highly transparent, nonhierarchical, antibureaucratic, and antitechnocratic organizational style.[34]

While the Alliance maintains offices, they are structured informally, with people moving in and out constantly, and most of the work does not take place in formal settings but through mobile communications. The informality and setting of the work in mobilities—communications over the phone and Internet, through constant movement of staff and personnel to meetings, including site visits by staff and by representatives of the communities themselves (often local activists travel to communities in other countries, and local communities host visits of members of communities from abroad)—creates a condition in which subjects learn to interact with others, creating a consciousness of respect and openness that creates this particular form of participatory subject.

One of the central activities of the Alliance, the central focus of the women of Mahila Milan, is encouraging a collective culture of savings, which is focused not on the immediacy of the project (savings is less about the immediate gain for the individual) but more focused on the long term, on "the importance of slow learning and cumulative change against the temporal logic of the project."[35] Indeed, this temporality and subjectivation is at the core of the Alliance's principle of federation:

> What is important to recognize here is that when Alliance leaders speak about a way of life organized around the practice of saving—in Jocklin's words, it is like "breathing"—they are framing saving as a moral discipline. The practice builds a certain kind of political fortitude and commitment to the collective good and creates persons who can manage their affairs in many other ways as well.[36]

Appadurai's essay was published in 2002, but we should note that the Alliance has remained and grown in the interim. According to SPARC's website, the Alliance now (March 2013) operates in over seventy cities in India and is networked with over twenty countries.[37] Homeless International reports that the NSDF now (again, March 2013) has over two million members in seventy-two towns and cities in India.[38]

The Alliance provides an example of what Partha Chatterjee calls "the politics of the governed" in "political society."[39] Political society is a heterogeneous space in which groups and communities form in circumstances of deprivation and oppression in order to resist and exploit the regulatory powers of the state and powerful corporations and groups (such as negotiating with power companies to legalize or otherwise accept siphoning off electricity into squatter settlements). The struggles are precarious, circumstantial, and tentative. They often stem from illegal populations outside of civil society, such as illegal squatters' developments in overcrowded global cities. Subjects in political society form associations to provide services for themselves (health care, housing, job training, etc.), to pressure the state to change laws or to grant them exceptions to the law so they can maintain their living quarters or technically illegal livelihoods (street vendors or cab drivers, for example), to negotiate recognition as a distinct population group in order to gain inclusion in state programs or to change the rules of those programs to better suit their needs.[40] In doing so, they "*give to the empirical form of a population group the moral attributes of a community.*"[41]

The subjects of political society

> do not relate to the organs of the state in the same way that the middle classes do, nor do governmental agencies treat them as proper citizens belonging to civil society. Those in political society make their claims on government, and in turn are governed, not within the framework of stable constitutionally defined rights and laws, but rather through temporary, contextual and unstable arrangements arrived at through direct political negotiations.[42]

The poor create for themselves an alternative moral and civic world as they negotiate the conditions and agencies that govern them. Rather than overturning the neoliberal governmental order or creating an alternative economy or passively accepting state administration as legitimated by polyarchal democracy, the poor in political society seek to turn the administration of their lives by the organs of governmentality to their advantage and needs. In doing so, the poor and others in most of the world are creating civic lives for themselves and struggling for inclusion on new terms in the civic life of the larger entities that govern them. They do so by reclaiming the spaces of their lives against the efforts of their governors to limit and orchestrate their movements.

The governed participate in globalization first as its remainders, conditioned by globalization, as when real-estate developers and speculators enclose places in the city in order to integrate them into the global capitalist economy that displaces large numbers, especially of the poor. But then they participate as protagonists who utilize the networks to create new strategies to further their goals. The Alliance studied by Appadurai, for example, exists locally and within networks with both NGOs and

UN agencies working on homelessness, housing, and sanitation, and the NSDF continually exchanges information and knowledge and meets with like organizations in over twenty other countries.[43] It participates in the Homeless International but is not defined or controlled by it. Again, Chatterjee describes the global dimensions of this activism well:

> There is a second answer to the question of how the results of local experiments may be replicated on a wider scale. Here, the local initiative does not attempt to be total and comprehensive; it does not seek to refashion the community in its wholeness. Rather, it seeks to develop specific practices with appropriate institutions. When successfully developed in a local context, these could acquire the form of a set of techniques which may be transported elsewhere after being released from their local constraints.[44]

These certain techniques can exploit, counter, manipulate, reinvest, the governmental practices of states and the global order and spread throughout the globe.

Chatterjee argues that the micro-democratic politics in political society involves an alternative conception of time-space from the representations of democracy as a unity of a singular form, as in neoliberal globalism.[45] Time is heterogeneous in the sense that different human associations do not all fit into a linear homogeneous time. The latter suggests that politics must be the same everywhere and that all forms of democracy can be understood in their relation to some form that is unfolding, perhaps unevenly but nevertheless as a naturalized identity, existing in a single time frame. Modernity has just one positive form. This is the underlying conception of neoliberal globalization. But democracy in globalization, as Chatterjee's argument suggests, is forming through the subjective actions of concrete actors in multiple forms dependent on the dense time/space framing in local settings and conditions. Democracy develops in local, historically contingent spaces, differently in different places.

While Chatterjee describes political society as a frame of the activities of the poor in India, it would seem relevant even in more affluent populations as well where governmentality targets population groups through regulation. He says, "As a matter of fact, it could even be said that the activities of political society in postcolonial countries represent a continuing critique of the paradoxical reality in all capitalist democracies of equal citizenship and majority rule, on the one hand, and the dominance of property and privilege, on the other."[46] We could cite here housing programs for gay men with AIDS in the 1980s and 1990s as an example when gay men organized to first be recognized as a population group eligible for city-subsidized housing and then to eliminate the AIDS-only wards in group homes that the city set up that wound up spreading the disease and reinforcing stereotypes of gay men.

Arguing that the Western idea of democracy is in crisis, its limits having been exposed and its promises undermined by its increasing preoccupation with a narrow instrumentalist and managerial governmentality, a similar argument to Sheldon Wolin's in *Democracy Inc.* that we discussed in chapter 2, Chatterjee contends that a new context has emerged for democratic politics among the poor and disenfranchised in postcolonial cities that can be replicated elsewhere. Therefore, the reimagining and perhaps reinvention of democracy in the novel participatory practices of the governed in states such as India promises not just potential new forms in postcolonial contexts but for democracy more globally as well:

> It is incumbent upon those who are still marginal in the world of modernity to use the opportunities they have to invent new forms of the modern social, economic, and political order. There are many experiments that have been carried out in the last hundred years or so. . . . It is worth considering whether many of these . . . might not in fact contain the possibility of entirely new forms of economic organization or democratic governance never thought of by the old forms of Western modernity.[47]

We have addressed examples in this chapter.

In this chapter we have seen democratic movements that form new democratic ways of being, new moral-political ways of living in self-conscious, direct confrontation with neoliberal globalism. We have also discussed others that are forming more modest yet robust democratic subjectivities in local struggles to resocialize and repoliticize their economies and to take control of the spaces in which they live. These involve negotiating the techniques of neoliberal governmentalization and are generating transversal networks that both create coalitions with like democratic communities both below and across the institution and power of the state and are projecting new techniques and ways of being democratic beyond Western democratic forms of polyarchy. In earlier chapters, we noted how democratic movements are emerging in response to neoliberal articulations of the state as nodes of global markets and corporate power, re-signifying democracy in the process (chapters 3 and 4), and how new imaginaries and experiments with transversal forms of liberal-democratic constitutionalism and the democratization of global governance are emerging to re-embed the global economy in liberal-democratic political projects (chapter 5). We have sought to stress this heterogeneity and heterodoxy of the democratic practices and subjectivities that are emerging in our rapidly globalizing world.

We have been guided throughout by our commitment to more participatory forms of democracy against the neoliberal contention that there is only one way to be democratic in the twenty-first century, an economic democracy in which individuals become privatized entrepreneurs who are largely passive participants in the rituals of polyarchal democracy. On the contrary, we argue that there is no single keystroke that sounds democracy in globalization, no wonder drug like the capitalist market that will produce it. New and inventive forms of participation are being invented and need to be cultivated. If some forms of global democratic constitutionalism and citizenship are to emerge and if new imaginings and ways of being democratic are to flourish in our global world, it will be as parts of counter-hegemonic projects taking various forms.

NOTES

INTRODUCTION

1. Francis Fukuyama, "The End of History," *National Interest* (Summer 1989). This was expanded into a best-selling book in 1992, as *The End of History and the Last Man* (New York: Free Press, 1992).

2. *Inaugural Addresses of the Presidents of the United States.* Washington, DC: U.S. GPO, 1989; Bartleby.com, 2001. www.bartleby.com/124/.

3. This seems to be a nonpartisan affair in the United States. In recent years, both the Democratic and Republican parties have created their own organizations, funded in large part by the NED, to promote democracy in other countries, such as the National Democratic Institute for International Affairs (NDI), currently headed by former secretary of state Madeleine Albright; and the International Republican Institute (IRI), currently headed by senator and former presidential candidate John McCain.

4. A good introductory collection is *Debating the Democratic Peace*, ed. Michael E. Brown, Sean M. Lynn-Jones, and Steven E. Miller (Cambridge, MA: MIT Press, 1996).

5. Michael Doyle, "Kant, Liberal Legacies, and Foreign Affairs," *Philosophy and Public Affairs* 12 (Summer and Fall 1983): 205–35, 323–53.

6. See Michael Doyle, ed., *Liberal Peace: Selected Essays* (London: Routledge, 2012); For a critical assessment, Susanna Campbell, David Chandler, and Meera Sabaratnam, eds., *A Liberal Peace? The Problems and Practices of Peacebuilding* (London: Zed, 2011).

7. See Milton Friedman, *Capitalism and Freedom: Fortieth Anniversary Edition* (Chicago: University of Chicago Press, 2002); Milton Friedman and Rose Friedman, *Free to Choose: A Personal Statement* (Boston: Mariner Books, 1990; original 1979).

8. David Held, *Democracy and the Global Order: From the Modern State to Cosmopolitan Governance* (Stanford, CA: Stanford University Press, 1995), 267.

9. Jan Aart Scholte, "Civil Society and Democratically Accountable Global Governance," *Government and Opposition* 39, no. 2 (Spring 2004): 211–33.

10. See Jürgen Habermas, *The Philosophical Discourse of Modernity* (Cambridge: Polity Press, 1987). For interesting works with similar purpose, see James Bohman, *Democracy across Borders: From Demos to Demoi* (Cambridge, MA: MIT Press, 2010); John S. Dryzek, *Deliberative Global Politics* (Cambridge: Polity Press, 2006).

11. Andrew Linklater, *The Transformation of Political Community: Ethical Foundations of the Post-Westphalian Era* (Cambridge: Polity Press, 1998); *Men and Citizens in the Theory of International Relations*, 2nd ed. (London: Macmillan, 1990); "Cosmopolitan Political Communities in International Relations," *International Relations* 16 (2002): 135–50.

12. William E. Connolly, "Pluralism and Sovereignty," in *Pluralism* (Durham, NC: Duke University Press, 2005), 131–60.

13. Marcos, "Chiapas: The Southeast in Two Winds," at http://flag.blackened.net/revolt/mexico/ezln/marcos_se_2_wind.html.

14. Taken from the Mondragon Corporation website at http://www.mondragon-corporation.com/ENG/Who-we-are/Introduction.aspx. For a broader discussion of the Mondragon collective, see J. K. Gibson-Graham, chapter 5 in *A Post-Capitalist Politics* (Minneapolis: University of Minnesota Press, 2006).

15. For a discussion of hegemony in these terms, see Antonio Gramsci, *Selections from the Prison Notebooks*, ed. and trans. Quintin Hoare and Geoffrey Nowell Smith (New York: International Publishers, 1971).

16. See, especially, R. B. J. Walker, *Inside/Outside: International Relations as Political Theory* (Cambridge: Cambridge University Press, 1993).

17. Benedict Anderson, *Imagined Communities*, rev. ed. (London: Verso, 1991); and Ronald J. Deibert, *Parchment, Printing, and Hypermedia: Communication in World Order Transformation* (New York: Columbia University Press, 1997).

18. For an insightful analysis of this point, see Bonnie Honig, *Democracy and the Foreigner* (Princeton, NJ: Princeton University Press, 2001).

19. This point has been central to Jacques Rancière's critique of liberal, and especially neoliberal, democracy. See, especially, his *Philosopher and His Poor*, ed. Andrew Parker, trans. John Drury, Corinne Oster, and Andrew Parker (Durham, NC: Duke University Press, 2004); and *Hatred of Democracy* (London: Verso, 2006).

20. The term is from Susan Strange, *Casino Capitalism* (Manchester, UK: Manchester University Press, 1997; original 1986).

CHAPTER 1

1. See, for example, James Madison, "Federalist no. 63," in Alexander Hamilton, James Madison, and John Jay, *The Federalist Papers*, ed. Ian Shapiro (New Haven, CT: Yale University Press, 2009), 320.

2. Robert Dahl, *On Democracy* (New Haven, CT: Yale University Press, 2000), 12–13.

3. See the critique of current democratic theory by Jacques Rancière, *Hatred of Democracy*, trans. Steve Corcoran (London: Verso, 2006).

4. Several important books that have reassessed the practice of democracy in Athens for political theory are: J. Peter Euben, John R. Wallach, and Josiah Ober, eds., *Athenian Political Thought and the Reconstruction of American Democracy* (Ithaca, NY: Cornell University Press, 1994); Josiah Ober, *Mass and Elite in Democratic Athens: Rhetoric, Ideology, and the Power of the People* (Princeton, NJ: Princeton University Press, 1989); Ober, *The Athenian Revolution: Essays on Ancient Greek Democracy and Political Theory* (Princeton, NJ: Princeton University Press, 1996); Moses Finley, *Democracy Ancient and Modern*, 2nd ed. (London: Hogarth, 1985); Ellen Meiksins Wood, *Peasant-Citizens and Slaves: The Foundations of Athenian Democracy* (London: Verso, 1997).

5. Ellen Meiksins Wood, *Citizens to Lords: A Social History of Western Political Thought from Antiquity to the Middle Ages* (London: Verso, 2008), 29.

6. Ober, *Athenian Revolution*, 4.

7. Simon Hornblower, "Democratic Institutions in Ancient Greece," in *Democracy: The Unfinished Journey, 508 BC to AD 1993*, ed. John Dunn (Oxford: Oxford University Press, 1992), 3.

8. Wood, *Citizens to Lords*, 33.

9. "The new divisions cut across tribal and class ties and elevated locality over kinship, establishing and strengthening new bonds, new loyalties specific to the polis, the community of citizens." Wood, *Citizens to Lords*, 35.

10. Hornblower, "Democratic Institutions," 15. The democracy and democratic ethos that emerged in ancient Athens was far from comprehensive, of course, and while the profound questions it raised and the notion of a community of politically equal citizens it established are of great significance in the modern democratic narrative, it is important to keep in mind that the Athenian citizenry excluded women, slaves, and metics (resident aliens). Cleisthenes seems to have assumed a citizenry of about 30,000 men—about a tenth of the population of Athens and surrounding Attica. Slaves accounted for a large percentage of the population, and the Persian Wars (490–479) and their aftermath increased the "alien" population to as many as 120,000.

11. J. Peter Euben, for example, has done very important work excavating the democratic political theory in the theater. See his *The Tragedy of Political Theory: The Road Not Taken* (Princeton, NJ: Princeton University Press, 1990). Also see Cynthia Farrar, *The Origins of Democratic Thinking: The Invention of Politics in Classical Athens* (Cambridge: Cambridge University Press, 1988).

12. Thucydides, *The Peloponnesian War*, trans. Walter Blanco, ed. Walter Blanco and Jennifer Tolbert Roberts (New York: Norton, 1998), 54.

13. Thucydides, *The Peloponnesian War*.

14. Aristotle, *The Politics*, ed. Stephen Everson (Cambridge: Cambridge University Press, 1988), 67.

15. Plato, *Republic*, trans. G. M. A. Grube, rev. C. D. C. Reeve (Indianapolis: 1992), book 8. (In fact, however, fourth-century Athens—the *Republic* was most likely written around 380—did not deteriorate into rule by a tyrant.)

16. For example, the Roman *populus*; the *populi* of the Renaissance Italian city-states; the "patriots" of the American war of independence; and/or the revolutionary "sans culottes" of the French Revolution.

17. In David Wootton, ed., *Divine Right and Democracy: An Anthology of Political Writings in Stuart England* (Indianapolis: Hackett, 1986), 286.

18. An excellent brief introduction to the Levellers is David Wootton, "The Levellers," in *Democracy: The Unfinished Journey, 508 BC to AD 1993*, ed. John Dunn (Oxford: Oxford University Press, 1992), 71–89.

19. In addition to *The Spirit of the Laws*, see "The Myth of the Troglodytes," in his earlier, fictional *The Persian Letters*. This is the myth of a tribe able to overcome a vastly superior enemy through mobilizing the subjective spirit of civic virtue that distinguished their community from other forms of government.

20. Montesquieu's argument for checks and balances is in the famous chapter 17 of *The Spirit of the Laws* on the English constitution.

21. Alexis de Tocqueville, *Democracy in America*, vol. 1, Henry Reeve translation, rev. and ed. Phillips Bradley (New York: Knopf, 1980), 202.

22. Tocqueville, *Democracy in America*, 203.

23. Tocqueville, *Democracy in America*, 199–206.

24. See, for example, Karl Marx, "On the Jewish Question," in *The Marx–Engels Reader*, 2nd ed., ed. Robert C. Tucker (New York: Norton, 1978), 26–52.

25. Alexander Hamilton, James Madison, and John Jay, *The Federalist Papers*, ed. Ian Shapiro (New Haven, CT: Yale University Press, 2009), 320.

26. See John Locke, *Second Treatise of Government* (New York: Macmillan, 1946).

27. See Michael Mandelbaum, *Democracy's Good Name* (New York: PublicAffairs Books, 2007), 99.

28. Mandelbaum, *Democracy's Good Name*, 103.

29. Mandelbaum, *Democracy's Good Name*, 101–2.

30. One such criticism from the moderate left was Christopher Lasch, *The Culture of Narcissism: American Life in the Age of Diminished Expectations* (New York: Norton, 1991; original 1979). From a more conservative point of view, see Daniel Bell, *The Cultural Contradictions of Capitalism* (New York: Basic Books, 1996; original 1976).

31. On this, see Irving Kristol, *Neoconservatism: The Autobiography of an Idea* (New York: Free Press, 1995), 35–37.

CHAPTER 2

1. Karl Polanyi, *The Great Transformation* (Boston: Beacon, 1954), 256.

2. FDR, cited in Jacob Hacker and Paul Pierson, *Winner Take All Politics: How Washington Made the Rich Richer and Turned Its Back on the Middle Class* (New York: Simon and Schuster, 2010), 306.

3. George Lakoff and Glen W. Smith, "Why Democracy Is Public: The American Dream Beats the Nightmare," *Reader Supported News*, July 29, 2011, http://www.reader supportednews.org/opinion2/277-75/6804-why-democracy-is-public.

4. Wendy Brown, "Neoliberalism and the End of Liberal Democracy," in *Edgework: Critical Essays on Knowledge and Power* (Princeton, NJ: Princeton University Press, 2005), 37–59.

5. Milton Friedman, *Capitalism and Freedom: Fortieth Anniversary Edition* (Chicago: University of Chicago Press, 2002); and Milton Friedman and Rose Friedman, *Free to Choose: A Personal Statement* (Boston: Mariner Books, 1990; original 1979).

6. Ludwig von Mises, *Human Action: A Treatise on Economics* (Vienna: Ludwig von Mises Institute, 1998), 270.

7. Daniel Yergin and Joseph Stanislaw, *The Commanding Heights: The Battle between Governments and the Marketplace That Is Remaking the World* (New York: Touchstone Books, 1999), 12.

8. Strange, *Casino Capitalism.*

9. These moderated neoliberal states remain "neoliberal" in that they remain committed to the capitalist marketplace as the keystone of the good modern society, in their facilitation of capitalist competition between firms and corporations, in their acceptance of the rules of global free trade, and in their ideological and institutional support for open export markets.

10. Robert Hunter Wade, "Globalization, Growth, Poverty, Inequality, Resentment and Imperialism," in *Global Political Economy*, 3rd ed., ed. John Ravenhill (Oxford: Oxford University Press, 2008), 377; and Branko Milanović, *Worlds Apart: Measuring International and Global Inequality* (Princeton, NJ: Princeton University Press, 2005), 53.

11. OECD, *Divided We Stand: Why Inequality Keeps Rising* (Paris: OECD, 2011), 4.

12. John Hills, *An Anatomy of Economic Inequality in the UK: Report of the National Equality Panel* (London: Centre for the Analysis of Social Exclusion, LSE, 2010), 1.

13. Susan George, "A Short History of Neo-Liberalism," Conference on Economic Sovereignty in a Globalizing World, Bangkok, March 24–26, 1999, http://www.global exchange.org/resources/econ101/neoliberalismhist.

14. Andrew Gamble, cited in Rosa Mulé, *Political Parties, Games and Redistribution* (Cambridge: Cambridge University Press, 2001), 100.

15. George Monbiot, "How the Neoliberals Stitched Up the Wealth of Nations for Themselves," *Guardian*, August 28, 2007.

16. David Harvey, *A Brief History of Neoliberalism* (Oxford: Oxford University Press, 2005), 16–17.

17. John Schmitt and Ben Zipperer, "Is the U.S. a Good Model for Reducing Social Exclusion in Europe?" *Post-Autistic Economics Review* 40 (2006).

18. Timothy Noah, "Can Domestic Policy Affect Income Distribution?" *New Republic*, March 13, 2012, http://www.newrepublic.com/authors/timothy-noah.

19. George Lakoff and Glenn W. Smith, "Why Democracy Is Public."

20. Michael Mandelbaum, *Democracy's Good Name: The Rise and Risks of the World's Most Popular Form of Government* (New York: PublicAffairs, 2007), xv.

21. Thomas Friedman, *The Lexus and the Olive Tree* (London: HarperCollins, 1999), 310–11.

22. David Harvey, *A Brief History of Neoliberalism*, 66.

23. William Robinson, "Globalization, the World System and Democracy Promotion," *Theory and Society* 25, no. 5 (October 1996): 623–24.

24. Sheldon Wolin, *Democracy Inc.: Managed Democracy and the Specter of Inverted Totalitarianism* (Princeton, NJ: Princeton University Press, 2010), 65.

25. Seymour Martin Lipset, Larry Diamond, and Juan Linz, eds., *Democracy in Developing Countries* (Boulder, CO: Lynne Rienner and the National Endowment for Democracy, 1989), xvi.

26. Robinson, "Globalization, the World System and Democracy Promotion," 625.

27. Joseph A. Schumpeter, *Capitalism, Socialism and Democracy* (New York: Harper Colophon Books, 1975), 297.

28. Robert Dahl, *A Preface to Democratic Theory* (Chicago: University of Chicago Press, 1956), 89.

29. A useful discussion on this is to be found in William E. Connolly, ed., *The Bias of Pluralism* (New York: Atherton, 1969).

30. Jacques Rancière, *Hatred of Democracy*, trans. Steve Corcoran (London: Verso, 2009).

31. Samuel Huntington, *Political Order in Changing Societies* (New Haven, CT: Yale University Press, 1968), 4–5.

32. Samuel Huntington, *The Third Wave: Democratization in the Late Twentieth Century* (Norman: University of Oklahoma Press, 1991).

33. William DiFazio, "Time, Poverty and Global Democracy," in *Implicating Empire: Globalization and Resistance in the 21st-Century World Order*, ed. Stanley Aronowitz and Heather Gautney (New York: Basic Books, 2003), 170.

34. On the "American Creed," see Samuel Huntington, *The Clash of Civilizations* (New York: Touchstone, 1996).

35. David Harvey, *A Brief History*, 66. Explicitly advocating this view also is Irving Kristol, *Neo-Conservatism: The Autobiography of an Idea* (New York: Free Press, 1995).

36. Wolin, *Democracy Inc.*

37. For an earlier perspective on this, see Carl Wright Mills, *The Power Elite* (Oxford: Oxford University Press, 1956).

38. Wolin, *Democracy Inc.*, 212.

39. Wolin, *Democracy Inc.*, 222.

40. Wolin, *Democracy Inc.*, 223.

41. Wolin, *Democracy Inc.*, 245.

42. Nothing much has changed in the Obama era, Wolin contends, because while the Democratic Party might seek to alleviate this state of affairs at the margins it will ultimately govern in favor of the capitalist market and of the big corporations in particular. In so doing, it will continue to manage American democracy in line with its elitist counterparts on its ideological right.

43. Wolin, *Democracy Inc.*, 261.

44. For example, as indicated in this chapter, see Wolin, *Democracy Inc.*; Robinson, "Globalization"; and Harvey, *A Brief History of Neoliberalism*.

45. Robinson, "Globalization," 642–43.

46. Robinson, "Globalization," 645.

47. Robinson, "Globalization," 647.

48. Roger Burbach, "The Tragedy of American Democracy," in *Low-Intensity Democracy: Political Power in the New World Order*, ed. Barry Gills, Joel Rocamora, and Richard Wilson (London: Pluto, 1993), 106.

49. Jennifer Mann, "Congress to Probe CIA-HAITI Ties: Reports Say Agency Financed Some Leaders Involved in Coup," *Los Angeles Times*, November 2, 1993; and Richard Cornwall, "CIA Helped Set up Terror Group in Haiti," *Independent*, October 7, 1994.

50. Anthony Lake, "From Containment to Enlargement." Johns Hopkins University School of Advanced International Studies, Washington, DC, September 21, 1993, http://www.mtholyoke.edu/acad/intrel/lakedoc.html.

51. Lake, "From Containment."

52. Lake, "From Containment."

53. Thomas Carothers, "The Clinton Record on Democracy Promotion," working paper no. 16, Carnegie Endowment for International Peace, September 2000, http://carnegieendowment.org/2000/09/12/clinton-record-on-democracy-promotion/2wrz.

54. Carothers, "Democracy Promotion," 2.

55. Condoleezza Rice, cited in Carothers, "Democracy Promotion," 2.

56. Rice, cited in Carothers, "Democracy Promotion," 2.

57. Mandelbaum, *Democracy's Good Name*, 179.

58. David Harvey, "Neoliberalism as Creative Destruction," *Annals of the American Academy of Political and Social Science* 610, no. 1 (March 2007): 25.

59. Harvey, "Neoliberalism as Creative Destruction," 25.

CHAPTER 3

1. Owen Jones, "Hugo Chavez Proves You Can Lead a Progressive, Popular Government That Says No to Neo-Liberalism," *Independent*, October 8, 2012.

2. Ali Rodriguez, Venezuelan foreign minister, cited in Randall Parish, Mark Peceny, and Justin Delacour, "Venezuela and the Collective Defence of Democracy Regime in the Americas," *Democratization* 14, no. 1 (2007): 226.

3. Steve Ellner, "Venezuela Reelects Hugo Chavez. What's Next?" *In These Times*, October 10, 2012, http://www.inthesetimes.com/article/13980/venezuelans_reelect_hugo_chavez/.

4. For a good summary of this reportage, see Lee Salter, "The Media's Misunderstanding of Venezuela: Hugo Chavez Is Definitely Going to Lose, Isn't He?" *New Statesman* 5 (October 2012), http://www.newstatesman.com/blogs/world-affairs/2012/10/.

5. Salter, "The Media's Misunderstanding."

6. Tamara Pearson, "Venezuela's Presidential Elections: An Imperfect-Victory," Venezuelaanalysis.com, October 8, 2011.

7. "Rumsfeld Likens Venezuela's Chavez to Hitler," Americas on NBC News.com, http://www.msnbc.msn.com/id/11159503/ns/world_news-americas/t/rumsfeld-likens-venezuelas-chavez-hitler/#.T6HE3e2H-JU.

8. Rebecca Stewart, "Rep. Connie Mack Blasts Venezuela's 'Thugocrat,'" CNN Politics, February 12, 2011, http://politicalticker.blogs.cnn.com/2011/02/12/rep-connie-mack-blasts-venezuelas-thugocrat/.

9. George W. Bush, cited in N. Scott Cole, "Hugo Chavez and President Bush's Credibility Gap: The Struggle against U.S. Democracy Promotion," *International Political Science Review* 28, no. 4 (2007): 499.

10. These insults were made in one of Chávez's regular TV appearances on March 19, 2006. See, "Chavez Blasts Bush as 'Donkey' and 'Drunkard,'" Free Republic, http://www .freerepublic.com/focus/f-news/1599346/posts. The "devil" claim is cited in "Chavez Tells UN Bush Is 'Devil,'" BBC News, September 20, 2006, http://news.bbc.co.uk/2/hi/ 5365142.stm.

11. Hugo Chávez, cited by William Kern, "President Chavez Criticizes Hillary Clinton as a 'Blond Condoleezza,'" *Moderate Voice*, March 6, 2010, http://themoderatevoice.com/.

12. Peter Romero, cited in Steve Ellner, "Venezuela's Foreign Policy," *Z Magazine Online*, November 2000, http://www.zcommunications.org/venezuelas-foreign-policy-by -steve-ellner.

13. Fernando Coronil and Julie Skurski, "Dismembering and Remembering the Nation: The Semantics of Political Violence in Venezuela," *Comparative Studies in Society and History* 33, no. 2 (1991): 311.

14. Daniel Hellinger, "Political Overview: The Breakdown of Puntofijismo and the Rise of Chavismo," in *Venezuelan Politics in the Chávez Era: Class, Polarization, and Conflict*, ed. Steve Ellner and Daniel Hellinger (Boulder, CO: Lynne Rienner, 2003), 35.

15. Hugo Chávez, cited in Margarita Lopez Maya and Luis Lander, "Popular Protest in Venezuela: Novelties and Continuities," *Latin American Perspectives* 32, no. 2 (2005): 100.

16. D. L. Raby, *Democracy and Revolution: Latin America and Socialism Today* (London: Pluto, 2006), 193.

17. Steve Ellner, *Rethinking Venezuelan Politics: Class, Conflict, and the Chávez Phenomenon* (Boulder, CO: Lynne Rienner, 2008), 128.

18. Steve Ellner, "The Chávez Election," *Z Net*, September 7, 2012.

19. Barry Cannon, *Hugo Chávez and the Bolivarian Revolution* (Manchester, UK: Manchester University Press, 2009), 60.

20. Steve Ellner, "Hugo Chávez's First Decade in Office: Breakthroughs and Shortcomings," *Latin American Perspectives* 31, no. 1 (2010): 81.

21. The poll results can be found in "The Discontents of Progress: As Latin Americans Become Less Poor, They Want Better Public Services," *Economist*, October 29, 2011, http:// www.economist.com/node/21534798.

22. Bolivarian Republic of Venezuela, Constitution of the Bolivarian Republic, 1999, 1.

23. Camila Piñeiro Harnecker, "Workplace Democracy and Social Conciousness in Venezuela," *Science and Society* 73, no. 3 (2009): 315.

24. Sujatha Fernandes, *Who Can Stop the Drums? Urban Social Movements in Chávez's Venezuela* (Durham, NC: Duke University Press, 2010), 86.

25. Harnecker, "Workplace Democracy," 315-16.

26. Steve Ellner, "The Chávez Election."

27. Greg Wilpert, *Changing Venezuela by Taking Power: The History and Policies of the Chávez Government* (London: Verso, 2007), 3.

28. Hugo Chávez, cited in Chris Carlson, "Venezuela Launches New Bolivarian Education Curriculum," Venezuelanalysis.com, September 19, 2007, http://www.venezuel analysis.com/news/2616.

29. Hugo Chávez, cited in J. Suggett, "Venezuelan Education Law: Socialist Indoctrination or Liberatory Education?" Venezuelanalysis.com, August 21, 2009, http://www.venezuelanalysis.com/analysis/4734.

30. Tom Griffiths, "Schooling for Twenty-First-Century Socialism: Venezuela's Bolivarian Project," Compare 40, no. 5 (2010): 613.

31. Barry Cannon, Hugo Chávez and the Bolivarian Revolution, 614.

32. Griffiths, "Schooling for Twenty-First-Century Socialism," 614.

33. Thomas Muhr and Antoni Verger, "Venezuela: Higher Education for All," Journal for Critical Education Policy Studies 4, no. 1 (March 2006), http://www.jceps.com/?pageID=article&articleID=63.

34. Bolivarian Republic of Venezuela, Constitution of the Bolivarian Republic, 1999, 4.

35. Thomas Muhr, "Counter-Hegemonic Regionalism and Higher Education for All: Venezuela and the ALBA," Globalisation, Societies and Education 8, no. 1 (2010): 50.

36. Tamara Pearson, "Chavez Rejects University Law," Venezuelanalysis.com, January 6, 2011, http://venezuelanalysis.com/news/5919.

37. Tom Griffiths and Jo Williams, "Mass Schooling for Socialist Transformation in Cuba and Venezuela," Journal for Critical Education Policy Studies 7, no. 2 (2009) 43–44.

38. Roger Burbach and Camila Piñeiro, "Venezuela's Participatory Socialism," Socialism and Democracy 21, no. 3 (2007): 194.

39. Sara Castro-Klarén, "Framing Pan-Americanism: Simon Bolivar's Findings," New Centennial Review 31, no. 1 (2003): 37.

40. Mark Weisbrot, Rebecca Ray, and Luis Sandoval, The Chávez Administration at Ten Years: The Economy and Social Indicators (Washington, DC: Center for Economic and Policy Research, 2009), 6.

41. Ewan Robertson, "Venezuela's Economic Growth Doubles 2011 Forecast," Venezuelanalysis.com, November 18, 2011, http://venezuelanalysis.com/news/6642.

42. Weisbrot, Ray, and Sandoval, The Chávez Administration at Ten Years, 7.

43. ECLAC, Social Panorama of Latin America 2011 (Santiago, Chile: UN Publication, 2011), 43.

44. Weisbrot, Ray, and Sandoval, The Chávez Administration at Ten Years, 93.

45. UNDP, Human Development Report, 2011, 132.

46. Charlie Devereux, "Venezuela Inflation Slows for Seventh Month on Import Surge," Bloomberg.com, July 3, 2012, http://www.bloomberg.com/news/2012-07-03/venezuela-inflation-slows-for-seventh-month-on-import-surge-1-.html; Peter Wilson, "Venezuela's Minimum Wage Hike No Match for Inflation," Bloomberg Businessweek, May 6, 2014, http://www.businessweek.com/articles/2014-05-06/venezuelas-minimum-wage-hike-is-no-match-for-inflation.

47. Steve Ellner, "Chávez Pushes the Limits: Radicalization and Discontent in Venezuela," NACLA Report on the Americas, July/August 2010, 7–42.

48. Ellner, "Chavez Pushes the Limits."

49. Steve Ellner and Daniel Hellinger, eds., Venezuelan Politics in the Chávez Era: Class, Polarization, and Conflict (Boulder, CO: Lynne Rienner, 2003), 220.

50. Phil Gunson, "Chávez's Venezuela," Current History, February 2006, 59.

51. Ali Rodriguez, cited in Parish, Peceny, and Delacour, "Venezuela and the Collective Defence," 226.

52. William Robinson, Latin America and Global Capitalism: A Critical Globalization Perspective (Baltimore: Johns Hopkins University Press, 2008), 499.

53. Joel Brinkley, "U.S. Proposal in the OAS Draws Fire as an Attack on Venezuela," *New York Times*, May 22, 2005; and Joel Brinkley, "Many in OAS Oppose U.S. on Plan for Democracy Panel," *International Herald Tribune*, May 23, 2005.

54. Brian Loveman, "U.S. Security Policies in Latin America and the Andean Region, 1990–2006," in *Addicted to Failure: U.S. Security Policy in Latin America and the Andean Region*, ed. Brian Loveman (Lanham, MD: Rowman & Littlefield, 2006), 50.

55. Jorge Valero, cited in Maria Luisa Azpiazu, "U.S. Faces Opposition in Push for OAS Role in Crisis Prevention," EFE News Service, June 3, 2005.

56. Tamara Pearson, "Venezuela's Proposed Social Charter Approved by OAS after 11 Years," Venezuelanalysis.com, June 5, 2012, http://venezuelanalysis.com/news/7036.

57. "Unasur Ministers Reach Consensus on a 'Democratic Clause,'" Merco Press, October 3, 2012, http://en.mercopress.com.

58. "Unasur Plans Ten-Year Infrastructure and Integration Projects," Merco Press, December 2, 2011, http://en.mercopress.com.

59. John Lindsay-Poland, "Retreat to Colombia: The Pentagon Adapts Its Latin America Strategy," *NACLA Report on the Americas* 43, no. 1 (2010): 23.

60. Jorge Castañeda, "Latin America's Left Turn: A Tale of Two Lefts," *Foreign Affairs* 85, no. 3 (2006): 28–43.

61. Castañeda, "Latin America's Left Turn," 38.

62. Greg Grandin, *Empire's Workshop: Latin America, the United States, and the Rise of the New Imperialism* (New York: Owl Books, 2007).

63. Douglas Schoen and Michael Rowan, *The Threat Closer to Home: Hugo Chávez and the War against America* (New York: Free Press, 2009), 4.

64. Mike Allen, "Marco Rubio: Obama 'Naive' about Chavez," *Politico*, July 11, 2012, http://www.politico.com/news/stories/0712/78385.html.

65. Mark Weisbrot, "Clinton's Latin American Clangers," *Guardian*, March 5, 2010, http://www.theguardian.com/commentisfree/cifamerica/2010/mar/05/hillary-clinton-latin-america.

66. Reyes Theis, "Venezuelan Govt's Ties to Iran and Cuba Have Not Served Its Interests," *El Universal*, December 19, 2011, http://www.eluniversal.com/nacional-y-politica/111219/venezuelan-govts-ties-to-iran-and-cuba-have-not-served-its-interests.

67. "'Leave Us Alone,' Chávez Fires Back," *El Universal*, December 20, 2011, http://www.eluniversal.com/nacional-y-politica/111220/leave-us-alone-chavez-fires-back.

68. Eva Golinger, "Wikileaks: Documents Confirm US Plans against Venezuela," Venezuelanalysis.com, December 17, 2010, http://venezuelanalysis.com/analysis/5870; and Eva Golinger, "CIA Announces New Mission in Venezuela and Cuba," Global Research, August 20, 2006, www.globalresearch.ca/PrintArticle.php?articleId=3015.

69. Eva Golinger, "USAID Closes Venezuela Program, Transfers to Miami," Venezuelanalysis.com, February 13, 2011, http://venezuelanalysis.com/analysis/5995.

70. N. Scott Cole, "Hugo Chavez and President Bush's Credibility Gap," 500.

71. Golinger, "USAID Closes Venezuela Program."

72. U.S. State Department, Press Release, "Rice Interview with Latin American Journalists," Scoop, June 8, 2005, http://www.scoop.co.nz/stories/WO0506/S00123.htm.

73. U.S. Department of State, "Remarks with Brazilian Foreign Minister Celso Luiz Nunes Amorim," March 3, 2010, http://m.state.gov/md137774.htm.

CHAPTER 4

1. The ANC government is an alliance of three core components: the ANC itself, the dominant component, the SA Communist Party (SAPC), and the Congress of South African Trade Unions (COSATU).

2. World Bank, *South Africa Economic Update: Focus on Inequality of Opportunity* (Washington, DC: World Bank, July 2012), viii.

3. Tony Karon confirms this using World Bank figures in "As South Africa Reels from Mine Shootings, Social Inequality Threatens to Undo the Post-Apartheid 'Miracle,'" *Time*, August 22, 2012, http://world.time.com/2012/08/22/as-south-africa-reels-from-mine-shootings-social-inequality-threatens-to-undo-the-post-apartheid-miracle/#ixzz2CAGyq1dR.

4. Aislinn Laing, "South African Whites Still Paid Six Times More," *Sydney Morning Herald*, October 31, 2012.

5. See Malcolm Sharara, "SA's Ticking Time Bomb," *News 24*, November 12, 2012, http://www.news24.com/.

6. World Bank, *South Africa*, 7.

7. World Bank, *South Africa*, viii.

8. For a broad and accessible discussion of this issue, see Naomi Klein, *The Shock Doctrine* (London: Penguin Books, 2007), chapter 10.

9. Chris Webb, "South Africa's Ruling ANC Party: Where Is the Left?" Global Research News, October 9, 2012, http://www.globalresearch.ca/south-africas-ruling-anc-party-where-is-the-left/5307655.

10. See Martin Plaut, "The Nation's White Elite—The Dog That Doesn't Bark," Norwegian Council for Africa, August 24, 2012, http://www.afrika.no/Detailed/22116.html.

11. Patrick Bond, "South African Political Economy after the Marikana Massacre," *Links*, October 18, 2012, http://links.org.au/node/3063.

12. Matthew Kavanagh, "South Africa's Freedom Charter at 50," *Z Magazine*, September 2005, http://www.zcommunications.org/south-africa-and-rsquo-s-freedom-charter-at-50-by-matthew-m-kavanagh.

13. Karon, "As South Africa Reels."

14. See Vishwas Satgar, "Reclaiming the South African Dream," *Red Pepper*, December 2011, http://www.redpepper.org.uk/reclaiming-the-south-african-dream/.

15. Sagie Narsiah, "Neoliberalism and Privatisation in South Africa," *GeoJournal* 57, no. 1–2 (May 2002): 3–13.

16. State assets transferred into private hands included the South African Broadcasting Corporation, Telekom, South African Airways, and the Post Office.

17. Lucien van der Walt, "After Ten Years of GEAR: COSATU, the Zuma Trial and the Dead End of Alliance Politics," Libcom.org, February 19, 2007, http://libcom.org/library/after-ten-years-of-gear-cosatu-the-zuma-trial-and-the-dead-end-of-alliance-politics.

18. Ishmail Lesufi, "Six Years of Neoliberal Socioeconomic Policies in South Africa," *Journal of Asian and African Studies* (2002): 289–91.

19. *Economist*, "Cry, the Beloved Country," October 18, 2012, http://www.economist.com/news/leaders/21564846-south-africa-sliding-downhill-while-much-rest-continent-clawing-its-way-up.

20. Tosin Sulaiman, "S. Africa FDI Plummets in First Half of 2012," *Reuters*, October 24, 2012, http://www.reuters.com/article/2012/10/24/ozabs-safrica-investment-idAFJOE 89N00D20121024.

21. *Economist*, "Cry, the Beloved Country."

22. *Economist*, "Cry, the Beloved Country."

23. *Economist*, "Cry, the Beloved Country."

24. Oupa Lehulere, "GEAR Blues on the Morning After," *South African Labor Bulletin* 23, no. 4 (1999): 36

25. Patrick Bond, *Talk Left, Walk Right: South Africa's Frustrated Global Reforms*, 2nd ed. (University of KwaZulu Natal Press, 2006), 16.

26. Kavanagh, "South Africa's Freedom,"

27. Dennis Brutus, cited in Kavanagh, "South Africa's Freedom."

28. This is Jay Naidoo, former general secretary of the SA Trade Union Congress and senior ANC leader, cited in Sudarsan Raghavan, "South Africa Loses Faith with the ANC," *Independent*, November 11, 2012, http://www.independent.co.uk/news/world/africa/south-africa-loses-faith-with-the-anc-8303778.html.

29. Peter Alexander, "A Massive Rebellion of the Poor," *Mail and Guardian*, April 13, 2012, http://mg.co.za/article/2012-04-13-a-massive-rebellion-of-the-poor.

30. This is from S'bu Zikode's, "We Are the Third Force," October 19, 2006, http://www.abahlali.org/node/17, which is regarded as the defining statement of the AbM.

31. Nigel Gibson, "Upright and Free, Fanon in South Africa, from Biko to the Shack-dwellers' Movement (Abahlali baseMjondolo)," *Social Identities* 14, no. 6 (November 2008): 683–715.

32. See Sarah Cooper-Knock, "Symbol of Hope Silenced," November 13, 2009, http://www.abahlali.org/node/6029.

33. This perspective is articulated by S'bu Zikode, in his "Opening Address," CUNY Graduate Center, New York, November 16, 2010, http://abahlali.org/node/7580.

34. Richard Pithouse, "The Thoroughly Democratic Logic of Refusing to Vote," South African Civil Society Information Service, April 2, 2009, http://eprints.ru.ac.za/1443/1/Pithouse_Thoroughly_Democratic.pdf.

35. Pithouse, "The Thoroughly Democratic Logic."

36. Patrick Bond, "How the Marikana Movement Stunned Neoliberal South Africa," *Counterpunch*, October 19–21, 2012, http://www.counterpunch.org/2012/10/19/how-the-marikana-movement-stunned-neoliberal-south-africa/.

37. Mphutlane wa Bofelo, cited in "'Black Boers' and Other Revolutionary Songs," Libcom.org, April 7, 2010, http://libcom.org/news/'black-boers'-other-revolutionary-songs-07042010.

38. There are a range of other parties at the national and regional level that can become significant in alliance arrangements. For a recent summary of Indian democracy, see Barbara Nelson and Assa Doran, "A Churning Democracy," *East Asia Forum Quarterly* 4, no. 1 (January–March 2012), http://press.anu.edu.au/wp-content/uploads/2012/02/whole2.pdf.

39. "The Man behind 'India Shining' Slogan," Rediff.com, April 2, 2004, http://www.rediff.com/money/2004/apr/02shining.htm.

40. Thomas Friedman, *The World Is Flat: A Brief History of the Twenty-First Century*, 2nd ed. (New York: Farrar, Strauss and Giroux, 2007).

41. Thomas Friedman, "India's Innovation Stimulus," *New York Times Sunday Review*, November 5, 2011, http://www.nytimes.com/2011/11/06/opinion/sunday/friedman-indias -innovation-stimulus.html?ref=thomaslfriedman&_r=0.

42. "World GDP," World Market Index, http://www.indexq.org/economy/gdp.php.

43. Paul Hannon and Sudeep Reddy, "China Edges out U.S. as Top Foreign-Investment Draw amid World Decline," *Wall Street Journal*, October 23, 2012, http://online.wsj .com/article/SB10001424052970203406404578074683825139320.html.

44. Hannon and Reddy, "China Edges out US,"; and Ruchir Sharma, "Broken BRICs," *Foreign Affairs*, November, December 2012, http://www.foreignaffairs.com/articles/138219/ ruchir-sharma/broken-brics.

45. Richard Douthwaite, *The Growth Illusion: How Economic Growth Has Enriched the Few, Impoverished the Many, and Endangered the Planet* (Totnes, Devon, UK: Green Books, 1999).

46. Gita Gopinath, cited in Tathagata Bhattacharya, "World Economic Forum 2012: Does the Indian Economy Need a Reboot?" IBN Live.com, http://ibnlive.in.com/news/ world economic-forum-2012-does-the-indian-economy-need-a-reboot/304372-61.html.

47. Praful Bidwai, "Two Decades of Neo-liberalism in India," *Daily Star*, August 4, 2011, http://www.thedailystar.net/newDesign/news-details.php?nid=197058.

48. Bidwai, "Two Decades of Neo-liberalism."

49. M. P. Singh and Krishna Murari, "The Impact of Neoliberalism on the Indian Polity," *Social Sciences*, August 27, 2011, http://www.socialsciences.in/article/impact-neo liberalism-indian-polity; and Sumit Ganguly, "Corruption Eating at India's Democracy," *East Asia Forum*, May 13, 2011, http://www.eastasiaforum.org/2011/05/13/corruption -eating-at-india-s-democracy-2/.

50. Bidwai, "Two Decades of Neo-liberalism."

51. Gopinath, cited in Bhattacharya, "World Economic Forum."

52. Bidwai, "Two Decades of Neo-liberalism."

53. Amartya Sen, *Poverty and Famines: An Essay on Entitlements and Deprivation* (Oxford: Clarendon, 1982); and Utsa Patnaik, *The Republic of Hunger and Other Essays* (London: Merlin, 2008).

54. Utsa Patnaik, "Neoliberalism and Rural Poverty in India," *Economic and Political Weekly*, July–August 2007, http://www.epw.in/aspects-poverty-and-employment/ neoliberalism-and-rural-poverty-india.html.

55. UNDP, *Human Development Report 2011*, http://hdr.undp.org/en/statistics.

56. Bidwai, "Two Decades of Neo-liberalism."

57. It still is, with Sonia Gandhi, widow of Rajiv Gandhi and the daughter-in-law of Indira Gandhi, as president of the Congress Party and of the governing coalition that chose Manmohan Singh as PM.

58. Singh and Murari, "The Impact of Neoliberalism."

59. Singh and Murari, "The Impact of Neoliberalism"

60. "Parliament at 60: How Rich Are Our Netas!" *First Post Politics*, May 16, 2012, http://www.firstpost.com/politics/parliament-at-60-how-rich-are-our-netas-311074.html.

61. The figures vary slightly. This is the figure presented by the World Bank in 2012, http://data.worldbank.org/indicator/NY.GDP.PCAP.CD.

62. Singh and Murari, "The Impact of Neoliberalism."

63. K. Chand, "Independence Day: India's Democracy Needs to Evolve," *Guardian*, August 15, 2012.

64. Singh and Murari, "The Impact of Neoliberalism."

65. For a range of views on Kerala, see Govinda Parayil, ed., *Kerala: The Development Experience* (London: Zed Books, 2000); Akash Kapur, "Poor but Prosperous," *Atlantic Monthly Online*, September 1998, http://www.theatlantic.com/past/docs/issues/98sep/kerala.htm; and T. Thomas Isaac and Richard Franke, *Local Democracy and Development: The Kerala People's Campaign for Decentralized Planning* (Lanham, MD: Rowman & Littlefield, 2002).

66. Shirin Shirin, "Economic Woes? Look to Kerala," *Foreign Policy in Focus*, December 10, 2008, http://www.fpif.org/articles/economic_woes_look_to_kerala.

67. There are 16 deaths per 1,000 births, as opposed to 32 per 1,000 nationally; Shirin, "Economic Woes?"

68. Stephen Shalom, "Lesson and Hope from Kerala," Z Commentaries, June 21, 1999, http://zcomm.org/zcommentary/lessons-and-hope-from-kerala-by-stephen1-shalom/.

69. On the literacy rate, see Dhritiman Gupta, "Kerala Budget 2012: Nearly Bankrupt but High Education Spends," *India Spend*, May 3, 2012, http://www.indiaspend.com/sectors/kerala-budget-2012-nearly-bankrupt-but-high-education-spends.

70. The figures on these categories come from Shirin, "Economic Woes?"; Amartya Sen, "The Kerala Difference," *New York Review of Books*, October 1991, http://www.nybooks.com/articles/archives/1991/oct/24/; and Kapur, "Poor but Prosperous."

71. Shirin, "Economic Woes?"

72. Kapur, "Poor but Prosperous." This has also been argued as the reason for the religious tolerance in Kerala, where the 60 percent Hindu community has, for the most part, joined Muslims (20 percent) and Christians (20 percent) in a cosmopolitan and secular political experiment.

73. Amartya Sen, in particular, has proposed this as the historical foundation for the subsequent Kerala experience, pointing to a philosophy and value system that have always been different from the Indian experience under British imperialism. See George Mathews, "Amartya Sen and the Kerala Model," *Hindu*, January 9, 2001.

74. Thomas Isaac and Franke, *Local Democracy and Development*.

75. Richard Franke and Barbara Chasin, *Kerala: Development through Radical Reform* (Oakland, CA: Institute for Food and Development Policy, 1994).

76. Franke and Chasin, "Development Through Radical Reform".

77. Bill McKibben, "The Enigma of Kerala," *UTNE Reader*, October 9, 2007, http://www.utne.com/archives/TheEnigmaofKerala.aspx.

78. Nachammai Raman, "How Almost Everyone in Kerala Learned to Read," *Christian Science Monitor*, May 17, 2005, http://www.csmonitor.com/2005/0517/p12s01-legn.html.

79. Franke and Chasin, *Development through Radical Reform*.

80. Thomas Isaac and Franke, *Local Democracy and Development*, 8–20.

81. Thomas Isaac and Franke, *Local Democracy and Development*, 1.

82. Thomas Isaac and Franke, *Local Democracy and Development*, 5.

83. There is, for example, a critical literature emanating from neoliberal economists at the Centre for Socio-economic and Environmental Studies (CSES) in Kochi, http://csesindia.org/publications.php. See K. K. George and Ajith Kumar, "Kerala: The Land of

Developmental Paradoxes," working paper no. 2, November 1997; K. K. George and K. K. Krishnakumar, "Centre-State Relations, Finance Commissions and Kerala's Fiscal Crisis," working paper no. 10, November 2003; K. K. George and K. K. Krishnakumar, "Kerala's Development Experience: Its Implications for Finance Commissions," working paper no. 21, 2009; and Michael Tharakan, "The Kerala Model Revisited: New Problems, Fresh Challenges," working paper no. 15, October 2006.

84. Soutik Biswas, "Conundrum of Kerala's Struggling Economy," BBC News Online, March 17, 2010, http://news.bbc.co.uk/2/hi/south_asia/8546952.stm. The upside of this situation is that educated Keralites are very employable and professional migrants remit significant amounts of money to be reinvested in the home economy (in real estate, new businesses, etc.). This is the view of Bill McKibben, "The Enigma of Kerala."

85. Jaidev Kumar, "Jobless No More?" *Hindu Business Line*, October 8, 2007.

86. Gupta, "Kerala Budget 2012."

87. Government of Kerala, "Kerala Budget 2012–13," March 19, 2012, speech by K. M. Mani, Minister for Finance, http://www.finance.kerala.gov.in/index.php?option=com_con tent&view=article&id=495:kerala-budget-2012-13&catid=18:state-budget&Itemid=32.

88. Gupta, "Kerala Budget 2012."

89. Bill McKibben, "The Enigma of Kerala."

90. Amartya Sen, cited in Dilasha Seth, "There's a Lot to Learn from Kerala in De-livering Quality of Life: Amartya Sen," *Business Standard*, January 5, 2013, http://www .business-standard.com/india/news/thereslot-to-learnkerala-in-delivering-quality-life -amartya-sen/497833/.

91. David Kotz, "Russia's Financial Crisis: The Failure of Neoliberalism?" *Z Magazine*, January 1999, http://www.zcommunications.org/russia-and-the-crisis-of-neoliberalism-by -david-kotz.

92. On the diverse "democratic" movement in Russia in the 1980s and early 1990s, see Peter Reddaway and Dmitri Glinski, *The Tragedy of Russia's Reforms: Market Bolshevism against Democracy* (Washington, DC: U.S. Institute of Peace, 2001); and Padma Desai, "Russian Perspectives on Reforms: From Yeltsin to Putin," *Journal of Economic Perspectives* 19, no. 1 (Winter 2005): 87–106.

93. Reddaway and Glinski, *The Tragedy of Russia's Reforms*, 236–60; and Naomi Klein, *The Shock Doctrine* (Camberwell, Victoria, Australia: Penguin, 2008), 220–22.

94. Klein, *Shock Doctrine*, 221; and Desai, "Russian Perspectives," 93–97.

95. Desai, "Russian Perspectives," 96.

96. Jeffrey Sachs, "What Is to Be Done?" *Economist*, January 13, 1990, http://www .economist.com/node/13002085.

97. Klein, *Shock Doctrine*, 231.

98. Reddaway and Glinski, *The Tragedy of Russia's Reforms*, 492–511.

99. Klein, *Shock Doctrine*, 231.

100. Perry Anderson, "Russia's Managed Democracy: Why Putin?" *London Review of Books* 29, no. 2 (January 25, 2007): 3–12, http://www.lrb.co.uk/v29/n02/perry-anderson/ russias-managed-democracy. Some of the most prominent oligarchs are Gusinsky, Po-tanin, Abramovich, Fridman, Khodorkovsky, and the now deceased Berezovsky.

101. Gavriil Popov, cited in Klein, *Shock Doctrine*, 222.

102. Klein, *Shock Doctrine*, 224.

103. Desai, "Russian Perspectives," 95. Given that the deficit then stood at 17 percent of GDP, the skepticism about doctrinaire neoliberalism increased, particularly among communist and nationalist MPs.

104. Kotz, "Russia's Financial Crisis."

105. Celestine Bohlen, "Yeltsin Deputy Calls Reforms 'Economic Genocide,'" *New York Times*, February 9, 1992, http://www.nytimes.com/1992/02/09/world/yeltsin-deputy -calls-reforms-economic-genocide.html.

106. Klein, *Shock Doctrine*, 226.

107. Others give the figures as around 500 killed and 1,000 wounded. See Klein, *Shock Doctrine*, 229. For more on the relationship between Yeltsin and the United States, see Reddaway and Glinski, *The Tragedy of Russia's Reforms*, 370–419.

108. Klein, *Shock Doctrine*, 229.

109. Including the right to choose the prime minister and the military hierarchy, even if the elected parliament objected to the choices, the power to veto any bill passed by the "people's" lower house (the Duma), and immunity from any impeachment proceedings emanating from the parliament.

110. This was the CEEB survey, conducted between 1990 and 1997, cited in Hannes Mueller, "Why Russia Failed to Follow Poland: Lessons for Economists," March 17, 2007, Department of Economics, London School of Economics, http://www.politik-salon.de/ files/hm_receo_2007.pdf.

111. Jeffrey Sachs, "What I Did in Russia," March 14, 2012, http://jeffsachs .org/2012/03/what-i-did-in-russia/.

112. Reddaway and Glinski, *The Tragedy of Russia's Reforms*, 524.

113. Simon Shuster, "Rewriting Russian History: Did Boris Yeltsin Steal the 1996 Presidential Election?" *Time World*, February 24, 2012, http://www.time.com/time/world/ article/0,8599,2107565,00.html.

114. Klein, *Shock Doctrine*, 239.

115. Klein, *Shock Doctrine*, 238–39.

116. Neal Ascherson, "Law v. Order," *London Review of Books* 26, no. 10 (May 2004): 22–24, http://www.lrb.co.uk/v26/n10/neal-ascherson/law-v-order.

117. Anderson, "Russia's Managed Democracy." As Anderson notes, even Stalin didn't have this strike rate.

118. Kotz, "Russia's Financial Crisis."

119. Reddaway and Glinski, *The Tragedy of Russia's Reforms*, 312.

120. On this, see Ben Goldby, "Russian Apartment Bombings: Coronation of the New Tsar?" *Sunday Mercury*, August 11, 2011, http://blogs.sundaymercury.net/thegrassyknoll/ 2010/08/russian-apartment-bombings-cor.html.

121. These descriptions are in Ascherson, "Law v. Order"; Anderson, "Russia's Managed Democracy"; and Klein, *Shock Doctrine*, 237.

122. Boris Nemtsov, cited in Desai, "Russian Perspectives," 102.

123. Anderson, "Russia's Managed Democracy."

124. This has seen Russia under Putin flexing its post-Soviet muscles, in the Ukraine and in Europe more generally during cold winters. See Paul Reynolds, "Russia: Bully or Just Applying the Rules?" BBC News Online, January 3, 2006, http://news.bbc.co.uk/2/hi/ europe/4577648.stm.

125. "Russia's Economy under Vladimir Putin: Achievements and Failures," *Riano-vosti*, January 3, 2008, http://en.rian.ru/analysis/20080301/100381963.html.

126. Anderson, "Russia's Managed Democracy."

127. This is Elena Gabitova, a sociologist in Siberia, cited in Simon Shuster, "See Putin Run: How the Prime Minister Is Relying on Russia's Heartland," *Time*, March 5, 2012, http://www.time.com/time/magazine/article/0,9171,2107534,00.html.

128. Ascherson, "Law v. Order."

129. See Steve LeVine, "The Last Free Oligarch," *Foreign Policy*, July 25, 2012, http://www.foreignpolicy.com/articles/2012/07/25/the_last_free_oligarch.

130. Ascherson, "Law v. Order."

131. Putin, cited in Ascherson, "Law v. Order."

132. Anderson, "Russia's Managed Democracy."

133. Ascherson, "Law v. Order."

134. For example, Anna Politkovskaya, shot dead in her apartment (2006), and Alexander Litvinenko, poisoned in London (2006) after serious claims about Putin and the war in Chechnya.

135. Tony Wood, "There Is No Alternative," *London Review of Books* 34, no. 4 (February 23, 2012): 11–14, http://www.lrb.co.uk/v34/n04/tony-wood/there-is-no-alternative.

136. Furman cited in Anderson, "Russia's Managed Democracy."

137. The Nashi are a "youth group," loyal to Putin, who are used to infiltrate protests, intimidate, and beat up protesters.

138. Wood, "There Is No Alternative."

139. Seen as promoting the rise of "Western" liberalism and internationalism and the weakening of Russian culture and nationalism.

140. *Economist*, "Building up the Castle Wall," June 13, 2012, http://www.econo mist.com/blogs/easternapproaches/2012/06/protest-russia; and Ellen Barry and Michael Schwirtz, "Arrests and Violence in Overflowing Rally in Moscow," *New York Times*, May 6, 2012, http://www.nytimes.com/2012/05/07/world/europe/at-moscow-rally-arrests-and -violence.html?_r=0.

141. Michael Schwirtz, "A Russian Protest Leader Takes Center Stage," *New York Times*, March 11, 2012, http://www.nytimes.com/2012/05/12/world/europe/sergei -udaltsov-russian-protest-leader-takes-center-stage.html.

142. Leon Aron, "Russia's Protesters: The People, Ideals and Prospects," American Enterprise Institute, August 9, 2012, http://www.aei.org/outlook/foreign-and-defense -policy/regional/europe/russias-protesters-the-people-ideals-and-prospects/.

143. Wood, "There Is No Alternative."

144. Paul Starobin, "The Putin Generation," *New Republic*, April 20, 2012, http:// www.newrepublic.com/article/world/magazine/102777/vladimir-putin-russia-protest -maxim-katz-moscow.

145. Susanne Sternthal, "Optimism in Diversity? Moscow's March of Millions," *Open Democracy Russia*, June 13, 2012, http://www.opendemocracy.net/od-russia/susanne -sternthal/optimism-in-diversity-moscow's-march-of-millions.

146. See Dmitri Travin, "Is Russian Protest Movement a Flash in the Pan?" *Open Democracy Russia*, June 4, 2012, http://www.opendemocracy.net/od-russia/dmitri-travin/ is-russia's-protest-movement-flash-in-pan.

147. See Anatol Lieven, "Mirage of the Putin Protests," *National Interest*, April 3, 2012, http://nationalinterest.org/commentary/behind-the-putin-protests-6722.

148. Thomas Friedman, "The Politics of Dignity," *New York Times*, January 31, 2012.

149. See Graeme Robertson, *The Politics of Protest in Hybrid Regimes* (New York: Cambridge University Press, 2011).

150. Charles Tilly, cited in Robertson, *Politics of Protest*, 10.

151. Jeffrey Sachs, *The End of Poverty* (New York: Penguin Books, 2005).

152. Anders Åslund, *Russia's Capitalist Revolution: Why Market Reform Succeeded and Democracy Failed* (Washington, DC: Peterson Institute, 2007).

153. See, Michael McFaul, "Russia's Crisis: Will Russia Survive Its Economic and Political Crisis?" NewsHour Online Forum, September 17, 1998, http://archive.is/aMY2.

154. Desai, "Russian Perspectives," 91.

155. Rogov, cited in Desai, "Russian Perspectives", 95.

156. Jack Matlock, *Superpower Illusions* (New Haven, CT: Yale University Press, 2010), 111.

157. Lawrence Summers, cited in William Keegan, *The Spectre of Capitalism: The Future of the World Economy after the Fall of Communism* (London: Radius Books, 1992), 109.

CHAPTER 5

1. See Thomas Friedman, *The World Is Flat: A Brief History of the Twenty-First Century*, 2nd ed. (New York: Farrar, Strauss and Giroux, 2007).

2. Fareed Zakaria, *The Future of Freedom: Illiberal Democracy at Home and Abroad*, rev. ed. (New York: Norton, 2007).

3. Manuel Castells, *The End of the Millennium* (Malden, MA: Blackwell, 1998), 370. Also see his *The Rise of Networked Society*, 2nd ed. (Malden, MA: Blackwell, 2000).

4. John Urry, *Mobilities* (Cambridge: Polity, 2007), 5–6, 7.

5. Arjun Appadurai, "Disjuncture and Difference in the Global Cultural Economy," in *Modernity at Large: Cultural Dimensions of Globalization* (Minneapolis: University of Minnesota Press, 1996): 27–43.

6. See the important Saskia Sassen, *Territory, Authority, Rights: From Medieval to Global Assemblages*, updated ed. (Princeton, NJ: Princeton University Press, 2006).

7. For an extensive analysis, see William Scheuerman, *Liberal Democracy and the Social Acceleration of Time* (Baltimore: Johns Hopkins University Press, 2004).

8. Seyla Benhabib, "Twilight of Sovereignty or the Emergence of Cosmopolitan Norms? Rethinking Citizenship in Volatile Times," *Citizenship Studies* 11, no. 1 (2007): 19–36.

9. Sheldon Wolin, "What Time Is It?" *Theory and Event* 1, no. 1 (1997), http://muse.jhu.edu/journals/theory_&_event/toc/archive.heml#1.1.

10. William E. Connolly, *Neuropolitics: Thinking, Culture, Speed* (Minneapolis: University of Minnesota Press, 2002).

11. One of the most important of these is the Chinese diaspora studied by Aiwa Ong, *Flexible Citizenship: The Cultural Logic of Transnationality* (Durham, NC: Duke University Press, 1999); and Aiwa Ong, *Neoliberalism as Exception: Mutations in Citizenship and Sovereignty* (Durham, NC: Duke University Press, 2006).

12. On the neoliberalism of the Obama administration, see Jamie Peck, "Decoding Obamanomics," chap. 6 in *Constructions of Neoliberal Reason*, 231–69. (Oxford: Oxford University Press, 2010).

13. SIPRI Military Expenditure Database (Stockholm: Stockholm International Peace Research Institute, 2013).

14. Simon Rogers, "US Military Suicides in Charts: How They Overtook Combat Death," *Guardian*, February 1, 2013, http://www.guardian.co.uk/news/datablog/2013/feb/01/us-military-suicides-trend-charts (accessed May 2, 2013).

15. See Howard Tumber and Jerry Palmer, *Media at War: The Iraq Crisis* (London: Sage, 2004).

16. Judith Butler, *Frames of War: When Is Life Grievable?* (London: Verso, 2010), xix, 15.

17. For an insightful analysis of the moral-democratic problematic of nuclear weapons, see George Kateb, "Thinking about Human Extinction (1): Nuclear Weapons and Individual Rights," "Thinking about Human Extinction (2): Nietzsche and Heidegger," and "Thinking About Nuclear Extinction (3): Emerson and Whitman," in *The Inner Ocean: Individualism and Democratic Culture* (Ithaca, NY: Cornell University Press, 1992), 107–71.

18. John Ellis, *The Social History of the Machine Gun* (Baltimore: Johns Hopkins University Press, 1986).

19. Useful here is Gabriel Kolko, *Centuries of War: Politics, Conflicts and Society since 1914* (New York: The New Press, 1995). Also see the classic study by William H. McNeil, *The Pursuit of Power: Technology, Armed Force and Society since AD 1000* (Chicago: University of Chicago Press, 1982).

20. A very useful history is Geoffrey Best, *Humanity in Warfare* (New York: Columbia University Press, 1983).

21. Paul Virilio, *Speed and Politics* (New York: Semiotext(e), 1983).

22. The most comprehensive description of these developments of cyborg and cyber warfare is P. W. Singer, *Wired for War* (New York: Penguin, 2009). Also see the special issue of the *Journal of Military Ethics* 9, no. 4 (2010), ed. George R. Lucas Jr. of the United States Naval Academy. The papers in this collection were drawn from the 10th Annual McCain Conference of the U.S. Service Academies and War Colleges.

23. United States Department of Defense, *National Security Strategy*, May 2010, 1–2, http://www.whitehouse.gov/sites/default/files/rss_viewer/national_security_strategy.pdf.

24. For a history of the development of this argument, from Montesquieu through Adam Smith, see Albert O. Hirschman, *The Passions and the Interests: Arguments for Capitalism before Its Triumph* (Princeton, NJ: Princeton University Press, 1977).

25. Immanuel Kant, *Political Writings*, 2nd ed., ed. Hans Reiss (Cambridge: Cambridge University Press, 1991), 93–130.

26. Bruce Russett, "The Fact of Democratic Peace," in *Debating the Democratic Peace*, ed. Michael E. Brown, Sean M. Lynn-Jones, and Steven E. Miller (Cambridge, MA: MIT Press, 1996).

27. His important essays have been collected recently in Michael W. Doyle, *Liberal Peace: Selected Essays* (London: Routledge, 2012). The quotation is from the introduction to this collection, p. 3.

28. Barry Buzan, Jaap De Wilde, and Ole Wæver, *Security: A New Framework for Analysis* (Denver: Lynne Rienner, 1997).

29. A very useful proposal in this regard is made by Michel Callon and others in the context of democratizing the politics of science by use of "hybrid forums" in which lay-persons with alternative perspectives on what appear to be scientific and technical issues are incorporated procedurally into deliberations and decision making. See Michel Callon, Pierre Lascoumes, and Yannick Barthe, *Acting in an Uncertain World: An Essay on Technical Democracy*, trans. Graham Burchell (Cambridge, MA: MIT Press, 2011).

30. Callon et al., *Acting in an Uncertain World*.

31. On the growth of this law, see Gunther Teubner, ed., *Global Law without a State* (Dartmouth, VT: Aldershot and Brookfield, 1997).

32. Karl Polanyi, *The Great Transformation: The Social and Economic Origins of Our Time* (Boston: Beacon, 1944, 1957), 71.

33. John Gerard Ruggie, "International Regimes, Transactions, and Change: Embedded Liberalism in the Postwar Economic Order," *International Organization* 36, no. 2 (1982): 386.

34. See David Held, *Democracy and the Global Order: From the Modern State to Cosmopolitan Governance* (Stanford, CA: Stanford University Press, 1995).

35. For this critique, see Jürgen Habermas, *The Postnational Constellation: Political Essays*, trans. Max Pensky (Cambridge, MA: MIT Press, 2001).

36. For the now classic argument that the democratic deficit arises out of the history of the Westphalian system, see Held, *Democracy and the Global Order*.

37. Jan Aart Scholte, "Civil Society and Democratically Accountable Global Governance." *Government and Opposition* 39, no. 2 (Spring 2004): 21

38. David Held, "Democracy and the New International Order," in *Cosmopolitan Democracy: An Agenda for a New World Order*, ed. Daniele Archibugi and David Held (Cambridge: Polity, 1995), 102. Also see Held on the problem of "communities of fate": David Held, "The Transformation of Political Community: Rethinking Democracy in the Context of Globalization," in *Democracy's Edges*, ed. Ian Shapiro and Casiano Hacker-Cordón (Cambridge: Cambridge University Press, 1999), 84–111.

39. There is already a large and growing literature on democratizing global governance. For a good introduction and summary, see Jan Aart Scholte, *Building Global Democracy? Civil Society and Accountable Global Governance* (Cambridge: Cambridge University Press, 2011). Also useful is Michael Barnett and Raymond Duvall, eds., *Power in Global Governance* (Cambridge University Press, 2005).

40. The literature in the debate of the form of the new international and global constitutionalism is large and growing. A good review, from a social democratic point of view, is Jean Cohen, *Globalization and Sovereignty: Rethinking Legality, Legitimacy, and Constitutionalism* (Cambridge: Cambridge University Press, 2012).

41. Benhabib, "Twilight of Sovereignty or the Emergence of Cosmopolitan Norms?" 10.

42. There is an increasing number of such arguments. For three, see: Habermas, *Postnational Constellation*; John S. Dryzek, *Deliberative Global Politics* (Cambridge: Polity, 2006); and James Bohman, *Democracy across Borders: From Dêmos to Dêmoi* (Cambridge, MA: MIT Press, 2010).

43. For the later argument, see Dryzek, *Deliberative Global Politics*.

44. For an argument that the "cosmopolitan democracy" arguments do not go far enough in overturning the statist presumptions of liberal-democratic theory, see Sofia Näsström, "What Globalization Overshadows," *Political Theory* 31, no. 6 (2003): 808–34. Also see Jens Bartelson, "Globalizing the Democratic Community," *Ethics and Global Politics* 1, no. 4 (2008): 159–74.

45. See, especially, Held, "The Transformation of Political Community."

46. Benhabib, "Twilight of Sovereignty," 22. For a particularly sophisticated analysis of the concept of global civil society, see John Keane, *Global Civil Society?* (Cambridge: Cambridge University Press, 2003).

47. The important theorist of social citizenship is T. H. Marshall, *Citizenship and Social Class and Other Essays* (Cambridge: Cambridge University Press, 1950).

48. Arjun Appadurai, *Fear of Small Numbers: An Essay on the Geography of Anger* (Durham, NC: Duke University Press, 2006), 6–7.

49. Exemplary here is the well-known "scarf affair" in France. Several Muslim schoolgirls were expelled from school for wearing religious garb (the hijab, a traditional form of Muslim head covering for women)—an action that violated the traditional French idea of citizenship as the secular attachment to the French nation and violated French laws that prohibited private display of religious symbols in public institutions. One of the more insightful is Seyla Benhabib in *The Claims of Culture: Equality and Diversity in the Global Era* (Princeton, NJ: Princeton University Press, 2002).

50. Again, there is a large literature on multinational/multicultural citizenship rooted in claims for recognition based on ideas of human or other rights of peoples that override those of nation-states. An especially good analysis of Canada is James Tully, *Strange Multiplicity: Constitutionalism in the Age of Diversity* (Cambridge: Cambridge University Press, 1995).

51. Urry, *Mobilities*, 35.

52. There is a vast literature now on diaspora and hybridity in collective identity. For a general introduction, see Jane Evans Braziel and Anita Mannur, eds., *Theorizing Diaspora: A Reader* (Malden, MA: Blackwell, 2003). On hybridity in identity and its implications for citizenship, see Stuart Hall, "The Local and the Global: Globalization and Ethnicity," and "Old and New Identities, Old and New Ethnicities," in *Culture, Globalization, and the World System*, ed. Anthony King (Minneapolis: University of Minnesota Press, 2011): 19–68; and John Tomlinson, *Globalization and Culture* (Chicago: University of Chicago Press, 1999). Also see the important works of Ong, *Neoliberalism as Exception* and *Flexible Citizenship*.

53. Dora Kostakopoulou, "Evolution of European Union Citizenship," *European Consortium for Political Research* 1680-4333/08 (2008): 285–95.

54. Paulina Tambakaki, "Agonism and the Reconception of European Citizenship," *British Journal of Politics and International Relations* 13 (2011): 567–85.

55. Étienne Balibar, "Europe, an 'Unimagined' Frontier of Democracy," *Diacritics* 33, nos. 3–4 (Fall–Winter 2003): 36–45. For a more extensive treatment, see Étienne Balibar, *We, the People of Europe? Reflections on Transnational Citizenship* (Princeton, NJ: Princeton University Press, 2004).

56. Rachel Donadio, "Fears about Immigrants Deepen Divisions in Europe," *New York Times*, April 12, 2011, http://www.nytimes.com/2011/04/13/world/europe/13europe.html?_r=0 (accessed June 5, 2013).

57. Balibar, "Europe, an 'Unimagined' Frontier of Democracy," 5.

CHAPTER 6

1. Susan Buck-Morss, *Hegel, Haiti, and Universal History* (Pittsburgh: University of Pittsburgh Press, 2009).

2. For an excellent description of the movements and their tactics, see Paul Mason, *Why It's Kicking Off Everywhere: The New Global Revolution* (London: Verso, 2012).

3. Jean-François Bayart, *Global Subjects: A Political Critique of Globalization*, trans. Andrew Brown (Cambridge: Polity, 2007), 182.

4. Bayart, *Global* Subjects, 177.

5. Michael Hardt and Antonio Negri, *Empire* (Cambridge, MA: Harvard University Press, 2000), xii.

6. Hardt and Negri, *Empire*, 393.

7. Hardt and Negri, *Empire*, 397.

8. Hardt and Negri, *Empire*, 396–400.

9. For a very useful critical alternative, see Saskia Sassen, "The Repositioning of Citizenship: Emergent Subjects and Spaces for Politics," in *Empire's New Clothes: Reading Hardt and Negri*, ed. Paul A. Passavant and Jodi Dean (New York: Routledge, 2004), 175–98.

10. Mainstream reaction to Occupy was in some cases sympathetic and in some hostile and even paranoid. At a press conference on October 6, 2011, President Obama described the Occupy Wall Street protests somewhat favorably but with a hint of condescension as "giving voice to a more broad-based frustration with how our finance sector works. . . . The American people understand that not everybody's been following the rules." Others were less positive. Then presidential candidate Mitt Romney called it "class warfare," and Newt Gingrich, former House Speaker, said, "I regard the Wall Street protest as a natural outcome of a bad education system, teaching them really dumb ideas." Reported by Meghan Neal, "Politicians React to the Occupy Wall Street Movement," *Huffington Post*, October 17, 2011, http://www.huffingtonpost.com/2011/10/17/occupy-wall-street-politician-reactions_n_1014273.html (accessed March 14, 2013).

11. Manuel Castells, *Networks of Outrage and Hope: Social Movements in the Internet Age* (Cambridge: Polity, 2012).

12. Principles of Solidarity, passed by the New York City General Assembly, September 29, 2011, http://www.nycga.net/resources/documents/principles-of-solidarity.

13. Just to cite an aggregate example, according to the U.S. Census Bureau, the median income of the lowest fifth of households in the United States has stayed roughly the same since 1970, and in 2011, it was lower than in 1973 ($11,239 in 2011 and $11,488 in 1973, in 2011 dollars). At the same time, the top 5 percent's has steadily increased, and has gone from $187,846 in 1973 to $311,414 in 2011, in 2011 dollars. Data available from U.S. Census Bureau, "Historical Income Tables: Income Inequality," http://www.census.gov/hhes/www/income/data/historical/inequality/index.html (accessed March 14, 2013).

14. Principles of Solidarity, Occupy Wall Street, http://www.nycga.net/resources/documents/principles-of-solidarity/ (accessed February 2, 2013).

15. See Todd Gitlin, *Occupy Nation: The Roots, the Spirit, and the Promise of Occupy Wall Street* (New York: HarperCollins, 2012).

16. On the American progressives, see Richard Hofstadter, *The Age of Reform* (New York: Vintage, 1960).

17. See a discussion of this tradition in David Held, *Models of Democracy*, 3rd ed. (Stanford, CA: Stanford University Press, 2006); and C. B. Macpherson, *The Life and Times of Liberal Democracy* (Oxford: Oxford University Press, 1978).

18. Ronaldo Munck, *Globalization and Contestation: The New Great Counter-Movement* (Cambridge: Routledge, 2006), 57–91.

19. For a detailed history of the World Social Forum, see Boaventura de Sousa Santos, *The Rise of the Global Left: The World Social Forum and Beyond* (London: Zed Books, 2006).

20. All quotations in the next two paragraphs are from the World Social Forum Charter of Principles, http://www.wsfindia.org/?q=node/3.

21. Charles Lindholm and José Pedro Zúquete, *The Struggle for the World: Liberation Movements for the 21st Century* (Stanford, CA: Stanford University Press, 2010), 101.

22. See G. Deleuze and F. Guattari, *A Thousand Plateaus* (London: Continuum, 2004). Hardt and Negri also use the Deleuzian term *rhizomatic* to describe the organization of the multitude in *Empire*.

23. References to Gibson-Graham are to J. K. Gibson-Graham, *A Postcapitalist Politics* (Minneapolis: University of Minnesota Press, 2006).

24. Hardt and Negri, *Empire*, xi.

25. The Basque region had remained relatively depressed and had suffered persecution stemming from the Spanish Civil War of the 1930s—the destruction made famous by Picasso's painting *Guernica*, the Basque town devastated by Hitler's bombing in support of Franco.

26. This information is from "Decalogue of CSR Commitments Mondragon, 2012," available on Mondragon's website: http://www.mondragon-corporation.com. It should be noted that only about half of the workers are co-op members, most in Basque, while the rest are contract/wage employees. This is one of the issues currently debated by the cooperative corporation as it has expanded globally and has been a point of some criticism. See Anjel Mari Errasti, Iñaki Heras, Baleren Bakaikoa, and Pilar Elgoibar, "The Internationalisation of Cooperatives: The Case of the Mondragon Cooperative Corporation," *Annals of Public and Cooperative Economics* 74, no. 4 (2003): 553–84. Also see the discussion in Gibson-Graham, *Postcapitalist Politics*, chapter 5.

27. Gibson-Graham, *Postcapitalist Politics*, 101.

28. Gibson-Graham, *Postcapitalist Politics*, 105.

29. Ana Lucía Fariña, "Bribri Women," *Cultural Survival Quarterly* 36, no. 1 (March 2012): 16–18. Also see Martha Honey, "Giving a Grade to Costa Rica's Green Tourism," *NACLA Report on the Americas* 36, no. 6 (May/June 2003): 39–46; and Marta Nel-Lo Andreu, "Organización y características del turismo rural comunitario en Costa Rica," *Anales de Geografía de la Universidad Complutense* 28, no. 2 (2008): 167–88.

30. Gibson-Graham, *Post-Capitalist Politics*, 88.

31. Arjun Appadurai, "Deep Democracy: Urban Governmentality and the Horizon of Politics," *Public Culture* 14, no. 1 (2002): 23. Appadurai has continued to study the Alliance and to follow its developments. See part 2, "The View from Mumbai," in *The Future as Cultural Fact: Essays on the Global Condition* (London: Verso, 2013), 113–214.

32. Appadurai, "Deep Democracy," 28.

33. Appadurai, "Deep Democracy," 32–33.

34. Appadurai, "Deep Democracy," 31.

35. Appadurai, "Deep Democracy," 30.
36. Appadurai, "Deep Democracy," 34.
37. Society for the Promotion of Area Resource Centers (SPARC), www.sparcindia
.org (accessed June 11, 2013).
38. "India: Society for the Promotion of Area Resource Centres (SPARC) and the Indian Alliance," Homeless International, http://www.homeless-international.org/our-work/
overseas-partners/india-sparc (accessed June 11, 2013).
39. Partha Chatterjee, *The Politics of the Governed: Reflections on Popular Politics in Most of the World* (New York: Columbia University Press, 2004); and Partha Chatterjee, *Lineages of Political Society: Studies in Postcolonial Democracy* (New York: Columbia University Press, 2011). All quotations are from the e-book edition downloaded from Apple iBooks store, 2013.
40. In this respect, Appadurai's description of the practice "precedent setting" in the Alliance describes one mode of this politics well. Appadurai, "Deep Democracy," 34:

> Underlying its bland, quasi-legal tone is a more radical idea: that the poor need to claim, refine, and define certain ways of doing things in spaces they already control and then use these practices to show donors, city officials, and other activists that their "precedents" are good ones and encourage such actors to invest further in them. This is a politics of show-and-tell, but it is also a philosophy of do first, talk later. The subversive feature of this principle is that it provides a linguistic device for negotiating between the legalities of urban government and the "illegal" arrangements to which the poor almost always have to resort, whether the illegality in question pertains to structures, living strategies, or access to water, electricity, or anything else that has been successfully siphoned out of the material resources of the city.

41. Chatterjee, *Politics of the Governed*, 57; italics in original.
42. Chatterjee, *Lineages*, 354.
43. For specifics, see Appadurai, "Cosmopolitanism from Below: Some Ethical Lessons from the Slums of Mumbai," in *The Future as Cultural Fact*, 197–214.
44. Chatterjee, *Lineages*, 182–83.
45. See the first of the Leonard Hastings Schoff Memorial Lectures by Chatterjee in *Politics of the Governed*, chapter 1.
46. Chatterjee, *Lineages*, 40.
47. Chatterjee, *Lineages*, 86.

SELECTED BIBLIOGRAPHY

Abbate, Janet. *Inventing the Internet*. Cambridge: MIT Press, 2000.

Anderson, Benedict. *Imagined Communities*. Rev. ed. London: Verso, 1991.

Andreu, Marta Nel-Lo. "Organización y características del turismo rural comunitario en Costa Rica." *Anales de Geografía de la Universidad Complutense* 28 (2008): 167–88.

Appadurai, Arjun. "Deep Democracy: Urban Governmentality and the Horizon of Politics." *Public Culture* 14 (2002): 21–47.

———. "Disjuncture and Difference in the Global Cultural Economy." In *Modernity at Large: Cultural Dimensions of Globalization*, 27–43. Minneapolis: University of Minnesota Press, 1996.

———. *Fear of Small Numbers: An Essay on the Geography of Anger*. Durham, NC: Duke University Press, 2006.

———. *The Future as Cultural Fact: Essays on the Global Condition*. London: Verso, 2013.

Archibugi, Daniele, and David Held, eds. *Cosmopolitan Democracy: An Agenda for a New World Order*. Cambridge: Polity, 1995.

Åslund, Anders. *Russia's Capitalist Revolution: Why Market Reform Succeeded and Democracy Failed*. Washington, DC: Peterson Institute, 2007.

Balibar, Étienne. "Europe, an 'Unimagined' Frontier of Democracy." *Diacritics* 33, nos. 3–4 (Fall–Winter 2003): 36–45.

———. *We, the People of Europe? Reflections on Transnational Citizenship*. Princeton, NJ: Princeton University Press, 2004.

Bartelson, Jens. "Globalizing the Democratic Community." *Ethics and Global Politics* 1, no. 4 (2008): 159–74.

Bayart, Jean-François. *Global Subjects: A Political Critique of Globalization*. Translated by Andrew Brown. Cambridge: Polity, 2007.

Benhabib, Seyla. *The Claims of Culture: Equality and Diversity in the Global Era*. Princeton, NJ: Princeton University Press, 2002.

———. "Twilight of Sovereignty or the Emergence of Cosmopolitan Norms? Rethinking Citizenship in Volatile Times." *Citizenship Studies* 11, no. 1 (2007): 19–36.

Bohman, James. *Democracy across Borders: From Demos to Demoi*. Cambridge: MIT Press, 2010.

Brown, Michael E., Sean M. Lynn-Jones, and Steven E. Miller, eds. *Debating the Democratic Peace*. Cambridge, MA: MIT Press, 1996.

Brown, Wendy. "Neoliberalism and the End of Liberal Democracy." In *Edgework: Critical Essays on Knowledge and Power*, 37–59. Princeton, NJ: Princeton University Press, 2005.

Buck-Morss, Susan. *Hegel, Haiti, and Universal History*. Pittsburgh: University of Pittsburgh Press, 2009.

Burbach, Roger. "The Tragedy of American Democracy." In *Low Intensity Democracy: Political Power in the New World Order*, edited by Barry Gills, Joel Rocamora, and Richard Wilson, 100–125. London: Pluto, 1993.

Burbach, R., and C. Piñeiro. "Venezuela's Participatory Socialism." *Socialism and Democracy* 21 (2007): 181–200.

Butler, Judith. *Frames of War: When Is Life Grievable?* London: Verso, 2010.

Buzan, Barry, et al. *Security: A New Framework for Analysis*. Denver: Lynne Rienner, 1997.

Callon, Michel, et al. *Acting in an Uncertain World: An Essay on Technical Democracy*. Translated by Graham Burchell. Cambridge: MIT Press, 2011.

Campbell, Susanna, David Chandler, and Meera Sabaratnam, eds. *A Liberal Peace? The Problems and Practices of Peacebuilding*. London: Zed, 2011.

Cannon, Barry. *Hugo Chávez and the Bolivarian Revolution: Populism and Democracy in a Globalised Age*. Manchester, UK: Manchester University Press, 2009.

Castañeda, Jorge. "Latin America's Left Turn: A Tale of Two Lefts." *Foreign Affairs* 85, no. 3 (2006): 28–43.

Castells, Manuel. *The End of the Millennium*. Malden, MA: Blackwell, 1998.

———. *Networks of Outrage and Hope: Social Movements in the Internet Age*. Cambridge: Polity, 2012.

———. *The Rise of Networked Society*. 2nd ed. Malden, MA: Blackwell, 2000.

Castro-Klarén, Sara. "Framing Pan-Americanism: Simon Bolivar's Findings." *New Centennial Review* 31, no. 1 (2003): 25–53.

Chatterjee, Partha. *Lineages of Political Society: Studies in Postcolonial Democracy.* New York: Columbia University Press, 2011.

———. *The Politics of the Governed: Reflections on Popular Politics in Most of the World.* New York: Columbia University Press, 2004.

Cohen, Jean. *Globalization and Sovereignty: Rethinking Legality, Legitimacy, and Constitutionalism.* Cambridge: Cambridge University Press, 2012.

Cole, Scott N. "Hugo Chavez and President Bush's Credibility Gap." *International Political Science Review* 27 (2007): 493–507.

Colton, Timothy, and Michael McFaul. *Popular Choice and Managed Democracy: The Russian Elections of 1999 and 2000.* Washington, DC: Brookings Institute, 2003.

Connolly, William E. *Neuropolitics: Thinking, Culture, Speed.* Minneapolis: University of Minnesota Press, 2002.

———. *Pluralism.* Durham, NC: Duke University Press, 2005.

Coronil, Fernando, and Julie Skurski. "Dismembering and Remembering the Nation: The Semantics of Political Violence in Venezuela." *Comparative Studies in Society and History* 33 (1991): 288–337.

Dahl, Robert. *On Democracy.* New Haven, CT: Yale University Press, 2000.

———. *A Preface to Democratic Theory.* Chicago: University of Chicago Press, 1956.

Deibert, Ronald J. *Parchment, Printing, and Hypermedia: Communication in World Order Transformation.* New York: Columbia University Press, 1997.

Deleuze, Gilles, and Felix Guattari. *A Thousand Plateaus.* London: Continuum, 2004.

Desai, Padma. *Conversations on Russia: Reform from Yeltsin to Putin.* New York: Oxford University Press, 2006.

———. "Russian Perspectives on Reforms: From Yeltsin to Putin." *Journal of Economic Perspectives* 19, no. 1 (Winter 2005): 87–106.

DiFazio, William. "Time, Poverty and Global Democracy," In *Implicating Empire: Globalization and Resistance in the 21st-Century World Order*, edited by Stanley Aronowitz and Heather Gautney, 179–98. New York: Basic Books, 2003.

Douthwaite, Richard J. *The Growth Illusion: How Economic Growth Has Enriched the Few, Impoverished the Many, and Endangered the Planet.* Totnes, Devon, UK: Green Books, 1999.

Doyle, Michael. "Kant, Liberal Legacies, and Foreign Affairs." *Philosophy and Public Affairs* 12 (1983): 205–35, 323–53.

———, ed. *Liberal Peace: Selected Essays.* London: Routledge, 2012.

Drèze, Jean, and Amartya Sen. *India: Development and Participation.* Oxford:, Oxford University Press, 2002.

———. *India: Economic Development and Social Opportunity.* Oxford: Oxford University Press, 1995.

Dryzek, John S. *Deliberative Global Politics.* Cambridge: Polity, 2006.

Dunn, John, ed. *Democracy: The Unfinished Journey, 508 BC to AD 1993.* Oxford: Oxford University Press, 1992.

Ellner, Steve. "Hugo Chávez's First Decade in Office: Breakthroughs and Shortcomings." *Latin American Perspectives* 31 (2010): 77–96.

———. *Rethinking Venezuelan Politics: Class, Conflict, and the Chávez Phenomenon.* Boulder, CO: Lynne Rienner, 2008.

Ellner, Steve, and Daniel Hellinger, eds. *Venezuelan Politics in the Chávez Era: Class, Polarization, and Conflict.* Boulder, CO: Lynne Rienner, 2003.

Errasti, Anjel Mari, et al. "The Internationalisation of Cooperatives: The Case of the Mondragon Cooperative Corporation." *Annals of Public and Cooperative Economics* 74, no. 4 (2003): 553–84.

Euben, J. Peter, John R. Wallach, and Josiah Ober, eds. *Athenian Political Thought and the Reconstruction of American Democracy.* Ithaca, NY: Cornell University Press, 1994.

Farrar, Cynthia. *The Origins of Democratic Thinking: The Invention of Politics in Classical Athens.* Cambridge: Cambridge University Press, 1988.

Fernandes, Sujatha. *Who Can Stop the Drums? Urban Social Movements in Chávez's Venezuela.* Durham, NC: Duke University Press, 2010.

Finley, Moses. *Democracy Ancient and Modern.* 2nd ed. London: Hogarth, 1985.

Friedman, Milton. *Capitalism and Freedom: Fortieth Anniversary Edition.* Chicago: University of Chicago Press, 2002.

———. *Free to Choose: A Personal Statement.* Boston: Mariner Books, 1990; original 1979.

Friedman, Thomas. *The Lexus and the Olive Tree.* London: HarperCollins, 1999.

———. *The World Is Flat: A Brief History of the Twenty-First Century.* 2nd ed. New York: Farrar, Strauss and Giroux, 2007.

Fukuyama, Francis. *The End of History and the Last Man.* New York: Free Press, 1992.

Gibson, Nigel. "Upright and Free, Fanon in South Africa, from Biko to the Shackdwellers' Movement (Abahlali baseMjondolo)." *Social Identities* 14, no. 6 (November 2008): 683–715.

Gibson-Graham, J. K. *A Post-Capitalist Politics.* Minneapolis: University of Minnesota Press, 2006.

Gitlin, Todd. *Occupy Nation: The Roots, the Spirit, and the Promise of Occupy Wall Street.* New York: HarperCollins, 2012.

Golinger, Eva. *The Chávez Code: Cracking U.S. Intervention in Venezuela.* Northampton, MA: Olive Branch, 2006.

Gramsci, Antonio. *Selections from the Prison Notebooks.* Edited and translated by Quintin Hoare and Geoffrey Nowell Smith. New York: International, 1971.

Grandin, Greg. *Empire's Workshop: Latin America, the United States, and the Rise of the New Imperialism.* New York: Owl Books, 2007.

Griffiths, Tom. "Schooling for 21st-Century Socialism: Venezuela's Bolvarian Project." *Compare* 40 (2010): 607–22.

Habermas, Jürgen. *The Philosophical Discourse of Modernity.* Cambridge: Polity: 1987.

———. *The Postnational Constellation: Political Essays.* Translated by Max Pensky. Cambridge, MA: MIT Press, 2001.

Hacker, Jacob, and Paul Pierson. *Winner Take All Politics: How Washington Made the Rich Richer and Turned Its Back on the Middle Class.* New York: Simon and Schuster, 2010.

Hardt, Michael, and Antonio Negri. *Empire.* Cambridge, MA: Harvard University Press, 2000.

Harnecker, C. Piñeiro. "Workplace Democracy and Social Conciousness." *Science and Society* 73 (2009): 309–39.

Harvey, David. *A Brief History of Neoliberalism.* Oxford: Oxford University Press, 2005.

———. "Neoliberalism as Creative Destruction." *The Annals of the American Academy of Political and Social Science* 610 (March 2007): 21–44.

Held, David. *Democracy and the Global Order: From the Modern State to Cosmopolitan Governance.* Stanford, CA: Stanford University Press, 1995.

———. *Models of Democracy.* 3rd ed. Stanford, CA: Stanford University Press, 2006.

Honey, Martha. "Giving a Grade to Costa Rica's Green Tourism." *NACLA Report on the Americas* 36, no. 6 (2003): 39–46.

Honig, Bonnie. *Democracy and the Foreigner.* Princeton, NJ: Princeton University Press, 2001.

Huntington, Samuel. *The Clash of Civilizations.* New York: Touchstone, 1996.

———. *The Third Wave: Democratization in the Late Twentieth Century.* Norman: University of Oklahoma Press, 1991.

Kateb, George. *The Inner Ocean: Individualism and Democratic Culture.* Ithaca, NY: Cornell University Press, 1992.

Keane, John. *Global Civil Society?* Cambridge: Cambridge University Press, 2003.

Klein, Naomi. *The Shock Doctrine.* London: Penguin Books, 2007.

Kristol, Irving. *Neoconservatism: The Autobiography of an Idea.* New York: Free Press, 1995.

Lindholm, Charles, and José Pedro Zúquete. *The Struggle for the World: Liberation Movements for the 21st Century.* Stanford, CA: Stanford University Press, 2010.

Linklater, Andrew. "Cosmopolitan Political Communities in International Relations." *International Relations* 16 (2002): 135–50.

———. *Men and Citizens in the Theory of International Relations.* 2nd ed. London: Macmillan, 1990.

———. *The Transformation of Political Community: Ethical Foundations of the Post-Westphalian Era.* Cambridge: Polity, 1998.

Lipset, Seymour Martin, et al., eds. *Democracy in Developing Countries.* Boulder, CO: Lynne Rienner and the National Endowment for Democracy, 1989.

Lucas, George R., Jr., ed. *Journal of Military Ethics* 9 (2010).

Macpherson, C. B. *The Life and Times of Liberal Democracy.* Oxford: Oxford University Press, 1978.

Mandelbaum, Michael. *Democracy's Good Name: The Rise and Risks of the World's Most Popular Form of Government.* New York: PublicAffairs, 2007.

Marshall, T. H. *Citizenship and Social Class and Other Essays.* Cambridge: Cambridge University Press, 1950.

Mason, Paul. *Why It's Kicking off Everywhere: The New Global Revolution.* London: Verso, 2012.

Matlock, Jack F. *Superpower Illusions.* New Haven, CT: Yale University Press, 2010.

Maya, Margareta López, and Edgardo Lander. "Popular Protest in Venezuela: Novelties and Continuities." *Latin American Perspectives* 32 (2005): 92–108.

Milanović, Branko. *Worlds Apart: Measuring International and Global Inequality.* Princeton, NJ: Princeton University Press, 2005.

Muhr, Thomas. "Counter-Hegemonic Regionalism and Higher Education for All: Venezuela and the ALBA." *Globalisation, Societies and Education* 8 (2010): 39–57.

Muhr, Thomas, and Antoni Verger. "Venezuela: Higher Education for All." *Journal for Critical Education Policy Studies* 4 (2006) (accessed January 14, 2014).

Munck, Ronaldo. *Globalization and Contestation: The New Great Counter-Movement.* Cambridge: Routledge, 2006.

Näsström, Sofia. "What Globalization Overshadows." *Political Theory* 31, no. 6 (2003): 808–34.

Ober, Josiah. *The Athenian Revolution. Essays on Ancient Greek Democracy and Political Theory.* Princeton, NJ: Princeton University Press, 1996.

———. *Mass and Elite in Democratic Athens: Rhetoric, Ideology, and the Power of the People.* Princeton, NJ: Princeton University Press, 1989.

OECD. *Divided We Stand: Why Inequality Keeps Rising.* Paris: OECD, 2011.

Ong, Aiwa. *Flexible Citizenship: The Cultural Logic of Transnationality.* Durham, NC: Duke University Press, 1999.

———. *Neoliberalism as Exception: Mutations in Citizenship and Sovereignty.* Durham, NC: Duke University Press, 2006.

Parayil, G., ed. *Kerala: The Development Experience.* London: Zed Books, 2000.

Parish, Randall, et al. "Venezuela and the Collective Defence of Democracy Regime in the Americas." *Democratization* 14 (2007): 207–31.

Patnaik, Utsa. *The Republic of Hunger and Other Essays.* London: Merlin, 2008.

Peck, Jamie. *Constructions of Neoliberal Reason.* Oxford: Oxford University Press, 2010.

Polanyi, Karl. *The Great Transformation: The Social and Economic Origins of Our Time.* Boston: Beacon, 1954.

Raby, D. L. *Democracy and Revolution: Latin America and Socialism Today.* London: Pluto, 2006.

Rancière, Jacques. *Hatred of Democracy.* Translated by Steve Corcoran. London: Verso, 2006.

———. *Philosopher and His Poor.* Edited by Andrew Parker. Translated by John Drury, Corinne Oster, and Andrew Parker. Durham, NC: Duke University Press 2004.

Reddaway, Peter, and Dmitri Glinski. *The Tragedy of Russia's Reforms: Market Bolshevism against Democracy.* Washington, DC: U.S. Institute of Peace, 2001.

Robertson, Graeme. *The Politics of Protest in Hybrid Regimes.* New York: Cambridge University Press, 2011.

Robinson, William. "Globalization, the World System and 'Democracy Promotion' in U.S. Foreign Policy." *Theory and* Society 25 (1996): 616–65.

———. *Latin America and Global Capitalism: A Critical Globalization Perspective.* Baltimore: Johns Hopkins University Press, 2008.

———. "Transformative Possibilities in Latin America." *Socialist Register.* London: Merlin, 2008.

Ruggie, John Gerard. "International Regimes, Transactions, and Change: Embedded Liberalism in the Postwar Economic Order." *International Organization* 36, no. 2 (1982): 379–415.

Sachs, Jeffrey. *The End of Poverty.* New York: Penguin Books, 2005.

Sassen, Saskia. "The Repositioning of Citizenship: Emergent Subjects and Spaces for Politics." In *Empire's New Clothes: Reading Hardt and Negri*, edited by Paul A. Passavant and Jodi Dean, 175–98. New York: Routledge, 2004.

———. *Territory, Authority, Rights: From Medieval to Global Assemblages.* Updated ed. Princeton, NJ: Princeton University Press, 2006.

Scheuerman, William. *Liberal Democracy and the Social Acceleration of Time.* Baltimore: Johns Hopkins University Press, 2004.

Schoen, Douglas, and Michael Rowan. *The Threat Closer to Home: Hugo Chávez and the War against America.* New York: Free Press, 2009.

Scholte, Jan Aart. *Building Global Democracy? Civil Society and Accountable Global Governance.* Cambridge: Cambridge University Press, 2011.

———. "Civil Society and Democratically Accountable Global Governance." *Government and Opposition* 39, no. 2 (Spring 2004): 211–33.

Schumpeter, Joseph A. *Capitalism, Socialism and Democracy.* New York: Harper Colophon Books, 1975.

Sen, Amartya. *Poverty and Famines: An Essay on Entitlements and Deprivation.* Oxford: Clarendon, 1982.

Shapiro, Ian, and Casiano Hacker-Cordón, eds. *Democracy's Edges.* Cambridge: Cambridge University Press, 1999.

Singer, P. W. *Wired for War.* New York: Penguin, 2009.

Sousa Santos, Boaventura de. *The Rise of the Global Left: The World Social Forum and Beyond.* London: Zed Books, 2006.

Strange, Susan. *Casino Capitalism.* Manchester, UK: Manchester University Press, 1997; original 1986.

Tambakaki, Paulina. "Agonism and the Reconception of European Citizenship." *British Journal of Politics and International Relations* 13 (2011): 567–85.

Teubner, Gunther, ed., *Global Law without a State.* Dartmouth: Aldershot and Brookfield, 1997.

Thomas Isaac, T., and R. Franke. *Local Democracy and Development: The Kerala People's Campaign for Decentralized Planning.* Lanham, MD: Rowman & Littlefield, 2002.

Tully, James. *Strange Multiplicity: Constitutionalism in the Age of Diversity.* Cambridge: Cambridge University Press, 1995.

Tumber, Howard, and Jerry Palmer. *Media at War: The Iraq Crisis*. London: Sage, 2004.

Urry, John. *Mobilities*. Cambridge: Polity, 2007.

Virilio, Paul. *Speed and Politics*: New York: Semiotext(e), 1983.

von Mises, Ludwig. *Human Action: A Treatise on Economics*. Vienna: Ludwig von Mises Institute, 1998.

Wade, Robert Hunter. "Globalization, Growth, Poverty, Inequality, Resentment and Imperialism." In *Global Political Economy*, 3rd ed. Edited by John Ravenhill. Oxford: Oxford University Press, 2008.

Walker, R. B. J. *Inside/Outside: International Relations as Political Theory*. Cambridge: Cambridge University Press, 1993.

Weisbrot, Mark, Rebecca Ray, and Luis Sandoval. *The Chávez Administration at Ten Years: The Economy and Social Indicators*. Washington, DC: Center for Economic and Policy Research, 2009.

Wilpert, Gregory. *Changing Venezuela by Taking Power: The History and Policies of the Chávez Government*. London: Verso, 2007.

Wolin, Sheldon. *Democracy Inc.: Managed Democracy and the Specter of Inverted Totalitarianism*. Princeton, NJ: Princeton University Press, 2010.

Wood, Ellen Meiksins. *Peasant-Citizens and Slaves: The Foundations of Athenian Democracy*. London: Verso, 1997.

Wootton, David, ed. *Divine Right and Democracy: An Anthology of Political Writings in Stuart England*. Indianapolis: Hackett, 1986.

World Bank: South Africa, Economic Update: Focus on Inequality of Opportunity. Washington, DC: World Bank, July 2012.

Yergin, Daniel, and Joseph Stanislaw. *The Commanding Heights: The Battle between Governments and the Marketplace That Is Remaking the World*. New York: Touchstone Books, 1999.

Zakaria, Fareed. *The Future of Freedom: Illiberal Democracy at Home and Abroad*. Rev. ed. New York: Norton, 2007.

INDEX

ABOUT THE AUTHORS

Jim George was senior lecturer at the Australian National University, where he taught international relations and international relations theory before retiring in 2012. He is the author/coauthor of five books, including *Discourses of Global Politics* (1994) and two editions of *Introduction to International Relations* (2007, 2012) and more than thirty articles in leading international relations journals. He taught international relations and international relations theory at the Australian National University for twenty-five years before retiring in 2012. He now lives in Canberra, Australia.

Stephen J. Rosow is professor of political science at the State University of New York at Oswego, where he teaches political theory and global studies. He is the author (with Walter Opello) of *Nation-State and Global Order* (1999, 2004), has edited books on critical international political economy and the future of the university, and has published articles on democratic theory, enlightenment political thought, and critical international relations theory.

CPSIA information can be obtained at www.ICGtesting.com
Printed in the USA
BVOW07s1548130714

358947BV00002B/3/P